Passport Stamps

SEARCHING THE WORLD FOR A WAR TO CALL HOME

Passport Stamps

SEARCHING THE WORLD FOR A WAR

TO CALL HOME

Sean D. Carberry

LAKE DALLAS, TEXAS

FIRST EDITION

No animals were harmed during the writing of this book.

Requests for permission to reprint material from this work should be sent to:

Permissions
Madville Publishing
P.O. Box 358
Lake Dallas, TX 75065

Author Photograph: CVS Pharmacy
Cover Design: Jacqueline Davis
Cover Art: Liz Davis

ISBN: 978-1-956440-55-3 paperback, 978-1-956440-56-0 ebook
Library of Congress Control Number: 2023936767

To Squeak, my little battle buddy who got me home, and to the memory of David Gilkey. You are missed every day.

Preface

> "A broken man has no place in polite society."
> —Dr. Mallard, *NCIS*

As a kid, "war correspondent" was never on the list of things I wanted to be when I grew up. I didn't become a journalist until I was 32, and even then, it was somewhat by accident. I had been a recording engineer and record producer in Boston and started looking for more stable work. I found a job as an audio engineer at WBUR, the Boston NPR station, and gradually found myself drawn to the content—the news and information—rather than the medium and technology.

Then 9/11 and the war in Afghanistan happened. Suddenly, being a war correspondent started calling to me out of a sense of public duty. I was in the business, and an important story was happening on the other side of the world. I felt compelled to experience it and communicate it back home.

However, it was not until 2007, when a traumatic personal experience made me question mortality and meaning in life, that I committed to traveling to the most deadly, dangerous, and depressing places in the world. My motives were a mix. On the altruistic side, I wanted to help inform the world what was going on and what it was all about. On the personal side, I needed to confront some things, prove myself, and do something that mattered that would validate me.

This book chronicles my journey from novice, in-over-my-head hack bumbling around places like Sudan and Iraq trying to earn my place among the pros, to full-time war correspondent in Kabul, where I was a pro with a story to cover and little to prove.

At its most basic, this work is a Bourdain-esque travel book that takes you on a tour of different countries and societies—many that will never show up on a vacation destination list. Essentially, this is the story behind the stamps in my passport. There are few five-star hotels and no Michelin Star restaurants described in these pages. There is a lot of dust, grit, ragged infrastructure, communication breakdown, weaponry, scary driving, and way too much food poisoning. There is also some of beauty, humanity, generosity, kindness, and more food poisoning.

The next layer is a behind-the-scenes look at conducting journalism in far-off places. It is a candid (and often self-deprecating and critical) discussion of the challenges of the craft and my steep learning curve of parachuting into unstable countries, places amidst or emerging from war, or nations about to plunge into conflict. There are near-catastrophic moments, and there is a lot of dumb luck, happenstance, and eventually some wisdom. On that level, it's a tale of wanting to be Ernie Pyle and often being Gomer Pyle.

Beyond that, this book is about universal human experiences—a journey to process loss and grief, to understand self-identity, and the search for purpose and a place where you feel at peace. It's the quest for "tribe." While my specific journey is unique, we are all on journeys of one kind or another, whether they are to move past or away from something, someplace, or someone or to move toward something, someplace, or someone.

Everything this book happened and happened as I describe to the best of my memory. The places and people are real, although a few names are not. There is violence, gore, profanity, sex, alcohol, abuse of prescription medications, discussion of suicide, and other unsavory activity that might be off-putting, but it's all part of the story.

Like most humans (and especially those of the expat temperament) I'm no saint. In the early chapters, I was often naïve, selfish, and a bit arrogant as I strove to establish myself in a competitive business. I was also dealing with some things, as you will read.

The last thing you need to know before turning the page is that I am a Gen X pop culture junkie. You will come across many references, some of which I explain, many I do not. Anyone who gets through this book without having to Google something, I owe you an adult beverage—preferably a Mai Tai at a Trader Vic's where we can discuss Warren Zevon (the soundtrack to this book) and Hunter S. Thompson (an influence).

Contents

Contents

Chapter One
20 Hours in Darfur

November 2007

KHARTOUM, Sudan — Everyone froze and stared at me bewildered as I entered the tiny restaurant near the center of Khartoum. I very well might have been the first white dude to wander unaccompanied into the place.

I took a spot in line among the Sudanese men wearing dusty white robes. They gradually eased back into conversation but kept an eye on me.

I approached the grimy counter and kitchen that wouldn't have passed a single health code in the United States. That was more enticing than deterring. I wanted the Sudanese experience.

Using the eight words of Arabic I knew, I ordered the traditional breakfast dish all the other customers were lined up for: fuul. The fact that I knew the name of the dish seemed to put the young men behind the counter at ease.

I handed over about the equivalent of a dollar in Sudanese pounds, and one of the servers handed me some bread and a metal bowl filled with fava beans cooked with garlic, lemon, and oil, and garnished with onion, tomato, and parsley.

I climbed a creaking ladder into a dingy 8-by-8-foot room where a group of five Sudanese men gestured for me to sit on the floor with them. One grabbed my bowl and dumped it into a larger bowl on the short, round table. He directed me to dig in.

There we sat eating the traditional Middle Eastern breakfast meal from the communal bowl. We ripped off pieces of bread and scooped up the brown mush with our unwashed hands. They spoke no English. I spoke no Arabic. It was authentic.

It was perhaps too authentic for my jaded western digestive system. I had to break into my Cipro stash the next morning to combat the microorganisms the meal sent rummaging through my innards. I was two-for-two on contracting food poisoning during my international reporting trips. It's one of the side effects of being an adventurous type who never says no to anything local or traditional.

After I finished breakfast and climbed out of the restaurant, I checked in with my fixer, Kambal. He was still in line at the government office that recorded passport information of visiting foreigners. I don't know why that information wasn't adequately captured at immigration at the airport, but apparently it wasn't, hence the extra bureaucratic step.

Fixers like Kambal are the backbone of international reporting. They are usually local journalists who work with foreign reporters and perform anything and everything from translation to arranging meetings to handling all local logistics like seemingly illogical passport registration activities.

Since Kambal was going to be tied up for a while with the oppressive Sudanese bureaucracy, I resumed my unsupervised roaming of the sand-covered streets among the sand-colored buildings.

I stumbled into a section of downtown where Jersey barriers blocked the streets. Inside the perimeter, the streets were covered with several inches of fine sand.

At the center of the cordoned off area was a tall building surrounded by an imposing security fence and festooned with all sorts of electronic gadgetry and antennae. I felt my sperm count decreasing from all the electromagnetic radiation. Turned out, it was the U.S. embassy.

I walked around the streets feeling it was probably the safest I could be in the city—which shows how naïve I was that I thought there would be little danger outside an American embassy in a country under U.S. sanctions and that had once hosted al-Qaeda. It was not a good time to be an American in Sudan.

I walked a block beyond the embassy and looked down one of the streets leading away from the building. With my back completely turned to the embassy, I took a picture of the street scene. I continued my oblivious roaming around.

Suddenly, I heard men yelling somewhere behind me. It wasn't a full-on ruckus, but a solid commotion. I turned and saw four angry Sudanese men in casual clothing wielding AK-47s. They were yelling and running toward me. They looked pissed, like someone had just stolen their car or insulted their mothers.

I assumed it was a coincidence and they were running toward something beyond where I was standing. I stepped aside so they could pass, but they stopped with their AKs pointed straight at me.

I was dumbfounded as they yelled at me in Arabic. I had no idea what to make of it. I had never had a gun pointed at me before, let alone four machine guns held by amped-up men in a nation with a long history of civil war and genocide. I was a mix of terrified and confused. Actually, I was so startled by it all that I was more confused than terrified. Since I hadn't done anything wrong (that I was aware of), I felt it was some sort of misunderstanding that should be easy to resolve.

One asked in English who I was and what I was doing. I calmly told them I was an American journalist. I showed them my temporary press credential from the Sudanese government. I assumed that would clear things up and they would send me on my way.

It did not and they did not. With their aged Kalashnikovs still trained on me, they asked for my passport, which was with Kambal several blocks away. I explained why it was not with me. I showed them my D.C. driver's license. I still didn't understand what the problem was. What the hell had I done that had set them off like that? For that matter, who the hell were they?

3

Finally, one of the men explained that they were local security for the embassy and that I had taken a picture "of" the embassy, which was prohibited. I pointed out that I took the picture "near" but not "of" the embassy. That was far too *Dead Poets Society* for them to grasp.

I tried to keep things light without being flip. I didn't think that taking a picture was an offense that warranted being shot in the street, but it didn't look like they were going to let me go, despite my Pee-Wee Herman ventriloquism attempt and Jedi mind tricks.

I was new to the whole traveling to dangerous, fragile nations thing. I had that narrow-minded, colonialist view of a white guy who had grown up in middle-class America. I viewed the men and the situation as almost cartoonish, and I couldn't believe I was being hassled for taking a picture. I assumed that I could simply reason my way out of whatever was going on—I thought my rules, my logic should apply on their turf. I was a dumbass who had a lot to learn.

Next thing I knew, they were parading me at gunpoint around the corner and down a narrow street. I was starting to get a bad feeling. It was dawning on me that I wasn't in Kansas anymore. I had no idea what rights I had, if any.

I walked along increasingly terrified, wondering if they were just taking me to the police chief's office so he could scold and throw a coffee mug at me, or if I was heading for a *Midnight Express* horror show.

They marched me up to a large metal door. They opened it and led me into a 10-by-15-foot concrete room with no windows and only the large metal door. There were four cots, a desk, and a small refrigerator. The men instructed me to sit on one of the cots. All but one left, and he sat at the desk with his weapon trained on me. I could see the safety was on and his finger was nowhere near the trigger, so I had that going for me.

He seemed calm and unconcerned, which calmed me. After a few minutes of silence, I decided to feel him out. I apologized for not knowing the rules and said I was a credentialed journalist, and I didn't take a picture of any of the embassy structures.

He spoke some English and responded with a reassuring tone. He said he was sorry to hold me there, but it was a requirement. He made it seem like things would be cool.

Even though I had no hostile-environment training—and not enough sense to know I should have taken said training prior to the trip—I had picked up enough from movies and TV to know that it's a good idea to make a personal connection with a would-be captor. So, I asked about him and his family to build a rapport. "How long have you worked for the embassy? How many kids do you have?" Stuff like that.

He answered, although I was too unnerved to pay attention and remember anything he said. I told him I lived in Washington, D.C. and worked for a small radio program. I babbled some more about how the people in Sudan seemed friendly and that I liked the country. I just wanted to keep a calm, friendly conversation going to humanize myself and gain his sympathy.

After about 30 minutes in the little jail, the other guards returned and marched me to a nearby office. I figured it was a good sign that we moved to a more comfortable setting rather than a full-on jail or dungeon.

They sat me down and interrogated me. They handed me a blank piece of paper and told me to write down my name, address, employer, age, gender, religion, height, weight, eye color, the color of every article of clothing I had on, my parents' names and addresses, and so on. After a while, it felt like the guy was simply thinking up anything he could without any kind of guide or legal mandate. He didn't ask my favorite color, but I was prepared to write down, "blue, no, yellow!"

They let me call Kambal. One of the armed guards took the phone and gave him directions to find us. I patiently wrote everything down as we waited for Kambal to bring my passport to prove my nationality. As we sat, we eased into casual conversation and it was clear there was no danger, nor any sanction. In fact, I started to get the feeling it was more about them covering their asses. They needed to be able to demonstrate to their bosses at the embassy that they took a security threat seriously and followed some sort of protocol if anyone asked.

Approximately 90 minutes after I was detained, Kambal arrived with my passport, which he couldn't register since he had to leave to rescue me. The security guys checked it out and chatted with Kambal. They made me pull out my camera and show them the photo (a crappy one of a generic sand-covered street with shuttered shops on each side) and delete it as they watched. They let me go with a warning. They apologized for the hassle, shook my hand, and said a friendly goodbye.

The whole time it was going on, I had my bag full of radio gear—cables, microphones, strange looking electronic things. The bag was in each of the two rooms with me the entire time, so it never left my eyesight. During the whole process, the Sudanese security guys frisked me, asked me for all kinds of personal information (like if I had rehabilitated myself), made me write down what color socks I was wearing, but they never searched my bag that literally had fucking wires sticking out of it. I wasn't about to suggest that they search it, but I was simply stunned that they detained me for taking a picture near the embassy, which was deemed a serious security risk, yet they didn't think it was important to make sure I wasn't carrying a fucking bomb in my bag. At that moment, I feared for the safety of the Americans working in the embassy.

That said, on just my second international reporting trip I had earned the "detained at gunpoint by local security forces" merit badge, so I was psyched about that.

It was inevitable that I would end up in a predicament like that in Khartoum. I mean, I was in one of the most press-unfriendly countries in the world. I had no training on how to report in hostile environments. In fact, it would be another three years before I attended a hostile environment course (an oversight, to put it mildly).

I was in Sudan to report a segment for the public radio program *America Abroad*. An upcoming episode was exploring the love-hate relationship between the United States and the United Nations. At the time, the United States was supporting the standup of a new UN peacekeeping mission in Darfur (that the Sudanese regime opposed). It was a rare example of the United States turning to and working with the United Nations. So, I was interviewing U.S., UN, and Sudanese officials in Khartoum and trying to get to Darfur to tour the new UN compound and interview personnel involved in the mission.

I was also in Sudan because I was new to the international reporting profession, and I was eager to join the ranks of journalists who covered the shit. So, despite having no practical experience or training—and only moderate street smarts at that time—I was jumping at opportunities to go to rough neighborhoods to prove myself and build street cred. Even though the genocide had peaked in 2003 and the "real" journalists had long moved on, I was aiming for badass points and journalism merit badges for reporting from Darfur.

Despite the reduced violence, the crushing bureaucracy still made reporting in Sudan and Darfur daunting for even the most seasoned journalists, let alone someone like me who at that time was pretty much the Mr. Bean of foreign correspondents. I was a mix of naïve, ambitious, and way too concerned with looking cool. Hence, I was stumbling into one predicament after another since arriving a few days earlier.

A few days earlier: I stood around outside the airport in the hot, dry night air looking for any sign of a driver waiting for me. As the only awkward white guy there, I figured my driver should have no problem spotting me. However, the only people who approached me were taxi drivers. I confidently waved them off since I had arranged for transportation in advance.

After 10 minutes, my confidence waned. I called my fixer and reported the situation. After a few calls back and forth, I received a call from my driver, who informed me he did not have a car. From my experience, the title "driver" required having a car, but apparently not in Sudan. My fixer instructed me to take a taxi to Ozone, a cafe and meeting place in the center of the city. He would meet me there.

I approached a row of battered and beaten yellow cabs of indeterminate origin. I walked up to the sorry vehicle at the front of the line and asked the driver to take me to Ozone.

He didn't speak any English. I repeated "Ozone" a few times, and he gave me the universal shrug of "Dude, I have no idea what the fuck you're saying."

Six other drivers huddled around us. They were all in their 20s and 30s and all spoke English. I explained where I wanted to go, and they spoke to the older driver in Arabic. The older gentleman seemed to understand the directions from the other drivers, so we threw my large bag on the roof rack of his tiny, ancient, and creaky yellow taxi (isn't that a Joni Mitchell B-side?) and set off for Ozone.

He drove around in what felt like circles for 30 minutes. He stopped to ask people on the sand-covered sidewalks for directions no less than eight times. I was shocked by that but would learn that it was standard practice in the Arab world where western-style street names and address systems do not exist. Directions often resemble, "Go that way really fast; if something gets in your way, turn."

The driver stopped yet again to ask for directions. The person he stopped on the sidewalk simply pointed across the street. Without realizing it, the driver had finally stumbled upon Ozone—an open-air cafe in the middle of a traffic circle.

I paid him and got out of the dusty and musty taxi, only to discover Ozone was closed. For 10 minutes I stood around alone in the dark with my luggage. Nothing at all suspicious about an American man in field clothing standing in the dark in the center of Khartoum with a large black duffle bag.

Eventually, my fixer arrived (on foot). He was around 30 and tall and husky with light-black skin and a mustache. His name was Ziryab, but he went by Jay. He was jovial and spoke first-rate English.

We flagged a taxi to my hotel, the Bougainvilla Guest house, which he had never heard of—not a good sign. The taxi driver had never heard of it either, but he drove off in the direction of where he suspected it might be. After more circling around and calling the hotel for directions, the driver found it. Jay looked at the hotel and then turned to me and asked who had booked me there—not a good sign.

I checked in and hauled my stuff to my room. It was a tiny and basic cell with two twin beds. There was a communal bathroom down the hall. I had clearly booked a room in a backpacker-style place, not the kind of establishment frequented by journalists and potential sources, or people who didn't wear patchouli.

It was getting late, and I was spent from the long journey from D.C. through Dubai to Khartoum, so I decided to stay there for the night and consider my options in the morning. I ordered some kebabs from a shack down the street and went upstairs to eat on the roof of the hotel.

The air was warm and dry—a pleasant change from Washington, or from the dank weather in Serbia and Russia on my trip the previous month. The city was rather dark with a minimal skyline.

As I pondered the night scene, the power cut out. That helped explain why the city and skyline seemed so dark. I downed my dinner as I watched surrounding neighborhoods darken and illuminate again like the runway in *Airplane*. As I walked down the stairs to my room, the sound of power generators faded in the distance.

The next day was a Friday. Like in most Muslim countries, that meant government offices and most businesses were closed. Jay took me to a couple of different hotels to see if there was something better than the guest house.

9

The streets were packed with cars, donkey carts, pedestrians, goats, and more cars. Buildings ranged from sheds and shacks to newer concrete and brick structures, most no more than three or four stories. Men and women walked together, and most, but not all women wore head coverings. Maybe a quarter of the men wore white *dishdashas*, or traditional tunics, and the rest wore pants and casual button-down shirts (untucked).

Aside from the yellow taxis of indeterminate origin, most of the vehicles were Toyotas with a periodic Volkswagen or Hyundai thrown into the mix. Small amounts of trash and debris lined the edges of the streets.

We passed a small restaurant. The name was Lucky Meal. The "M" was a yellow double arch. It was an unmistakable poaching of the McDonald's logo and as close as you could get to an American chain restaurant in the sanctioned country. I gathered that the owners had not seen *Coming to America*. Hence, they missed the opportunity to name it McDowell's.

We visited the VIP International Hotel, a definite step up with its modern construction, air-conditioned rooms, moderately stable WiFi, and en suite bathrooms. It was centrally located and had some guests working for international organizations, so that would be my new base.

We returned to the guest house to check out. When the red-haired German woman at the desk presented me the bill, I handed her a credit card. She paused, clearly taken aback by the gesture. She gave me a look that simultaneously said, "What are you doing? Are you an idiot?" and "We might have a problem." She told me that they did not take any credit cards—no one in Sudan did. She explained that under international sanctions, they were cut off from the likes of Visa and MasterCard. For that matter, they were cut off from any western banks or ATMs.

You'd think I would have clued into that detail before getting on a plane to Sudan for an eight-day reporting trip with about $250 in my pocket and four different credit and debit cards in my wallet. At least a red flag should have gone off the night before when I checked in and she didn't ask for a credit card.

I sat in a state of mild shock and mentally soiled a pair of underwear. Between the taxi rides and meals so far, paying the hotel bill in cash was going to leave me with about $20 in my pocket.

I didn't want to make a scene and didn't want to give her any more reason to think I was an idiot, so pulled a Nathan Thurm (Martin Short *SNL* character from when the show was still funny) and brushed it off like I knew what I was doing while in my head saying, "I know that. Of course I know that. It's so funny you think I wouldn't know that."

Then, I confidently pulled out cash and paid the bill like I had things under control. Jay and I left and as we walked out, I was saying in my head, "Shit shit shit, oh shit, how the hell am I going to get money and get through the rest of my trip?"

I had never faced a situation like that before. How the hell had I not learned before the trip that western credit and debit cards would be of no use? I was so cocky in my preparation before the trip that I was only concerned with how cool I was going to be for going to Darfur. I talked to people who had been to Sudan and Darfur to get the rundown on all the bureaucracy and permissions needed, but I just assumed that the all-American credit card commanded respect throughout the world.

My panic attack continued as Jay and I drove across town to the VIP hotel. I checked in thinking I was going to have to sneak out in the middle of the night to avoid paying the bill.

I settled into my room and frantically researched options for accessing money. I was more than relieved to discover that Western Union operated in Sudan and was the primary means for getting money in the country. I changed the pair of underwear in my mind.

I called my office in Washington and sheepishly informed all the 20-somethings there that their intrepid, badass (more like dumbass) correspondent was unaware that credit cards did not work in Sudan.

They told me that the boss was away for a couple of weeks, and he was the only one able to access the business account.

Fortunately, they spared me any additional humiliation and emptied their pockets and came up with $300 on the spot and ran to the closest Western Union office to send it to me. That would buy me a few days.

The next day Jay drove me to the Western Union office at a nearby mall to retrieve my cash. I can't express how much of a relief it was. It felt like a girlfriend saying, "Turns out I'm not pregnant."

From the mall we headed into downtown Khartoum. The traffic was epic. I had never seen anything like it before. It was like the gridlock of people trying to flee New York City in a zombie apocalypse movie minus the screaming. The day before was the Muslim world's equivalent of Sunday, which was why the traffic was rather mild that day.

Since Jay had a full-time job, he couldn't work with me every day, so he brought in reinforcements. Kambal was also around 30 and leaner and with darker skin than Jay. While he was completely professional, he struck me as having a bit of a mischievous streak, which I liked.

Kambal and I spent the next couple of days shuttling between government offices confronting a level of bureaucracy straight out of the movie *Brazil*. We endured multiple trips to the passport registration office and the Ministry of Information. Office hours seemed to change every day. The specific individuals who had to process my various forms always managed to leave early.

For my Darfur travel permit application, I needed to submit 5 passport photos, and of course I only had 4 with me. At least I had already learned that you should always carry extra passport photos on foreign reporting trips. Fortunately, the Ministry of Information was able to process my press card on the spot, so I was legally allowed to interview people and take pictures (although apparently not near the U.S. embassy).

Kambal and I headed off to a market in town so I could get the worst (both in terms of my pose and the photo quality) passport pictures of my life. They weren't as bad as a Nick Nolte mugshot, but close. From there we headed back to my hotel so I could make some calls—including a call to my girlfriend to send me some more money since my office in D.C. was closed.

After completing that business, Jay drove me to the office of a British-educated Sudanese PR consultant named Ahmed who was advising the government. He agreed to an on-the-record interview.

Ahmed was probably in his late 30s and had a shaved head and glasses. He spoke at length about the government, the history of the conflicts in the country, the UN mission and other topics relating to Sudan, the United States, and the United Nations. The gist of it was that the U.S. sanctions were the source of most of the problems in the country, that there was strong evidence that only 9,000 people had been killed in Darfur, and the numbers included those who died of disease or famine to artificially inflate the death count and make the situation seem worse than it was (at the time, the UN said more than 200,000 had been killed in the genocide). Ahmed argued that the international community was somewhat racist and anti-Islamic and needed to back off, eliminate sanctions, allow Sudan to fix its problems, and then come in to invest in the oil industry to help the country grow its economy.

It was an interesting intellectual argument, but it was bullshit as far as I was concerned. The reality was, Sudan's problems happened on its watch—everything from the civil war, the period when al-Qaeda camped out in Sudan, and the Darfur genocide—so there was no compelling argument whatsoever that if the international community backed off and ended the sanctions that the government would suddenly play nicely and solve its issues on its own. President Omar al-Bashir was a war criminal according to just about everyone who wasn't in the Sudanese government.

We debated for 45 minutes. After, Ahmed complemented me for my critical listening skills and for all my questions that picked apart the logic and causality he asserted in his arguments. That further signaled to me that it was simply an exercise in spin, and he was trying to sell me a narrative that I would report to the benefit of Sudan.

I had interviewed American politicians before, so I was accustomed to hearing pitches and treating them for what they were. However, that was the first time I had been subject to an aggressive messaging campaign by a foreign PR agent, let alone one working for a government under sanctions for sponsoring terrorism and conducting genocide. It felt almost sleazy to have such serious matters of human rights and security reduced to a sales pitch like that. It was another eye-opening moment about how the world works and how lobbying and hustling take place. Going forward, it would not phase me when foreign officials would attempt to co-opt me and use my reporting as a vehicle to deliver their (often bullshit) messages to the United States and the international community.

OK, now we're caught back up to the start of this chapter when I was detained outside the embassy. The following morning, I started with a dose of Cipro and then went to the U.S. embassy to interview the *charge de affaires* (since the two countries did not have formal diplomatic relations and there was no ambassador to interview). As I was being escorted in by a young foreign service officer, I explained to him what had gone down the day before and told him the embassy might want to review some of its security protocols. I was nonplussed by how non-nonplussed he was by my tale. I guess they assumed the local security guys were cannon fodder and they relied on the Marines inside the perimeter if any shit went down.

That evening, the fixers and I went on an adventure to procure alcohol. Sudan was hardcore when it came to Islam, and alcohol was as *haram* (forbidden) as anything could be. But as we all know, making something illegal does not eliminate all demand, and where there is demand, there is supply. You just have to know where the supply is, and my guys did.

We drove through dusty streets under cover of darkness into a remote corner of the city and pulled up at a modest house. I felt a little giddy that I was doing something devious and badass.

A man invited us inside and we sat in the nicely furnished living room. It had the awkward feel of meeting the parents of your prom date. Jay and Kambal chatted with the man and then went off into another room of the house while I waited.

A few minutes later, they came back and presented me with options for purchase. One was what looked like an IV bag filled with clear liquid and was alleged to be some sort of schnapps from Uganda. Another option was a pint bottle with a suspicious label stating it was "Zed Pineapple" from Tanzania. There were a few other equally odd and terrifying options. Khartoum was clearly the land of the misfit alcohols, where all the bottles from around the world that were too weird or terrible to drink ended up sitting in a warm bedroom waiting to be rescued by third-tier journalists—like me—who were not connected enough to tap into diplomatic stashes.

As tempted as I was by the mystery IV bag, I went with the bottle of Zed, and paid the man $40. It was probably at least five, if not ten, times the original cost of the alcohol in Tanzania—empirical evidence of the law of supply and demand. The fixers and I departed with our stash and went to an outdoor *shisha* cafe. We ordered juice drinks and subtly spiked them with our pineapple liquid.

We consumed our beverages and huffed down some applemint *shisha*. From there, we went to a local pool hall, and I had a moment of alcohol-induced competence and ran the table a couple of times.

Through it, we maintained eyesight, did not grow any new hair anywhere, and our livers did not leap out of our bodies screaming. All in all, it was a fun and successful evening—far more "normal" than I expected in what I smugly viewed as a backward and dysfunctional country. I also earned the "sneaking around to procure forbidden alcohol" merit badge.

I spent the next couple of days running around doing

interviews in Khartoum while monitoring progress on my Darfur travel permit. One night, Kambal and I went to an outdoor Ethiopian restaurant for dinner only to stumble into a wedding reception. The family invited us to celebrate.

A DJ played music through a distorted and cracking PA system. The women wore brightly colored dresses and head scarves. Henna tattoos covered their hands. The men wore pants—ranging from jeans to shiny dress pants—and button-down shirts. I could see from the wrinkle patterns on some of the men's shirts that they had been purchased and opened from their packaging that day.

The men looked casual and frumpy next to the glimmering women. I was wearing a maroon Gap T-shirt and khaki linen pants, so I wasn't exactly dressed for a wedding reception, not that I had any idea I would stumble into one.

Sudan was the second poorest country I had been to at that point. In 2003, I traveled to Mali to attend a music festival (headlined by Robert Plant) in the middle of the desert north of Timbuktu. It was the first time I visited an undeveloped place, and the first time I had been somewhere that had just emerged from domestic conflict.

It was the place that pierced my privileged American bubble and showed that there are people around the world living with next to nothing who are nonetheless happy, at peace with themselves and their lives, and incredibly generous. That trip made me slightly less jaded—slightly. So, when I saw the people in Khartoum having a great time at a wedding party that probably cost the same as a centerpiece at an American wedding table, I felt neither surprised nor guilty about how little they had.

The family encouraged me to take all the pictures I wanted, and guests posed with each other and with me. I was humbled by their generosity and friendliness. As a cynical, American Gen X'er, it was difficult to process unconditional hospitality like that. Part of me expected them to ask for something in return.

In the coming years as I spent more time in the Middle East,

I would grow accustomed to the culture of hospitality and learn not to question it. But that night I was suspicious why people welcomed in a stranger from a wealthy country imposing sanctions on their country.

Technically, I didn't crash the wedding since they invited me into their party. However, for merit badge purposes, I told people that I crashed a wedding in Sudan.

The next day was a Thursday, and the day before I was scheduled to return to Washington. At 10:45 that morning, I received my travel permit for Darfur. It did not seem like a coincidence that I received the permit the day before I was scheduled to leave the country—a fact that the officials processing my permit request knew. As I later learned from conversations with other journalists, that kind of thing was a common tactic in the region. If the government issued the permit, they could say they were being cooperative, even if they issued it when it was too late to exercise the permit.

However, I was not going to come that far, get that close, and not set foot in Darfur. Kambal and I went to the Emirates office in Khartoum to bump my return flight a couple of days.

After changing my flight home, we went to a travel agent to purchase a ticket to Darfur since I didn't have time to arrange for a UN flight. Nova Airlines was the only option. It was a disconcerting name.

Kambal dropped me at the airport. After a mild flap over a missing stamp on my paperwork from one government office or another, airport officials allowed me to board the flight.

I walked out onto the tarmac and approached the white-and-red Nova 737. Once I got about 50 feet from the aircraft, I had second thoughts. I could see that the plane was spent. It looked hand-painted, and there were chips and cracks all over the body.

I haltingly walked up the steps. I contemplated pulling the plug, but I had come too far to turn back just because I was about to fly on a plane that should have been grounded a decade prior.

Inside the seats were filthy, and the fabric worn, torn, and shot. Seats and overhead bins were taped and tied. It smelled like a shoe. I took my seat and tried to remember if my tetanus shot was current. I looked up and saw that the signs were written in English and Chinese. What that told me was that the plane had belonged to a Chinese airline and had been flown to the point it no longer passed Chinese standards, and then the Chinese government dumped it on Sudan.

I was the only western-looking person on the plane—all the diplomats and NGO workers were far too smart (or prohibited by their security regulations) to fly Nova. As the plane taxied to the runway and took off, I did my best to ignore the strange sounds and smells.

Ten minutes into the flight, things quieted down to the point that I could let my mind wander. It had been a draining week of bureaucracy, detention, mild food poisoning, and some levity over my credit card blunder. It was a grind having to navigate it all and do so under a tight deadline. But it was also kind of fun to navigate and pass through the traps.

I've always loved travel and exploration, and Sudan was foreign in every respect. There was so much to take in, sights, sounds, smells—although some I could live without—and it was exciting and challenging to be improvising my way through such a different society and culture. That said, I was mostly ignorant and lucky in my bumbling through the bureaucracy. I rarely knew what I was doing and was reacting to situations rather than controlling them.

I felt immense pressure to deliver a great story to justify the trip. I had to prove to myself and to America Abroad Media, my employer of three months, that I was worthy of sending to far flung places to report complicated stories. I had been hired as senior producer with the mandate to make the monthly one-hour international affairs program more radio friendly (that was a low bar). Field reporting was part of the job description, but the small organization had limited funds. I had a trip budget of $5k (that had to cover all transportation, lodging, meals, telecom expenses, and fixer/translator expenses) and had to come home with solid material to justify the expense.

I also felt I had to prove myself to other journalists. There were a lot of people dreaming of and vying to be foreign correspondents, and a shitload of people who would have killed to have my job, even though it was for a program that no one I knew had heard of when I joined the organization. As much as I was thinking about a future of moving onto a larger and more reputable organization, I also had to watch my back. Like Wall Street, Hollywood, or politics, the foreign correspondent world is cutthroat and competitive and there's no shortage of people— from type-A, sociopathic narcissists to bleeding-heart altruists— looking to get into the game.

The plane started to descend, and I returned my focus to hoping the aged beast would make it to the ground in one piece. Somewhat amazingly, we landed safely. I hurried off the plane and got on the bus to the "terminal" looking back at the aircraft half expecting it to burst into pieces like the Bluesmobile in front of the Cook County Building.

My contact picked me up and drove me through the sandy streets past small walled compounds to his house. I dropped my bags and then wandered to "downtown" El Fasher to explore.

I started with the *souk* (market). It was like the local markets in Mali. Stall after stall of people selling fruits, vegetables, mystery meats, textiles, large tins of oil, and other wares. It seemed thriving, if not vibrant.

I soaked in the sights, sounds, and smells. I was in the moment. Despite my mild OCD, I love the chaos and energy of local markets in the Middle East and Asia. I have never encountered anything close to it in the United States.

After touring the market, I roamed the town. People and animals gathered along the trash-strewn banks of El Fasher Lake. Trees looking like something from a Dr. Seuss book emerged from the middle of the lake. Exotic birds hovered above in the

Golden Hour sunlight. It was all quite striking and beautiful—almost *Land of the Lost* (the original, not the Will Ferrell travesty—seriously, has that guy ever played a character who isn't a bombastic idiot?). Looking at it all, it was easy to forget that nearby were enormous displaced-persons camps housing tens of thousands of people who fled the violence and genocide that had started in 2003.

The sun was creeping toward the horizon, so I decided to head back to my lodging. I shot more photos as I walked along the unpaved road from the town to the house where I was staying.

Suddenly, I heard men yelling. I turned to see two men emerging from a small shop. They approached me angrily. Seriously? What the fuck now? Not again.

They spoke a little bit of English, which frankly shocked me. What would drive locals in Darfur to learn English, and how and where did they learn it?

I didn't have long to ponder that before I had to deal with the more pressing matter, which was their complaint that I was taking photographs. Unlike the embassy episode, I was certain I was in the right. That said, I was panicked about how it was going to play out.

They yelled at me asking who I was and demanding that I delete the photos. I asked them who they were and what authority they had to harass me. I realized I probably wasn't going to get too far with that approach since at the end of the day, there were two of them and it was their turf. They did not answer my questions. I told them I was a reporter and I had papers and permits. I showed them my press card, Darfur permit, and my passport. I was pissed that I had to pull out my papers for a couple of random dudes on the street.

They examined the documents.

As if someone had flipped a switch, the two men smiled and welcomed me. They said they had a small gallery of some sort and asked me if I would come see it with them. As hospitable as it all seemed, I was furious and amped up on adrenaline. I politely declined. As I walked away, they again welcomed me and said I could visit them anytime.

I couldn't process the encounter. How could they go from such hostility and looking like they were ready to rip my arms off to then treating me like a relative they hadn't seen in years? It was beyond me. In the coming years, I would experience situations like that countless times and learn to anticipate and master the routine of going from chest thumping to bonding like some kind of primate ritual. Nonetheless, in that case, I found little to take away from the encounter and walked off fuming and wanting to punch someone in the head.

I returned to the house and got cleaned up to head to … a party. One of the NGOs operating in the area was having a gathering. I had no idea what to expect, but I wasn't about to pass up an opportunity to witness a "crisis party" and to mine the event for contacts, information, and maybe some other action.

Emergency Sex is a book that came out in 2004. The crux was that people in the aid and development communities use alcohol and sex to cope with the stresses and horrors they witness and experience. That was hardly a revelation, but the book caused a stir for talking openly about debauchery in the aid community and undermining the chaste and altruistic image of the Tom Tuttles and Beth Wexlers of the world.

Anyhow, I wanted in on the debauchery. A taxi picked me up and drove through the darkness—and I mean hardcore desert darkness—to a small glowing and throbbing block house. The image of the whore house in the *Beetlejuice* model town popped into my head.

I entered the single-story house and there were dozens of foreigners and a few locals imbibing a variety of spirits and carrying on loudly as music blared in the background.

There was a gorgeous young American foreign service officer recently posted to El Fasher. She was surrounded by half the men at the party. Obviously, the guys had not seen *A Beautiful Mind*. Since I had, I knew to ignore her and look for less-contested prey.

Yes, as I mentioned earlier, I had a girlfriend at the time. However, it was a rebound relationship, and I was in a weird emotional headspace—more on that later—so I was a scoundrel and on the prowl.

I mingled awkwardly and fell into conversation with a few people. While no one questioned who I was or why I was there, I was feeling self-conscious and insecure. Some of the people at the party had spent years, even decades, working in hostile environs. They had seen and survived a lot of shit.

I was a neophyte with zero street cred. Yes, I had navigated all the obstacles necessary to make it to El Fasher on my own, which was not insignificant. But I was making it up as I went along. I had ambition and just enough street smarts and ability to think on my feet to get by in a weird place.

Anyhow, I was living my first "war story." I didn't want to reveal to the party guests that I was in the process of losing my hostile environment virginity. So, I quietly went about my business and acted like I belonged there. I felt a little like a spy, so I had that going for me, which was nice.

I convinced one aid worker to step outside for an interview. I felt a bit conflicted about discussing the pain and suffering of the local population at a party where the people there to help the locals were drinking and carrying on seemingly without a care. That was just the first of countless parties I would attend in failed states and conflict zones, and while that icky feeling would fade over the years, part of me always felt it was insulting to be drinking and chasing women as the locals suffered. Although, it clearly never bothered me to the point that I would turn down an opportunity to drink and chase women in war zones.

That interview would turn out to be the only one I would conduct in Darfur. The next morning the general in the UN mission I was to meet called in sick. There was no one else to escort me around the UN facilities or to discuss the new peacekeeping mission. I didn't have a permit to enter the camps or interview local government officials. All I could do was have a driver take me around the perimeter of a camp so I could surreptitiously take pictures from the car.

And just like that, my time in Darfur was up. A week of fighting through bureaucracy and anticipation, and all I got was one interview, a party, and shaky pictures of a camp.

Nova managed to get me back to Khartoum in one piece and my fixers met me and took me to the office of the minister of communication and administration. It was my final interview before heading home that evening.

I sat in the minister's office with him, my fixers, and two other mysterious Sudanese men who did not identify themselves. I was pretty crispy from the chaos of the trip, and the minister's bullshit talking point answers to my questions were pissing me off.

The more we talked, the more I felt my blood pressure rising. Despite having interviewed countless American politicians and having confronted every interview trick—the pivot off your question to "what the real issue here is," the filibuster, the strict adherence to talking points—his use of those tactics was getting under my skin.

As we were wrapping up, I remarked that he did not answer my questions and that he did not address the criticisms and accusations that people were levying against his government (it was stupid and naïve to think he would). He laughed. The other men in the room laughed. My blood was boiling, and those men were laughing about how they managed the interview and did not admit any wrongdoing on the part of a government accused of genocide and other crimes and human rights violations.

I packed up my gear in a huff, stifling my raging urge to punch one of the men in the head. In hindsight, part of what I was experiencing was the cumulative stress of operating in a tough place where I was repeatedly confronted and challenged and where there was a constant threat of danger. I wasn't aware of the impacts of those stressors at that time. Over the years, that feeling would become my normal idle.

Jay and Kambal transported me to the airport. I vented and rambled like Walter Sobchak the entire drive.

I thanked the guys profusely and gave them my remaining cash, not that there was much. I couldn't possibly express my gratitude to them. They bent over backward to accommodate me and to make sure I was safe and had everything I needed. They bought me meals, took me to their homes to meet and talk with their families, and largely put their lives on hold for a week to tend to me.

They did that essentially for free—I paid for meals when they would let me, and gas and hard expenses, but they would not take money from me for their time. They felt they were performing a public service by helping me report and inform the international community about their country and its criminal regime. It was fucking humbling.

The trip was a success insofar as I made it in and out of a difficult country without injury or arrest—just a brief detention. I had enough material for a story, but not nearly what I had hoped to get while I was there. The bureaucracy was too overwhelming for the time I had to travel. Had I another week to spend there, I probably could have accomplished most of my wish list.

I had been extremely lucky in getting a visa so quickly and getting the Darfur travel permit in a reasonable timeframe as well. But I couldn't pull everything off as hoped in the time I had.

That was the reality of my situation—based on the production demands and the budget of the radio program, I could travel for 7 to 10 days. Darfur was not a location you could get in and out of in that timeframe. But I was not going to let details and logistical challenges stand in the way of my ambition.

And as a result, I joined the club of journalists who had "covered" Darfur. Sure, I was there three or four years after the peak of the crisis, I was there for all of 20 hours, I didn't accomplish much more than go to a party, but it was still a dangerous place and I dipped my big toe into it—OK, maybe my pinky toe. Mission accomplished from the "I've been to Darfur" bragging rights perspective.

The lesson I should have learned from the trip was that I still had a lot to learn about operating in hostile environments. Instead of focusing on that, I was busy scheming my next brush with danger.

Chapter Two
The Call of the Tribe

The Sudan trip gave me a taste of the danger, unpredictability,
and excitement of reporting in hostile environments. It was a
jump into the deep end of the pool without floaties. I was hungry
for more.

Unfortunately, my personal ambitions of running around
war zones and failed states did not always align with the editorial
needs of the monthly radio program. There were many important
topics to cover around the world, and not all were wars or stories
that would get me in the shit.

After Sudan I traveled to Egypt and Taiwan. The Egypt
assignment was basically a puff piece on U.S. public diplomacy
efforts—outreach, education, and exchange programs designed to
make Egyptians like America. It was a wonky story, although I
would come to learn that America Abroad Media was into wonky
and had an ulterior motive of promoting America's image and
interests in Muslim countries—in other words, conducting public
diplomacy. Even though it was kind of a lame story, it was an
opportunity to visit Egypt.

Cairo was loud and polluted as expected—constant car horns
and black gook that accumulated in your nose. It gave me the
chance to see the pyramids and the Khan al-Khalili *souk*. I also
discovered the legendary Sakara King 10 percent alcohol beer at a
little hotel I stayed at in El Minya, a small city on the Nile about
200 miles south of Cairo. I downed a couple of pint cans of the
potent potable while watching a flopping contest, I mean a soccer

match, on the TV of the hotel's outdoor lawn bar and emailing my friend and legendary mixologist Brother Cleve about the beverage, of which he had heard but never encountered in person. I finally had one up on him in the drink department.

In Taiwan I gathered my story on the triangle of tension between the United States, China, and Taiwan with little difficulty while enjoying night markets, massages, and Chinese New Year in Taipei. The only potential danger came from a few mystery foods I ate, but I did not need to break out the Cipro. The story focused heavily on notions of identity—how there is a spectrum of Chinese versus Taiwanese identity in Taiwan.

In the two years leading up to joining America Abroad Media, I had developed a fascination with notions of identity and identity politics. So, I was in my intellectual happy place exploring how identity played out in Taiwanese politics and relations with mainland China.

After those two trips, I got to take another shot at danger: Colombia. I traveled there to report on the foreign policy and state building efforts of the Catholic church and the Holy See—the Vatican's governmental and diplomatic arm.

My aspiration was to be badass and get out into the jungle to tangle with guerrillas and narcos. I wanted to see communities caught in the crossfire between government militias and coked-up Marxists. I wanted war stories. Again, I was consumed with building my reputation and impressing people with tales of daring do, and I wanted to do that essentially at the expense of the people of Colombia who were victims of the violence and danger. While I wasn't completely unsympathetic or un-empathetic to the plight of people in difficult environments, it was far from the top of my mind in the early days of my international reporting career.

I wanted to tell important stories that would help people in places like the jungles of Colombia, but I wanted my stories to help me impress people and advance my career. That was hardly unusual in the business, but not the most appealing of qualities. I matured over time.

Anyhow, while I did visit Bogota's Ciudad Bolivar mega slum and I spent a few days in the jungles of the poverty- and violence-stricken Choco region, I didn't see any action. The most dangerous thing I did was taking a woman I met in a Bogota nightclub back to my hotel and had to run around the streets at 2 a.m. to find an open pharmacy selling condoms—through a drawer in a bulletproof window like a bank teller.

In both Cairo and Bogota, I had the opportunity to go out drinking with the expat foreign correspondents. In each case, I was envious. They were experienced correspondents some of whom had lived in several foreign cities, and most had seen shit. They were closely knit groups of adventurous internationalists—they were tribes.

That's what was calling to me at that moment in my life—the foreign/war correspondent tribe. There was a mix of freedom, danger, competition, and fellowship to it all. The adventure of visiting strange places and seeing weird things, of meeting fascinating, and sometimes terrifying people, of battling through bureaucracy and language barriers to find truth, of living and telling stories: that was what had drawn them to Bogota and Cairo, and that's what I was chasing.

Cliche as it is, 9/11 set that chase in motion. I was early in my journalism career as a producer for *The Connection*, an NPR show produced at WBUR in Boston. In the fall of 2001 as U.S. forces were pursuing al-Qaeda in Afghanistan, I often spent mornings dialing satellite phones trying to reach people on the ground in Afghanistan to get them on the program. I was typically calling one of the Karzais or one of the handful of rockstar foreign correspondents covering the special forces and Afghan militias driving out the Taliban.

That lit the fire in me. Talking to Dexter Filkins, Sarah Chayes, or Anthony Shadid over spotty connections as they vividly described the Afghan landscape, the fighting, the history in the making: I was envious. Yes, I was doing my part as a young—in my career at least—journalist to help inform the American public what was taking place over there. However, I couldn't help but feel that sitting in a studio and talking to the people in the field who were risking their lives to tell incredible stories was not where I wanted to be.

Some journalists feel that investigative reporting is the highest calling in field. Others believe political or finance reporting is most impactful or fulfilling. In the fall of 2001, I came to believe that war reporting was the pinnacle. I felt that to matter as a journalist, it was my professional obligation to get out there and cover the story. While I had no training or experience that qualified me to be out in the field, I felt that was where I needed to be and by sitting on the sidelines, I was inadequate as a journalist.

That was consistent for me. In whatever career or activity I engaged in, I immediately wanted to be at the top of the field, regardless of my capabilities. For example, in high school, I had dreams of being an Olympic gymnast, even though my peak potential would have been as an alternate on a Division III college team. So, getting over my skis was nothing new.

I was also seduced by the romanticized tales and images of the journalist life in war zones. There was a mystique, a sense of adventure and excitement to it. There were bonds forged in the bunkers and bars of Beirut, Baghdad, and the Balkans. I craved the intensity of the experience.

I felt that way every day for the next couple of years. The fighting continued in Afghanistan, and I was stuck in an overly air-conditioned control room in Boston. Then came the invasion of Iraq and correspondents flocked to that country as I sat in the studio and once again called them on satellite phones. In the spring of 2003, WBUR sent Dick Gordon, the host of *The Connection*, to Iraq for two weeks. He had years of experience as a foreign correspondent covering conflicts—the experience I was then desperately seeking. I raised my hand and volunteered to field produce on the trip.

I was told it was too hairy of a situation to break in a virgin. I played the "everyone has to have a first trip to a war zone" card, but my appeal went nowhere. Looking back, it raised the question of how someone builds the skills and gets ready to deploy to a war zone. Yes, there are training courses and experience to gain in hostile places that are below the level of war, but at some point, you have to lose your virginity. That said, how many experienced correspondents would choose to go into battle with a trainee rather than an experienced hand? From where I sit now, I wouldn't have taken me to Baghdad then either.

Dutifully, I stayed behind and did my part from the studio, all the while feeling more and more like Mister Roberts sitting on The Bucket. I find it interesting that when I first saw that movie as a young teenager, I was drawn to that character and his longing for action, to do his part for the cause, to matter and make a difference. Obviously, I wanted a different ending for myself than he got.

Finally, in summer 2007, after a few more twists and turns in life (including a devastating breakup), I came across a job posting from America Abroad Media. It was a small, obscure organization I had never heard of, nor had I heard its radio program, *America Abroad*. It was a monthly, hour-long international affairs program distributed by Public Radio International.

It didn't matter that I hadn't heard of the show (or that most of my friends in the public radio world hadn't heard of it, and those who had thought it was some sort of State Department project). What did matter was that they needed a producer who could make the program more "radio friendly" and travel around the world to gather material. At that point, I was an experienced producer who wanted to travel the world.

I applied, got the job, and moved to D.C. Within a couple of months, I was hopping on planes to weird places and chasing my dream of joining the war correspondent tribe.

Chapter Three
Seeking Closure in Lebanon

July 2008

BEIRUT — I arrived in the evening of July 5. I climbed into a beat-up Mercedes and the driver delivered me to my girlfriend's ex-boyfriend's apartment on a hill in the upscale Achrafieh neighborhood of East Beirut. We were all friends, so it was cool.

My first full day in the city was a Sunday, and since Lebanon has a Monday through Friday workweek unlike the Sunday through Thursday workweek of other countries in the region, I had the day to myself. I set out on my usual routine of walking around to get the feel for the place, and to find a SIM card.

I started out wandering the streets near the apartment. The architecture was strongly French-Mediterranean with 4-to-6-story buildings ranging in color from white to sand with balconies surrounded by ornate metal railings. They were mostly clean and in good repair. The streets and sidewalks were clean and as it was a Sunday morning, things were quiet.

Despite being the most religiously diverse country in the Middle East, Beirut was (and still is) rather segregated with Muslim neighborhoods in the west of the city, Christian ones in the east. Expats are largely split between the Hamra neighborhood in the west and Gemmayze and Achrafieh in the east. Those neighborhoods are densely packed with shops, restaurants, and bars.

I made my way to the center of the city, which had been the

so-called "Green Line" between warring sides during the civil war. By summer 2008, the downtown had been largely rebuilt into an upscale but soulless re-imagination of Beirut. Shops, restaurants (including the ubiquitous Dunkin' Donuts), and offices (private and government) occupied the neo-Mediterranean tan buildings that tried hard but felt inauthentic.

Several older, bombed-out buildings still stood downtown, providing a stark contrast and reminder that Lebanon is often a veneer of glitz and excitement overlain on tectonic geopolitical plates that can jolt into violent spasms with little warning. Construction billboards surrounded several blocks and depicted renderings of the glamorous new buildings that would someday rise out of the city's ashes.

Roman ruins also lay in-between the new buildings and civil war relics. Within a single block you could see ancient ruins, a church, a mosque, burned out French Mandate buildings, and modern construction—all part of the charm and appeal of the city.

From there, I wandered westward along the Corniche. Families were out swimming and fishing on the rocky coastline. I continued along to the western limit of the city and followed the coast south to the scenic Raouche Rocks before turning back in the direction of Achrafieh.

Along the way I passed a Hard Rock Café. I'm honestly not sure what possessed me to stop. I generally despise anything blatantly commercial or artificial. I think that might have been what called to me, a morbid curiosity to see such a cliché and artificial construct in a city famous for its history and culture. Also, it was hot as balls outside, and I needed a beer to cool off.

Inside it was like any other Hard Rock, bedecked with memorabilia and full of young people enjoying beers and burgers. I grabbed a seat at the bar, ordered a beer, and stared at the TV showing a Wimbledon match.

I quickly fell into conversation with an American Lebanese man at the bar next to me. Karim was maybe 30 with black curly hair and glasses. He worked in finance in London and was visiting family for the first time in many years. He said he had stayed away because of the years of instability and uncertainty after the civil war.

In 2008, Lebanon finally resolved two years of political crisis in the wake of the 2006 war with Israel and formed a new government. That brought a level of calm that made Karim feel it was safe to visit. It's also why I was there at that time. The formation of the new government provided a timely opportunity to report on the structural and historic reasons Lebanon was (and still is) such a fragile state, prone to political paroxysms and episodes of violence or all-out war.

It didn't take us long to get onto the topic of identity. His Christian parents had grown up in Lebanon, but he was born in the United States. He felt pulled in different directions about who he was and how he identified. While solidly American and not having lived through any of the conflict in Lebanon, the country, its people, and his family were an integral part of who he was, to the point where he wondered what his true "home" was.

Of course, I brought up my ex and the tale of that relationship, how it altered the course of my life, and that I was in Lebanon as much to do journalism as to seek closure.

Cue the harp music and visual blur to indicate a flashback/reveal sequence:

In 2005, I went to grad school to study public administration. The day after graduation in June 2006, I was on a plane to Dubai for a summer internship at the Dubai School of Government.

Dubai is the EPCOT version of the Middle East—it's all artificial glitz with no real culture. Seriously, I learned how to downhill ski in a Dubai mall. Meanwhile, there were wars going on just short flights away in Iraq and Afghanistan. Israel and Lebanon went at it that summer, yet I was watching it all from the comfort of the biggest artificial city outside of Las Vegas.

That summer I wrote papers on governance and political reform. My research and writing immersed me in Arab politics, culture, and notions of identity. That knowledge and experience proved critical the moment I got home, but not for reasons I would have expected.

The day after I returned to Boston, a grad school classmate invited me to join him and another classmate for drinks. I arrived at Grafton Street in Harvard Square and linked up with Ben, a chiseled former Navy aviator. We ate and caught up while waiting for our other friend Lawrence, a tall Peruvian bon-vivant.

As we ate, two women entered and walked around the bar. One was a tall, exotic-looking brunette wearing a tight lilac T-shirt. She had the face of a Greek goddess, an athletic frame, and brown eyes that radiated tremendous depth, complexity, and intrigue. I was captivated. The two women settled along the wall across the room, and I didn't let the goddess out of my sight.

Lawrence arrived and joined us at the table. The two women saw him and walked over to join us. One was his date, and the other (the one who caught my eye) was apparently a setup for Ben. I was the fifth wheel—at least to start.

I quickly started chatting with my infatuation. We'll call her Layla. I mentioned to her that I had just returned from a summer in Dubai where I was writing about Arab politics and identity. That got her attention. I noticed that she had an accent and asked about it. She explained that she was Lebanese-Palestinian and lived in Beirut until she was eight, and then her family fled the civil war and moved to southern California.

"So, how do you identify?" I asked. She lit up to the question. It started a deep conversation about identity and the concept of tribe—in the literal sense of ethnic/ancestral tribes and the broader sense of the human need for a feeling of belonging. She was passionate, candid, and quick-witted. I was transfixed as she spoke about her upbringing.

We closed the bar and went to Ben's nearby apartment for more drinks. That's where it began. Layla and I snuck a kiss on the couch.

The next weekend, we went on our first date—a Red Sox game. I was all in. She was beautiful, very smart—top of her class at UCLA, Fulbright scholar—witty, well-traveled, a polyglot, and endlessly fascinating.

Part of what fascinated me about her was how she wrestled with her identity. She struggled to reconcile her Palestinian and Lebanese identities as they each had implications in shaping her. Her father was Palestinian Christian, which afforded much better status in Lebanon than that of Palestinian Muslims, but Palestinian Christian was still not Lebanese. Then, the Lebanese Christian side of the family added other identity dynamics to the mix.

To be wrestling with all of that as a child as an identity-fueled civil war raged, and then to be uprooted and moved to the United States, how could that not create internal tensions and questions about where you belong, what community or "tribe" with which to identify? She described how during college she associated with a Muslim student group because it was the closest thing to a tribe she could find where she felt herself and surrounded by kindred.

I couldn't begin to understand her experience, but I related to the longing and the need to find some sort of "place" where you felt at home—a tribe. Looking back over my life, I was constantly seeking and drawn to tightly knit groups of people that had bonds forged in some deep, common experience.

I grew up in suburban, white, upper-middle-class America, which was so vast and bland of an identity that it didn't create any sense of closeness or kinship. That's likely why everyone in that world was seeking or joining groups of some kind—"tribes." Church, sports teams, band, drama club, cliques: they were all tribes of a sort that people joined and found community and a shared sense of identity.

At Lehigh University I found myself drawn to the Kappa Alpha Society. KA initially seemed like a fun group of guys, but I discovered there was a mystical quality to KA. It was the first social fraternity in the United States, and it was also a literary society. It was founded at Union College in 1825 by young men who could be described as seekers. They were students of philosophy, literature, and theology. They would sneak around campus and hold meetings in attics where they smoked pipes, sang songs, wrote and read poetry, and discussed life. They were the original Dead Poets Society.

In college, I embraced and embodied the KA ethic. I spent countless late nights engaged in deep conversations with brothers about the meaning of life, who we were, where we were going, and of course booze and sex. KA was my tribe in college.

In the years after college, I wandered in and out of different tribes. There was the Saturday X-Night tribe of moshers at the club Axis in Boston. There was the tribe of musicians playing the Toad, Lizard Lounge, and Sally O'Brien's circuit in Cambridge and Somerville. Next was the public radio tribe in Boston.

In the fall of 2006 and into 2007, Layla became my tribe. We traveled, introduced each other to our respective worlds, and went to dinners and parties hosted by her extended family. I brought her out to see and meet my local musician tribe.

What probably sealed the deal for me as much as anything was when I made her watch *Young Frankenstein*, and she loved it. I had found my match. She was my Rushmore.

I wanted to be where she was. I wanted the nights in the kitchen trying to perfect Asian wrinkled string beans, the black-tie holiday party when we looked like we walked off the set of a James Bond movie, scuba diving in Nicaragua, and saying goodbye in the morning and feeling the anticipation of seeing her at the end of the day.

I wanted to spend my life in the moment that she was. Afghanistan, Iraq, and the draw of being a foreign correspondent that had animated me for years before I met Layla faded. That relationship became my animating passion in life. I didn't need anything else.

She did.

What I did not see coming, especially at the time when I was about to ask her to move in with me, was that her sense of identity would be the undoing of our relationship. Deep down, she needed to be with someone from her tribe, which I was not. I was a placeholder.

While I thought we could and did work together as people who could relate to questioning identity in general and searching for tribe, it was only a matter of time before she would come across a Lebanese expat with whom she could feel "at home."

Out of the blue in May 2007, it started with, "I think we need some space." My heart froze. Layla didn't really define it beyond that. We spent a few more days together, and I thought it was a blip and we were fine. Then, she followed with, "I think we should see other people." The shoe dropped. She had met someone from her tribe. She said she felt the need to explore that possible connection and had to be free of me to do it.

A few days later I sat in tears as I watched her pack up her stuff at my place. I tried every appeal I could think of to convince her to reconsider. I felt the air being sucked out of my chest as she put her bags in the trunk of her car and drove off.

The feeling was as much physical as emotional. I felt shaky from the constant adrenaline and other chemicals the heartbreak was surging through my body. I felt that panic/anxiety sensation where if I sat still, my life force would simply fall out of me and that would be it. It was like the shark species that have to swim continuously to oxygenate, I felt that if I stopped moving, I would die.

I took up running as one way to try to release it. I barely ate. Sleeping was almost impossible. I lost 15 pounds in the first month after the breakup—technically, that was a good thing, but still.

Once that relationship was over and it was clear there wasn't a thing I could do to change her mind, I had to get the fuck out of Boston. There was no way in hell I was going to stick around the scene of the emotional crime.

My thoughts and feelings were raging in a variety of directions. I was feeling a death wish. The urge to run around wild places and war zones came coursing back. I wanted to see Fallujah and Helmand up close and personal. She had turned me into Johnny

Ringo—I had a hole in the middle that I needed to fill with death, destruction, and danger.

I also felt a strong need to travel to Lebanon to understand the factors that made her who she was and led to our demise.

Two other things happened that summer that added emotional upheaval to my life and shaped me going forward. First, on July 4, my step-grandmother committed suicide. It was a shock, but when I stepped back and thought about it, it made some sense. She had felt alone and empty since my grandfather passed some 20 years prior, something she had once confided in me. She turned to international travel to fill the void, just as I was setting out to do.

In 2007, the years and miles were catching up with my step-grandmother. Her body was struggling to keep up with the rigors of traveling the world, and that was one of the factors that led her to pull the plug.

She and I had not been that close until I was an adult and started traveling to strange and interesting places. That was her comfort zone and what allowed us to bond. We communicated frequently when I was living in Dubai about the oddities of the place—ridiculous malls, camel races, night golf. We had a kinship. Right before my relationship ended, my grandmother came to Massachusetts, and she, Layla, and I spent a day on Martha's Vineyard. I realized after her suicide that the trip was part of her farewell tour—seeing relatives one last time and visiting a few places she had not yet seen, such as the Vineyard.

That created a painful nexus. My last memory of my grandmother was a beautiful May day I spent with her and Layla on the Vineyard. A week later, Layla bailed and five weeks after that, my grandmother killed herself.

To process the grief, I turned to writing music. I hadn't written a song since the days after another difficult breakup in 1994. In the process, I discovered that all my cassette tapes of songs I had written and recorded dating back to high school had disappeared. It wasn't an extensive collection, but I had written and recorded at least 20 songs and instrumentals, many that I had long forgotten and could not recreate.

I retraced steps through different places I had lived over the years. To this day, I don't know what happened, but my artistic creations were nowhere to be found.

Something that had been a central part of who I was in my teens and twenties—my identity—and my creative output was gone. Another part of me died the moment I realized my music was lost. It added even more fuel to need to travel to the most dangerous places in the world to flirt with death to feel alive. At the same time, given my step-grandmother's suicide, I was contemplating whether I needed to stick around, but I decided I wasn't done yet.

Amid my flailing, I found the America Abroad Media job and dove into as much danger as I could. I was finally on the path to realizing the dream of doing the war journalism I was called to after 9/11. But there was an additional, personal dimension to it. I needed excise demons and fill holes. I was in search of a new tribe.

So, there's the reveal, the backstory of why I was running around chasing death and women in a desperate attempt to process profound grief, loss, and uncertainty about who I was and where I fit in the world. Well, there's one other nugget to the story though that still makes my head spin when I think about it.

The night I met Layla, I was jet lagged as I had just returned from Dubai. At one point while we were at the bar, I decided I was cooked and left to catch the last Red Line train that left Harvard Square around 12:25 am. I entered the station, swiped through the turnstile, and walked up the platform to the train. I was maybe 20 feet from the front car when the door shut, and the train pulled away.

I stood there contemplating my options. I decided that since I was going to have to take a taxi home regardless, I might as well go back to the bar. I rejoined the group, and that led to the beginning of the relationship without which my war correspondent journey never happens. If I get to the station 10 seconds earlier, I make the train and probably never see Layla again. It was a real-life example of the movie *Sliding Doors* and a reminder of how a seemingly insignificant thing—missing a subway train—can change the course of your life. It's like the infamous coin toss that killed Ritchie Valens.

Anyhow, I missed the train, the relationship happened, it ended, and I was searching for a new tribe that made me feel the way I did with Layla. That tribe could be a single person (a new partner) or a community—war correspondents or expats. I was simultaneously chasing both, and as of the summer of 2008, I was making more progress toward the war correspondent tribe.

In less than a year on the job, I had touched down in Serbia, Kosovo, Russia, Dubai, Sudan, Egypt, Taiwan, Miami, Colombia, Chicago, and South Korea—some cool stamps in my passport. I was producing some solid radio stories on interesting subjects. The radio program was improving each month and distribution was increasing.

Most of my friends and family were jealous of my travel. A lot of other journalists were jealous. Yet, it wasn't filling the void. I was having profound and memorable moments, seeing once-in-a-lifetime things, but I was doing most of it alone and in-between trips I was returning to an emptiness and inner sadness despite having a loving girlfriend who I had met right after I moved to D.C. She was a feisty and fun Syrian woman (the closest substitute I could find for Layla), but she was a rebound and destined to end up relationship roadkill.

Now, I did not go full-on Ted Striker and lay all that on Karim—remember him, the guy at the Hard Rock in Beirut? I gave him the Cliff Notes version. I told him that I had been in a serious relationship with a Lebanese-Palestinian woman and was devastated when she left me for a man from her tribe. I explained to Karim how that drove me to want to understand identity struggles in general, but specifically in the Lebanese context. He said he too wondered whether he ultimately needed a Lebanese partner to feel connected and complete—to feel at home.

In a weird way, it was helpful to hear that. It made me feel like I was doomed from the start with Layla and there wasn't anything I could have done to change the outcome. It wasn't my fault. It was cold comfort.

I felt a kinship with Karim. We were having a deep, honest conversation about questions of where we belonged in the world. Who were we? What or who would make us feel at home? Was there a destination for either of us, or was it going to be a constant journey and search?

On one level, I was energized by the conversation because it was the first time I was able to speak candidly about Layla with someone who could understand. On another level, the conversation reminded me how lost I still was. Deep down, I wanted to return to the tribe of Layla. Part of me didn't want to be on the quest I was on—roaming around the world on my own trying to find myself and a new tribe. It was thrilling, but also daunting and kind of terrifying.

And there was the emotional conflict of being in Layla's home turf without her. I needed to be there to try to understand who she was and what happened to me, but I desperately wanted her holding my hand and taking me around the city to show me her world. It was kind of like hanging out with your ex's best friend as a way to try to feel some sort of connection again and to secretly hope it could lead to reconciliation.

Eventually, the discussion got a little too heavy and I had to shake it off like Steve Martin and John Candy in the pillow scene of *Planes, Trains, and Automobiles*. Karim and I returned to talking about Wimbledon and the party scene in Beirut. I finished my beer and wandered outside to grab a taxi.

I returned to the apartment, showered off the day's sweat, and then wandered down the hill to check out Kayan, one of the quieter bars in Gemmayze popular among expats and young Lebanese.

It was just right. It had that brownish hue and intimate feel of a Parisian or Manhattan bistro where you'd expect to run into a Hemingway or Burrows.

I took a seat at the well-stocked bar, ordered an Almaza beer, and took in the scene. It was quiet and only a few of us sat at the bar. As I was alone, I fell into conversation with Mazen the bartender.

He was a bright 21-year-old university student. It didn't take long for the conversation to get deep. I explained that I was a journalist working on a program about Lebanon's fragile, identity-based construction and its unfortunate history as a proxy war battlefield.

Mazen represented a significant demographic in Lebanon. He was a young Shia Muslim who considered himself secular, but he was a strong supporter of Hezbollah. He said that he supported them not for religious reasons but because they were the only ones standing up to Israel for its treatment of Palestinians (like many Lebanese, he had Palestinian relatives) and its conflicts with Lebanon. While he wanted no part of Hezbollah's religious leanings and criticized its often-destabilizing role in domestic politics, he felt the Lebanese government and military were simply too passive regarding Israel.

Mazen made drinks and I drank and snacked on pickled carrot slices. We chatted until it was closing time. I made my way back up the hill to the apartment, settled into bed, and let the sights, sounds, and conversations of the day soak in. My mind raced with joy that I had finally made it to Beirut, fascination with the city and the people I met, and longing to talk about all of it with Layla. I anticipated I would probably have that reaction once I got to Beirut. The question was what to do with it and how to process it. That night, I took the easy way out: avoidance, aka Ambien.

The next morning, after visiting the Ministry of Information to get my government press card, I traveled to Dahiya, the largely

Shia suburb south of Beirut to get press credentials from Lebanon's other "government": Hezbollah.

Their press office was in a dense urban neighborhood. The energy there was edgy and tense. It was a poor area that did not see tourists or strangers other than journalists. Unlike downtown Beirut, in Dahiya all the women wore headscarves. I felt everyone stared at me with an air of suspicion.

I entered an uninviting building and told the young woman at the front desk I wanted permission to speak with Hezbollah personnel and to do reporting in Hezbollah-controlled territory. She directed me to a small grayish-blue waiting room. I sat in a worn-out fabric chair and filled out some paperwork as an ancient TV in the room ran Hezbollah's Al-Manar news station.

I returned to the desk and presented my credentials and explained the nature of my reporting. The people in the office were gruff, but not hostile. The woman at the desk told me to expect a call in a day or two with a response.

I spent the next couple of days taxiing from meeting to meeting to interview academics, analysts, and current and former officials. We spoke about the fragile political structure in Lebanon, born out of a 1943 pact that distributed power and representation proportionally across 18 recognized sects. Since 1989, power has been divided 50-50 between Christians and Muslims, and the allocation of seats in parliament by sect is fixed. Even though the demographics have changed over the years (a decrease in Christians, increase in Shia) the political system remains fixed. As a result, power struggles routinely emerge, and the government often collapses as it did from 2006 to 2008.

After dinner one night, I sat in the apartment with my head again spinning—partly from the Arak (Lebanon's ubiquitous anise liquor), and mostly from the volume of information I had been absorbing about Lebanon and how that made me think about Layla. I knew that the odds were close to zero that I would ever have the chance to talk about it with her, not that I really knew what that would accomplish for either of us. What did I want at that point, just to say, "Hey, look, I've been there and understand it all now?" It wasn't going to change a damn thing for her. It was all on me to process and figure out what to make of it. Yes, deep down I still wanted her back, to put the missing piece of me back into place. But I knew that wasn't going to happen. I drifted off to sleep feeling unresolved.

The next morning, my driver and fixer Khalid picked me up to take me to Saida, a major city south of Beirut. Khalid looked to be in his late 40s and exuded a grizzled wisdom. His glasses-covered eyes peered with the focus and intensity of a bird of prey. He had worked as a driver and fixer for much of the expat press in Lebanon at one time or another. He knew his shit. We rolled south in his yellow Mercedes, and he delivered me to the office of the mayor of Saida.

I interviewed Mayor Abdel-Rahman Bizri about the complex dynamics of Saida, a Sunni city with the largest population of Palestinians in Lebanon and surrounded by Shia and pro-Hezbollah communities. He said their mutual support of the Palestinian cause and disdain for Israel united the different populations.

From the mayor's office, I was taken to the home of a senior Palestinian official who lived near the Ain el-Helweh refugee camp. Sadly, the audio of that interview did not survive, nor do I have clear notes of that interview. He was a significant figure in the Palestinian political hierarchy and might have overseen the camp, but I'm not positive about that.

What I do recall vividly was that he did not believe I was a journalist. "I know I am not speaking with a reporter," he said through the translator, "I know who I am speaking to." He leaned close and gave me a non-wink wink.

He was convinced I was some sort of government agent and so he kept telling me to "deliver messages" to Washington about the plight of the Palestinians. I couldn't disavow him of his belief—as far from reality as it was—but I will never forget sitting across from him in the ramshackle little kitchen of his apartment and how he would lean toward me with a gleam in his eye as he thought he was doing back-channel diplomacy with the United States. I felt cool.

After we wrapped up our conversation, several people escorted me into the camp, the largest of the many in Lebanon. Since I was unable to get into the camp in Darfur, it was my first refugee camp. You never forget your first one.

The most concise description of the camp I can think of is jerry-rigged.

The place looked medieval in the sense that the buildings all had upper floors cantilevered over the ground floors, and most of the upper floors had been built as additions as the camp expanded. All the buildings looked improvised. Built from cinderblocks, some had smooth plaster finishes, others raw blocks.

Streets angled and curved with no rhyme or reason. Alleyways snaked this way and that.

What was most striking was the tangle of electric and phone wires hanging precariously from every façade, overhang, and post. It looked like the NASA experiment in the '90s that exposed spiders to toxic substances to examine the impact on their web-making. The haphazard wiring looked like spiders on a mix of chloral hydrate caffeine. Fortunately, I'm only mildly OCD, so I could tolerate it for a short period, but the visuals of the streets made my head hurt.

Camp residents said they were frustrated by the continued limbo in which they lived. Most still had hopes of returning to a Palestine of some kind. Some just wanted to settle into Lebanon, but that would not be an option since it would upset the sectarian balance. One person I met was a 19-year-old with thin stubble and a strong non-Palestinian accent. As a child his parents sent him to live with relatives in Texas. He said his family and friends in the camp made fun of him for speaking both English and Arabic with a drawl. It fucked with my head to be in a refugee camp in Lebanon talking to a Palestinian who sounded like Mike Nesmith as he described the overwhelming nature of life in the camp—constant noise, crowded streets, people living on top of each other, the heat, and smells ranging from fresh bread to rotting trash.

After an hour of roaming the Terry Gilliam-esque dystopia of the camp and fending off the urge to be depressed by the conditions, Khalid hauled me back to Beirut. I showered and dressed for dinner. I was joining some friends and friends of friends at a nice, hip restaurant in Gemmayze. From one extreme to another—that's Lebanon for you.

All the metaphors, similes, and aphorisms are overused: a study in contrasts, a case of extremes, paradoxical, whatever… But the fact is, Lebanon is a place of amazing contrasts, contradictions, and conundrums (mostly political, but some of the women too—but we'll leave that aside). The country exhibits staggering beauty—mountains, valleys, coastlines (and the women)—but some of the ugliest scenes imaginable—refugee camps, scars of war, extreme poverty.

The dinner was slightly awkward in that my current girlfriend's ex was the organizer. While there wasn't anything awkward between him and me, there were a couple of beautiful women in our party, and under other circumstances I would have tried to spend the night with at least one of them. Alas, I had to maintain appearances.

During dinner, the conversation turned to Lebanese identity, go figure. It was initially lighthearted as everyone made fun of the Druze woman at the table for being a member of a cult. The Druze faith is a bizarre (well, I consider all faiths bizarre) amalgam of Christianity, Islam, Buddhism, and other beliefs including reincarnation. To many people, it is a cult, although several steps shy of Scientology and Tom Cruise shit.

The conversation turned more serious, and I told the tale of Layla. The two Lebanese women in the group nodded knowingly. They both said that they would date any ethnicity but would end up marrying Lebanese men. They said the small Lebanese population in the world and the importance of sectarian identity in Lebanon compelled them to keep within their tribe. It was more cold comfort.

That dinner was another moment when I confronted imposter syndrome. Like in Cairo and Bogota, I was sitting at a table of seasoned hacks who had spent a lot of time living and working in the Middle East. They were part of the Beirut tribe and years ahead of me career-wise. I was trying not to overcompensate for my lack of experience during the conversation. I mean, it was a huge fucking deal for me to be sitting there in Beirut on a reporting trip. It was a "holy shit, I can't believe I'm doing this!" kind of moment, but I had to carry myself at the table as if it were just another day at the office.

Part of the problem for me was that I had started my journalism career at age 32, so I had a decade less experience than others my age. People looked at me and assumed I was on par experience-wise because of my age, so I felt the need to show I knew my shit. That was a factor in why I had been pushing so aggressively in my first year on the job to see shit and collect merit badges so I could fit in and be respected.

That said, that night in Beirut I was certainly more confident than when I was in Darfur or hanging out with the tribes in Cairo and Bogota. I had completed a few more trips, had produced some solid stories, and was learning more tricks of the trade. I was no longer a toddler, but I hadn't hit puberty as a foreign correspondent either.

A couple of days later, Khalid and I set out north to the city of Tripoli—not to be confused with the Libyan capital, which I would visit three years later. The 50-mile drive wound along the coastline to the angsty city. Tripoli has long been a flashpoint in Lebanon, and clashes had been taking place in the city for about a month leading up to my visit, hence I was hoping to see some action.

Tripoli's Jebel Mohsen neighborhood is home to Lebanese Alawites who align with Syria and Hezbollah. Across Syria Street from Jebel Mohsen is the Bab al-Tabbaneh neighborhood, which is home to anti-Syrian Sunnis and some seriously radical Islamists. The two sides fought during the civil war. That section of Lebanon tended to be a microcosm of the regional dynamics. When tensions ratchet up between Lebanon and Syria, or Hezbollah and Israel, clashes often break out along Syria Street in Tripoli.

We met up with an imam from Bab al-Tabbaneh who accompanied us on a driving and walking tour of the street. He pointed out scorched and bombed-out buildings on each side and recounted the recent fighting. Fighters armed with machine guns and RPGs had battled on and off for more than a month, killing a handful of people and wounding dozens.

Shell casings and some bullets from AK-47s lay amongst the trash and debris in the road. Acrid smells of recently burnt buildings wafted through the air.

The imam explained that during the recent fighting each side burned apartment buildings of the other side. As you would expect, each side blamed the other for starting the clashes. The Sunnis painted themselves as poor, simple people just trying to make a living. They said that the Alawites of Jebel Mohsen started the most recent round of violence.

We encountered some of the Sunni fighters. As we spoke, Khalid started getting tense. He said the men were dodgy. They were not making a lot of sense and Khalid had concerns we could end up shot or kidnapped. We were starting to attract more attention and more men were coming out of buildings to gather around us.

We continued down Syria Street until even my nascent Spidey-sense started to feel like we were getting suspicious looks. The recent clashes had not come to a clear or decisive end and tensions were still high.

Deep down I was hoping for some "bang bang." I mean, I didn't visit one of the most dangerous places in the country for no reason. I was hoping for some action to make my radio story more compelling, and to earn the firefight merit badge.

Alas, I listened to Khalid and (to a lesser extent) my gut, which both said we had overstayed our welcome on the street and should get out of town. As much as I was always hoping for action for the experience and to make my stories more compelling, I really did not want to end up with a black hood over my head in the trunk of an old Mercedes. We piled into Khalid's car and made our way out of Tripoli as the sun began to set.

The next day, I was off to Syria. The 70-mile drive to Damascus climbed over the mountains and through the Beqaa valley, home to the paradoxical mix of vineyards and Hezbollah supporters, in other words, acetic and ascetic. From there, it was through Arizona-like terrain until the city limits of Damascus. Being stuck in a car for a couple of hours with a driver who did not speak English provided quiet time.

I wish I could say I had some sort of breakthrough. I didn't. It was more of the same. I was largely doing the work I wanted to be doing. I was traveling the world to eye-opening places and seeing sometimes the best but often the worst of humanity. I was seeking one of two things: a new Layla or a full-time overseas job where I could become an official member of a tribe. Of course, I wanted both, but I figured that one or the other would quiet my mind and soul for a while. I had no control over whether or when I would meet a new partner, but I had some control over the job. I had to focus on doing impactful reporting and showing that I knew what I was doing to open doors. Reporting from Syria wasn't going to hurt as it was difficult for journalists to get in, and I was lucky to have the right connections. It was another merit badge.

We reached the border and had no problems exiting the Lebanese side. Entering Syria took 30 minutes as the border officers didn't believe my visa was real and I had to call my embassy contact in D.C. to get someone in Damascus call the border goons and talk them off the ledge. That said, it would have been disappointing and inauthentic if there wasn't a minor crisis at the border and the possibility of not making it into Syria.

I spent the week running around doing a mix of tourism and journalism. I hit the essentials: the Old City, Ummayad Mosque, and the ruins in Bosra and Palmyra, the latter I'm glad I was able to see before ISIS occupied it and ruined a lot of the ruins.

My fixer and I bounced around the city meeting with political analysts, current and past government officials, and some locals to discuss the complex nature of relations between Syria and Lebanon. Wassim was a young, sharp, chain-smoking journalist who knew how to walk the line between doing independent reporting, and not pissing off Big Brother.

As we went from taxis to cafes to offices, there was one constant: smoke. I was aware going in that Syria was one of the heavier smoking countries in the region, but holy fuck I was not prepared for the constant haze of cigarette smoke.

I easily smoked two packs a day passively. Taxi drivers smoked. Restaurant employees smoked. People smoked in elevators. People smoked while in line at shops to buy cigarettes. Interviewees would smoke as I talked with them. I felt like and smelled like a fucking ashtray the whole time I was in Damascus. It would have been comical if it weren't so sickening to a non-smoker. I soldiered on with my work, watering eyes and all.

At some point amid our scurrying between meetings, Wassim received a phone call. It was the principal's office, aka the *mukhabarat* or security services. Something we did tripped their radar and we had to make an appearance.

I had expected a run in given Syria's notoriously tight grip on media and speech. While I was operating above board with the proper visa and was making no attempt to sneak around or speak with any unauthorized individuals, I knew at some point that an official would try to put the fear of God into me and remind me that I was on a short leash.

Wassim and I dutifully appeared at the ministry of information and entered the office of a stern but pretty woman in maybe her early 30s. We sat down and she delivered us a warning.

For the life of me, I can't remember what alleged foul we committed. It was most likely a minor offense like failing to notify the Ministry of Information ahead of time about some of the people we were interviewing or otherwise failing to get "permission" for something. It was not Wassim's first offense, and like all local journalists, he was on a first-name basis with the ministry and security personnel.

We took our wrist slap and left. Of course, I was feeling proud of earning another merit badge for getting called in for a scolding by the Syrian thought police. Granted, in Syria it was more of an achievement to complete a reporting trip without a call to the principal's office, but I still felt it added to my street cred to have that box checked.

And with that, it was time to return to Beirut. I completed my last two interviews in the city and then finessed an invitation to the grand reopening of the Hotel Riviera's beach club.

The party was packed with gorgeous women dressed to the nines, men ranging from studly to slovenly, loud music, and copious amounts of alcohol. I interviewed the overly made-up marketing director at the party, and she gave a vivid description of the importance of partying in Beirut and how for the previous two years the scene had been subdued by the political crisis and fears of a return to conflict. The party was a kind of "coming back out" event for the city and a return to form.

Sadly, for me, I was unable to fully immerse myself in the party as I had to catch a 2 a.m. flight back home. So, I enjoyed as much eye candy as I could and started thinking about the next chance I would get to party in Beirut.

After I returned home and slowed down, I dug in trying to process everything. For a year I had been yearning to get to Lebanon to help me understand the devastating end of my relationship and to find some sort of closure. Instead, I felt more conflicted after the trip.

I came away with a deeper understanding of the country and its identities. I understood how the socio-political system caused people to develop a sectarian identity as strong, if not sometimes stronger, than their national identity.

I saw and felt the deep need to be with those of your tribe—

especially when you are removed from it by living outside of Lebanon. In that regard, I saw that it was inevitable that Layla was going to leave me as soon as she encountered a viable candidate from her tribe.

On an intellectual level, I could rationalize that I was doomed from the start and never had a fighting chance in that relationship. The flip side was I felt more connected to Layla and felt like we had much more of a foundation to build something together. We didn't share the same identity or tribe, but we shared an understanding of the need for it and how it drove us, and with that we could have empathized with each other and formed our own tribe out of that shared understanding.

I was better able to understand my own struggles and how in so many chapters of my life I was driven by a quest for tribe without being fully aware of it. I was always drawn to and happiest in "tribal" settings like summer camp, my small-group trip to Denmark, my fraternity, the late-night crowd of musicians and service industry people in Boston, or my grad school classmates.

After Lebanon, I was seeing much more clearly that we are all inherently tribal. We all define it differently, but it is simply human nature to seek kindred spirits and fellow travelers. We crave that commonality and safety. Obviously, there are plenty of downsides to tribalism (as evidenced by U.S. and global politics in recent years), but it's in our DNA.

Bottom line, I was just as broken after the trip as before, but I had a better understanding why I was broken. So, I was still stuck with a gaping soul wound and would have to find something or someone else to fill it. Until I found the latter, the former was going to be chasing death around the world in search of a tribe.

Chapter Four
Stumbling Around Serbia

October 2007

BELGRADE, Serbia — A gruff 50-something taxi driver with buzzed hair approached me as I exited Belgrade airport. He spoke solid English and seemed to have a low Travis Bickle quotient. We negotiated a bit over the rate, and I decided to take a chance with him.

As soon as I got in the car, he turned to me and said, "CIA?" Given the history between Serbia and the United States, it was no surprise that Serbs assumed a single American man of military age wearing cargo pants and carrying technical-looking luggage was an operative.

I told the driver that I was a journalist and was in town to report on the soft-power conflict between Russia and the United States in the region. In particular, I was exploring how Russia was siding with Serbia in opposing Kosovo's imminent independence bid that the United States supported.

America Abroad was producing a show on the deteriorating relationship between Russia and the United States. I had chosen Serbia and Kosovo as the subject of my segment because it was the headiest destination I could come up with to show a foreign policy standoff between the two powers.

I was hoping to earn badass points for traveling to a rough neighborhood even though it was long past the heady days when the real correspondents roamed around the Balkans covering the brutal wars. I knew that serious journalists would be unimpressed by the fact I was traveling to Serbia and Kosovo in 2007, but I hoped the average person back home would think it was a big deal.

A little Ferris Bueller fourth wall break here. Serbia was my first trip for *America Abroad*, so everything in this chapter took place before the events of the previous chapters. Even though it was my first trip, I didn't feel it was the right starting point for the narrative. I contemplated cutting it altogether, but Putin's invasion of Ukraine changed that. My 2007 reporting on the chilling relationship between Russia and the United States provides some context for what has played out in Ukraine. Back to the story.

The taxi driver was unconvinced by my explanation of why I was in Serbia. Regardless, he apparently didn't care if I was CIA and continued talking candidly.

He said he was tired—tired of the years of conflict and political and economic struggles and he just wanted the problem to go away. He said Serbia should just let Kosovo go to get things over with, even though he and everyone he knew felt that in principle Kosovo should remain Serbian.

A quick journalism hack: taxi drivers are fantastic sources. I mean, what do they do all day? They drive around listening to the radio and talking to people from all walks of life. They have their fingers on the pulse of a society. Two other great sources of atmospherics are barbers and bartenders. A lot of reporters will get a haircut as soon as they arrive in a new country. Hence, I was chatting up the driver to get everything I could out of him to help me get my bearings on the mood in Serbia and where people's heads were.

We pulled up to the dumpy Union Hotel. I paid the driver the agreed price and he handed me his card. I survived my first taxi ride as a parachuting international journalist.

I checked in, dropped my bags, and commenced the obligatory

walkabout to get the feel for the city. The main pedestrian street was near my hotel. It was bustling with the typical assortment of shops, cafes, vendors, and people doing what they do on temperate Saturday afternoons in a European city.

The only European cities I had visited were London, Paris, Rome, Copenhagen, and a couple of other cities in Denmark. Belgrade was none of them. While it had some ornamental buildings that exuded a sense of age and history, it lacked the grandeur of the major European cities. Many of the buildings were bland, socialist designs covered in wart-like air-conditioning fans. A lot of the structures were simply tired with worn facades coated with soot.

The people wore dark colors with that modern slim "European" look. I quickly noticed that the women were generally tall and fit with dark features and piercing eyes like Stana Katic, Claudia Black, or Cote de Pablo—basically my kryptonite. However, most of them were also walking arm in arm with tall, fit men, meaning I was of no interest to the women.

I wandered around in a mild daze looking at all the women. Their features and coloring reminded me of Layla. It was like Mr. Smith in *The Matrix*: she was everywhere I looked. It stung.

I felt alone despite being in a crowded city. I was finally doing what I had been chasing since 9/11 and the invasion of Afghanistan—I was traveling the world, exploring weird places, and producing radio stories about it. Yet, I felt an emptiness, an isolation. As much as I wanted that life, that experience, I was only there because a door to a different life had slammed in my face in summer 2007 when Layla bailed. I kept trying to shake it off and get back into the moment, to feel energized by the adventure of exploring a place not many Americans visited. However, all the tall, dark, and beautiful women just gnawed at my wounds.

That night I wandered my way into a tiny bar across the street from the towering Cathedral of St. Sava. The bar was dark and the music way too loud. A black-and-white photo of Al Pacino hung behind the bar and an electronic dartboard flashed away on the far wall.

I ordered a Jelen Pivo beer and quickly fell into conversation with the five locals there—one of whom was a tall, dark, and beautiful woman who was of course there with her husband—who never stopped eyeing me suspiciously (can't say I blamed him). We talked politics—Serbian, U.S., Russian, and European—for about four hours. The gist: Serbs were frustrated by the U.S. involvement in the status of Kosovo, frustrated by U.S. foreign policy in general, reluctantly accepting of Russian support in the Kosovo negotiations—people liked having an ally but didn't trust Russia's motives—and just tired of all of it.

The couple put me on the spot to explain U.S. foreign policy during the Balkan wars. While I had done a little research before the trip, I was hardly an expert. All the activity in the Balkans took place during my twenties when I was focused on music, motorcycles, street hockey, and women (well, I'm still focused on those things). I was oblivious to international affairs in my twenties. If someone had floated the idea of being a foreign correspondent, I would have laughed. After all, I got a D in my only international relations class in college. Life lesson—never say never, unless you're Sean Connery, in which case cut your losses with *Diamonds are Forever*.

I bluffed my way through conversation until 5 a.m. when the bartender fell asleep on the bar. Time to go.

The next day, I wandered out to the pedestrian street and Kalemegdan Park. Along the way I stopped at a store to buy some camouflage.

I was clearly sticking out as American and more than once I had been asked if I was a spy. So, I found a clothing store and picked out a Scandinavian-style jacket—one of those dark grey, slim-fit military-looking (M-65 style) things so common in Europe that no one gives a second look to anyone wearing one. I figured it might help me blend in.

I continued to Kalemegdan. The park and fortress stand on a point of the city overlooking the junction of the Sava and Danube Rivers. The sprawling grounds include gardens, monuments, fountains, a Military Museum, observation posts along the fortress perimeter, and tennis courts in what used to be a section of the moat.

I started doing the most awkward and uncomfortable form of journalism there is—approaching strangers, shoving a microphone in their faces, and asking them politically sensitive questions. Due to my extremely small travel budget and minimal experience reporting in foreign countries, I had not hired a fixer. So, I did not have a local to help soften my approach to strangers in a country where Americans were at best tolerated and at worst loathed.

I approached a few people, most of whom had no desire to say anything on the record to a sketchy American. I ended up chatting with a popcorn vendor who spoke a little English. He introduced me to a 15-year-old boy who spoke English and the kid offered to walk around the park with me and translate—a free fixer.

One woman we interviewed was a 19-year-old Serb from Pristina—the capital of Kosovo. The short, pretty woman with blonde-dyed hair (a rarity in Belgrade) began to tear up when she said she doubted she would ever be able to go home to the place she was born once Kosovo was an independent country. From her perspective, Serbs would not be welcome in an independent Kosovo and her family would have to leave their homes and move north to live in Serbia.

On a human level, I was moved by her emotion and her plight—she faced a life-altering circumstance. However, my cynical journalist brain was really thinking, "yes, this is going to be a powerful bit of radio." Any journalist who claims they don't experience that duality on the job is selling something.

Eventually, my free fixer had to go home for dinner, and I packed up my kit for the day. I felt like I had some decent material and some raw perspectives. Not a bad start.

The next morning, I hopped a cab to the bus station and purchased a ticket for the 9:30 a.m. bus to Mitrovica, Kosovo.

Mitrovica was, and is, a divided city in Kosovo. The Ibar River splits the city between north and south. The north is Serbian even though the entire city is within Kosovo. The south is Albanian.

Mitrovica was a hot spot during the 1999 Kosovo war and most of the Serbs living south of the river fled to the north. NATO Kosovo Force (KFOR) peacekeepers deployed to Mitrovica along with UN police.

Deadly ethnic clashes continued to break out after the war. After Kosovo declared independence in 2008, things heated up as there was a significant Serbian population in northern Kosovo, and the Serbs did not recognize Kosovo as an independent nation. It was all rather predictable and could have been avoided had everyone agreed to draw the borders such that the Serbs in Kosovo would not end up as an ethnic minority in an independent Kosovo. Of course, others would argue it could have been avoided by keeping Kosovo as part of Serbia. Easier said than done.

The bridge in Mitrovica across the river was my objective and would be the opening scene and metaphor in my story. My other objective of course was to visit a place with a history of violence to help build my street cred.

I boarded the bus, which was no older than the late '80s, and seemed solid, initially. However, under braking, there was a horrendous rattle and shuddering from the rear end that had me wondering how long it would be before the axle would fall off in the middle of the road. None of the passengers spoke English, and several emitted aromas I could not identify for the life of me. It was authentic.

After nearly seven hours, the bus rolled into Mitrovica. I got off at what looked like the main drag in town. I didn't think to arrange for a fixer or a local contact who could serve as a guide or ambassador for me. I was improvising. I was an idiot.

I wandered up the street looking for a café or bar where I could talk with people. I walked into a pub and the bartender said he was willing to talk but couldn't as he was working alone and too busy. He told me my best bet was to head down the street to the UN police office and ask them for suggestions.

I casually sauntered into the police station carrying my two suspicious looking bags and told them I was a journalist looking for people in town I could interview about Russia. I was either telling the truth or was a real-life Maxwell Smart—or both. Either way, the officer gave me the hairy eyeball and directed me to the Dolce Vita Café next to the bridge.

I walked back through town and into the café. I asked a few people if they wanted to talk. One athletic-looking 18-year-old named Zoran volunteered. He was passionate about Serbian territorial integrity and very concerned about the prospects for the future in Mitrovica. He said he was afraid to cross the bridge to the Albanian side because he was convinced he'd be assaulted. I was of course saying to myself, "That's a money quote."

He described himself as a regular teenager who loved everything that cool guys love. He said he hated politics. He just wanted Serbia to keep its land and he was a fan of Vladimir Putin because he was standing behind Serbia. "Only Putin understand us," he said, "I love him, he's so strong."

I could see how visceral it was for him. In his eyes, the international community was seeking to divide Serbia and take a big chunk of the country. Should Kosovo become independent, the border would be far to the north of Mitrovica, meaning the whole city would be part of Kosovo and if Zoran wanted to stay in his hometown, he'd end up living as a minority in Kosovo. Hence, his passion for Putin. There he was pouring his heart out and getting emotional over a potentially life-changing political situation, and I was giddy because he was giving me great material.

To be fair to myself, I was there to tell an important story and make the audience aware of some serious shit playing out in a place most were unfamiliar with, so of course I wanted compelling material to make them pay attention and understand the stakes. Of course, I also wanted compelling material so my boss and other journalists would take notice. I mean, who wants to do mediocre work in any profession? Admittedly, it is a weird duality to feel kind of gleeful when you hear someone expressing tremendous pain and angst. It is a part of the job that I was just learning, and it would only grow more complicated and affect me in many ways in the coming years.

After we chatted, I stepped out into the chilly fall air and looked at the Mitrovica bridge. To this day, people refer to the bridge as one that divides, rather than connects, two communities. Serbs backed by Russia on one side, and Albanians backed by the United States on the other. It was journalistic poetry.

I spent the rest of the afternoon strolling back and forth across the bridge in the on-and-off rain in a feckless search for UN or NATO people I could interview. People kept directing me to other people to talk to get permission to conduct interviews, and I was going in circles getting the Heisman everywhere I went.

It was sinking in that I had been half-assed in my prep work. I hadn't hired a fixer who would have done the legwork and arranged the necessary contacts and permissions ahead of my arrival in Mitrovica. I naïvely assumed I could show up in a divided town under the control of a NATO peacekeeping force and speak to people on the spot about sensitive matters. Sometimes ambush tactics are the best approach in journalism, but I didn't have the experience at that point to know one way or another. I was just bull-in-the-china-shop-ing my way along, and it wasn't paying off—shocking.

It was getting dark, and the rain wasn't fucking around anymore. I asked some UN folks to help me find a taxi to Pristina. Eventually, a taxi showed up that the UN guys said would be safe. The driver didn't speak any English, and of course I had to pee as soon as we hit the road.

Fortunately, the ride only took about 45 minutes. We arrived at the Grand Pristina Hotel. The establishment was impressive in size and scale, if not appearance. The lobby wasn't bad looking, and the elevators were quite modern. My room, however, hadn't been updated since the '70s, but it had a certain modernist, yet retro, panache.

It had the vibe of spook central and oozed Cold War charm. Talk about a place where "if the walls could talk." Of course, the walls were probably still listening and the place crawling with spooks and agents of all kinds, and even if not, everyone figured it was. I was starting to enjoy the feeling of everyone assuming I was a spy.

The next morning, I visited the Russian chancery to interview Russia's top diplomat in Kosovo, Andrei Dronov. The middle-aged Russian was quite personable, well spoken, and candid about Russia's interests. We chatted for about 30 minutes, and by the end of the conversation it was clear to me that Russia saw itself as a player again and that it would use all international norms and bodies to assert itself on the world stage. For example, if Kosovo declared independence without agreement from Belgrade, Russia would view that as a violation of Serbian sovereignty and international law that could serve as a demonstration effect for pro-Russian enclaves in Georgia, Ukraine, or other former Soviet states to declare independence and align with Russia. And guess what, that's exactly what played out in the 15 years since that conversation.

After the interview, I returned to the hotel, checked out, and walked across the street to the University of Kosovo. Students roamed the campus exuding a relaxed and friendly vibe—a different sensation than the streets in Belgrade. The women were equally attractive as those in Belgrade with long brunette hair (although more curly hair than in Belgrade), dark eyes, and angular facial features like Layla. More paper cuts doused with lemon.

Students I interviewed expressed similar thoughts—Russia was not really concerned about Kosovo. It was simply an opportunity for Putin—suffering from geopolitical penis envy (my words)—to thump his chest in front of the west and declare that Russia was a world power again. The students were unanimously happy to have U.S. support. It was sadly refreshing to find a place in the world in 2007 where people were happy with U.S. foreign policy.

I walked back to the main drag and hopped a taxi back to Mitrovica. I interviewed a UN official who was originally from Hungary and had been in and out of Kosovo for years. We stood in the middle of the bridge as the bespectacled bureaucrat explained the standoff between Russia and the United States that metaphorically played out on the bridge. I stood there pleased with myself as he described the setting and gave me what I thought was a vivid opening scene to my story.

To kill time before catching the bus back to Belgrade, I wandered up a hill in North Mitrovica to check out an Orthodox church. As I stood next to the church looking south, I could hear the call to prayer in the distance. I spotted a mosque in the center of South Mitrovica, and I stood there absorbed in the contrast. It was powerful on a variety of levels—the church on the hill looking across the river to the Muslim side of the divided city. The notion of people living on opposite sides of a 50-foot-wide river having such animosity toward each other had been purely academic to me until that moment. I had not been anywhere in the world where there was such a stark divide and hostilities going back centuries.

Mitrovica was my introduction to the nature of "the shit." It was the first of countless times I would see and experience that kind of ethnic and religious divide that led to conflict as I would travel over the coming years to places including Lebanon, Israel, Iraq, Northern Ireland, and Cyprus where simply crossing the street (perhaps through razor wire and checkpoints) could transport you across historic battle lines. That moment in Mitrovica was the second step in my nascent journey into understanding ethnic and tribal identity politics in the world. A journey launched by having my heart broken by a woman who grew up living those internal and external conflicts.

I walked back down the hill to a row of buses on the north side and waited for the 5 p.m. bus. By 5:20, I realized there was no 5 p.m. bus to Belgrade. I couldn't determine whether I had misread the schedule—likely—or whether the scheduled bus simply didn't show—equally likely.

I had two options, find a place to crash for the night and try the bus the following day, or find a cab willing to drive 250 miles to Belgrade. I located a group of taxis and explained to the ruffled old men smoking and chatting that I needed a ride to Belgrade. Most threw up their hands making gestures to the effect of, "are you nuts?" Several of them chatted and then one indicated he was willing. Of course, he spoke no English. One of the other drivers helped me negotiate a 140 euro fare and explained to my driver the name of my hotel in Belgrade.

We set off in his 20-year-old maroon Mercedes sedan and I sat in the passenger seat transcribing interviews on my laptop. The driver, who was the Serbian version of Jim Ignatowski with his wild hair, floppy jowls, and quirky expressions, would periodically motion to me to put my electronic gear away as we passed checkpoints.

The drive languished. Since we couldn't talk, I tried to get as much work done as I could, but it was difficult as my eyes became progressively more irritated by the driver's chain smoking. About four hours or so into the drive, Jim started running out of steam. He began nodding a bit and weaving on the road. I tried to ignore it and trust that he was in control. But it continued and I started to panic. Was this stranger going to veer off the road and kill us both? My pulse started racing. Just then, he nodded and drifted toward the side of the road. The only thing I could think to do was to yell "coffee!" He jerked his head up, nodded, and made an Ignatowski-like grunt.

He pulled into a small plaza and downed a cup of coffee and inhaled a couple of cigarettes. After the coffee break, he managed to stay awake for a while, but then started nodding off and weaving again, driving my testicles up into my armpits in fear. I was barely keeping it together. I was trying to decide whether to offer to drive or ask him to pull over and let me out. It seemed like standing alone alongside a dark highway in the middle of nowhere in Serbia was safer than continuing with him.

Instead, I periodically spoke loudly as if I were trying to have a conversation, but I just needed to wake him up. We proceeded that way until we reached Belgrade. He had never driven there before and had no clue where to go. Fortunately, he had the sense to pull over at a taxi stand and ask the drivers there how to get to my hotel. I decided I was better off paying him there and hopping in one of the other cabs.

I unclenched, peeled my fingernails from the seat of the Mercedes, and got out of the car with panic adrenaline surging through me. I hopped in the Belgrade taxi and the driver immediately asked me if I was FBI as we made our way to my hotel. I told him I was CIA. Why not give the people what they want?

My last night in Serbia I went out to dinner with a grad school classmate. We went to a little shack clinging to the hillside above the Danube. Inside was dark, uneven wood-plank construction with aging fishing nets hanging from the walls and ceiling. The tiny restaurant was packed with about 30 people, including a pair of musicians playing acoustic guitars and alternating between Serbian folk music and classic western pop and rock.

We ate a couple of different dishes made from fish caught in the river that day. I thought the food was great, but it would turn out not to like me very much.

The next morning, I woke up feeling a little off. That's never a good thing in general, but especially when you have to fly. I broke out the Cipro. I then called the taxi driver who had taken me from the airport into Belgrade and asked him if he could take me to the airport and give me a bit of a driving tour along the way.

He took me around the city and pointed out all the destroyed buildings from the U.S.-led bombing campaign in 1999. Talk about open wounds. Some of the buildings were in the center of the city and were barely standing. It was the first time I had seen in person the impact of military weaponry. It was eerie to see bombed-out buildings in an otherwise peaceful and "normal" city.

We continued to the outskirts of the city so I could see the Chinese embassy that the United States "accidentally" bombed (China of course accused the United States of deliberately hitting the facility). The building, surrounded by a black metal fence and with its windows blown out, stood like a beige ghost in an abandoned neighborhood. It was a haunting monument to history.

We continued to the airport. I paid and thanked the driver who was still convinced I was CIA. It felt kind of cool to be accused of being a spy. It made me feel like I was a real foreign correspondent and that I was in the game.

Unfortunately, my trip to Serbia didn't end with my flight out of the country. The fish bacteria tagged along. A week or so after I returned to D.C. the bacteria gained the upper hand and sent me to the ER for a course of IV fluids and antibiotics. While going to the hospital was not a priority international journalism merit badge to earn, I got that one out of the way on my first trip.

Chapter Five
Getting Embed in Iraq

August 2008

KUWAIT — The inside of a C-130 looks like an unfinished basement—wires, cables, hydraulic lines running everywhere, and exposed metal framework throughout. It kind of makes you think twice about flying—if you got on a commercial jet and saw how much mechanical, electrical, and hydraulic crap there was, you'd panic about how many things could possibly break or go wrong and run screaming for a train. Seriously, there are so many wires, cables, hoses, metal thingies—thingies that could be years beyond their useful life or repaired with chewing gum or... Well, let's not go down that road. Suffice to say, the inside of a C-130 is primitive and chaotic looking.

The engines ramped up to a thunderous roar, and the plane lurched forward. You learn a quick physics lesson during takeoff in a C-130. Since you are sitting in seats running parallel to the direction of travel, the cargo netting serving as your seat back is useless. The force of acceleration throws you sideways and you must reach above and behind you to grab the netting to hold yourself upright.

The climb out of Kuwait was long and steady, but the flight was surprisingly smooth. In addition to the 72 of us sitting in the cargo area and the two pallets of bags, there were two crewmen in the back. Each one was seated on a wooden perch hanging from straps attached to the framework—they looked like parakeets in a cage. During the flight the two sat there and joked with each other.

I fell into a light doze for the first two-thirds of the flight. Then, there was a dramatic change in the disposition of the plane. I felt G-forces, but my senses were so wonky because of sitting sideways and not being about to see out the windows that I couldn't tell exactly what direction we were banking. I opened my eyes and got a small dose of reality.

The airmen who had been casually sitting on the perches all flight were now wearing flak jackets and strapped into harnesses. They were facing out the windows and wearing night-vision goggles. They had turned into spotters looking for hostile threats as we approached Baghdad.

Then, the descent got real. It was the steep, corkscrewing approach you've no doubt heard about. It never quite felt like the sensation of the initial drop of a roller coaster, but it was jarring. We went through a few steep declines, corkscrewing merrily away (I kept thinking about *The In-Laws*: "serpentine, serpentine!"). A couple of times I could feel blood rushing from my head in directions I couldn't quite determine, and I got slightly dizzy. At one point we banked so heavily that I could see the lights of the city below rush past the window—I could swear we were past the point of being perpendicular to the ground in that turn. In one sense it was all somewhat fun—but given the reason why we were flying so aggressively, that dampened some of the enjoyment.

Then there was the landing. There was no doubt, not the slightest question whatsoever when we hit the ground. It was like a lion hitting a gazelle—swift, strong, and decisive. That landing made even the roughest commercial landing I had experienced feel like a feather landing on a pool of water. I sat and did a Terminator-like internal system check to make sure all my spinal discs were still intact.

With that, I was on the ground in Baghdad—finally the chance to experience the shit.

America Abroad was producing a program about post-conflict stabilization and reconstruction. One of the vehicles the United States had developed to carry out stabilization work in Iraq and Afghanistan was the Provincial Reconstruction Team (PRT). They were interagency teams of military personnel with State Department and USAID staff who were co-located in provinces and districts in Iraq and Afghanistan. Their mandate was to work with local communities to develop and construct projects that would improve security and stability and enhance the legitimacy of local and national governments. Fascinating topic and much has been written over the years about the PRT model and how effective they were or weren't. That's for another book. The important thing here is that I had an excuse to travel to Iraq to embed with the military and finally get my ass into a war zone.

Being my first embed, I was not fully prepared for the volume of paperwork and amount of time needed to apply for, negotiate over, and get approved for an embed. Fortunately, I had a well-placed grad school classmate, LTC Rudy Burwell, who was the point person in the U.S. Army's media office in Baghdad. While Rudy was getting ready to rotate out, he was able to grease the skids.

Still, I had to fill out applications, provide multiple letters from my media organization, submit all manner of identification, and explain in detail my proposed story and why I should be granted an embed. Applying for a mortgage was less complicated. Well, given that was right before the housing crash, maybe that's not the best comparison since a pulse was all that was needed to get a mortgage then, and I'm pretty sure you could get a waiver of that requirement too.

Anyhow, I spent weeks submitting the required materials and emailing back and forth with Baghdad to get everything approved. Part of the challenge was that to embed, you had to find a unit willing and able to take you in during your proposed timeframe. Of course, I wanted to embed with a PRT in one of the dangerous places like Fallujah or Anbar. Let's face it, the PRT story was soft—it was focused on civil affairs, not combat activities. I wanted to use the story as a vehicle to get as close to combat and finally see the scary shit.

The only PRT that could host me during my time window was in Baghdad and based at the massive Victory Base Complex. It was about as safe as you could get in Iraq at the time. I finally got to do an embed in Iraq and it was one with training wheels and floaties.

Still, it would get me into the country. I went about getting body armor and all the kit I would need for the trip. I won't lie, I was psyched to finally need body armor. As boxes arrived at the office I was like a little kid in the weeks before Christmas. I was finally going to join the club of journalists who reported in Iraq. Yes, it was five years after the start of the war, and the worst of the violence had passed by the time I was going to touch down, but I was finally getting into the game.

With all my approvals, documents, and kit organized, I set out for Baghdad. As you can guess, given my inexperience, there was going to be something I didn't get properly sorted out before the trip. It was my military flights.

As I would learn, navigating the obscure and unnecessarily confusing world of military transportation is an art. The short of it is, if you book properly in advance, you can get reserved seats and a confirmed day if not flight time. If you don't book properly in advance, you are stuck in a particular hell called Space Available (Space-A), which is the military equivalent of standby, and that can result in days of waiting for a seat. Guess which category I fell into…

After a commercial flight from D.C. to Kuwait, I entered the arrival hall and quickly found my Army handler. We piled into a dusty SUV and set off for Camp Ali al-Salim, which was basically a giant bus station in the middle of the desert. Soldiers, contractors, and journalists would hang out there while waiting for seats on C-130s or C-17s to fly into Iraq or Afghanistan.

The drive took about 45 minutes and I saw about as much as there was to see in Kuwait—some houses along the highway, and then desert. Kuwait is easily the least interesting Gulf country.

We arrived at the camp, and the sergeant gave me the run-down of all the things I needed to do to get my ass on a plane to Baghdad. I hit the mess hall for dinner, sat in the media transit office for a while doing work, and then crashed early.

I had a wonderful night trying to sleep in the standard eight-bunk tent where the lights stayed on, and people were transiting in and out all through the night. Even though I took an Ambien, I managed only four hours of restless sleep. Having to get up to pee was fun—climb off the top bunk, put on shoes, and walk out of the tent in the hot night air to one of the lovely, aromatic latrines with an internal temperature of about 110F. It was the kind of situation that made you get good and desperate to go before you decided to get up and go through all the hassle. I'll spare you a detailed description of the smell of the hot latrines but suffice to say it was a scent you do not forget.

Like many things the military did, the Space-A flight process was complicated, opaque, and a complete fucking pain in the ass. You strolled into the "terminal" tent and signed up with the Air Force to request a seat. Then, you'd show up to roll calls at 6:30 a.m. and 8 p.m. and sit around in the giant bus-station-like tent waiting to get called for a flight. When I signed up, I was number 60 on the list. The first day I was at the camp, there were four flights going to Baghdad with five seats available in all.

You had to be prepared to spend a lot of time sitting in uncomfortable seats in the giant, dark tent full of tired and cranky soldiers and contractors. The other side of that coin was the fact that time spent there meant less time on the ground in Iraq since I had a firm deadline to get back to D.C.

I endured two days of sitting through roll calls and at one point loading onto a plane only to get off and start the process over again due to a mechanical problem. Finally, I got on a flight to Baghdad.

I got off the plane at Baghdad International Airport and entered the military terminal to request a helicopter flight to Landing

Zone Washington in the Green Zone. Fortunately, I only had to wait an hour before they called my name.

I threw on my gear, lined up, and walked out to the landing strip. Two Black Hawks approached. They landed, people off-loaded, and then we were escorted on board. I strapped in trying to look like I was a master of the five-point seatbelts and not give away that it was my first time in a military helicopter. "First time in a limo, doctor?" "First time in a limo this small…"

We took off with the other bird following along, and we flew in a path I certainly couldn't follow in the dark. It seemed like we went in a big circle and landed almost where we started (I later realized that was pretty much the case). Baghdad at night was an unremarkable sight—at least the area we covered. A few lights here and there, no discernible landmarks or characteristics—but what was I expecting anyhow, Paris?

I entered the trailer at LZ Washington, and one of the staffers there called the press center to have someone pick me up. About 10 minutes later a specialist arrived and drove me to the office—it was approaching 1 a.m. and the streets of the Green Zone were empty, and frankly rather haunting. Only a few security personnel were out, and otherwise it looked the deserted setting of a zombie film.

We entered the press center checkpoint. I went through security (all the security workers there were contractors from Peru). The lieutenant on duty showed me to the bunks in the media lounge, I took a quick shower, checked email, and crashed.

The next morning, I received my press credentials after being fingerprinted and retinal scanned—yes "retinal" not the other r-word, but I thought that was a possibility too. I spent the day trying to contact State Department personnel, attending a press conference about the developments of the Iraqi Navy (I was picturing a bunch of guys wearing floaties in pedal boats), and otherwise trying to be productive while waiting for my helicopter flight to Camp Liberty.

While waiting in the trailer for my flight, a mild bit of chaos ensued. Someone came in saying that a group of Georgian soldiers would be scrambling through to get on a flight since they were being redeployed back to Georgia to deal with a little conflict with Russia (the first shoe dropping in the wake of Kosovo's independence as discussed in the previous chapter).

A few minutes later, two Georgian soldiers entered the trailer along with a Georgian priest. He was in full Orthodox attire—black robe, a funny hat, gold jewelry, long grey beard, and of course a desert camouflage flak jacket. They were in and out of the trailer too quickly for me to process the scene and dig out my camera to take a picture. Suffice to say, the image of an Orthodox priest in religious vestments and body armor waddling onto a Black Hawk is forever etched in my mind.

Eventually, they called my flight, and I boarded the helo. The flight was relatively short—7 to 8 minutes—and then I got off at Landing Zone Liberty. When I got off, I realized I had no idea where I was going or how I was getting there.

I went into the trailer to ask what was going on and no one knew anything. I just assumed that on an embed there would be people waiting for me and holding my hand at each stop.

I dug out some papers, made a couple of calls on the base phone, and learned that a sergeant was going to pick me up, but apparently the people in the embed office didn't bother to give me a copy of my transit orders or any other information about my point of contact.

I finally found the sergeant who drove me to Camp Liberty—home away from home for the 2nd Brigade Combat Team of the 101st Airborne Division. He checked me in, dropped off my stuff in my trailer, and we hit the dining facility (DFAC) for dinner.

It was an impressive facility—much larger and better stocked with food than the DFAC at the dump of a base in Kuwait. The walls were adorned with all kinds of Americana—mostly '50s era. The food was reasonable, although I was glad I was only going to have to live with it for five days rather than 15 months.

The next morning, I hounded the public affairs team about setting up a visit to Fallujah or some other dangerous location to see a second PRT. We didn't make much headway before it was time to attend a weekly meeting where the PRT members and some of the other brigade personnel discussed objectives and reviewed ongoing initiatives. I wasn't allowed to record the meeting, which was fine since it was boring as hell and full of eye-straining and mind-numbing PowerPoint slides.

The next day, I went on my first "mission" outside the wire. I loaded into a hulking Mine-Resistant Ambush Protected vehicle (MRAP) with several members of the PRT and we slowly made our way out of the base and into the city. I glued myself to one of the tiny windows in the vehicle and snapped pictures of the largely empty streets. Most of the shops were closed, and there were very few cars or people out and about. We passed stretches of blast wall and razor wire and a variety of derelict and damaged buildings. We passed a few shops that were open and selling furniture, household items, enormous watermelons, tires, cooking oil, and rotisserie chicken. Some of the streets were reasonably clean, others covered in dust, debris, and trash. Some side streets were blocked off with hulking piles of dirt and rubble, presumably to prevent car bombs from entering the streets.

We parked in a small street in the Mansour district and exited the hulking vehicle. On one side of the street was a nice strip of median with vibrant plants and tall palm trees growing out of planter boxes. If you just looked in that direction, it seemed like a quiet, clean neighborhood and you wouldn't think it was a war zone.

On the other side of the street, however, was a six-foot-tall wall of concrete blast panels partially painted with scenes of blue skies and palm trees. A long coil of razor wire ran along the ground in front of the blast wall. It was more like the image of Baghdad I was expecting. Inside the wall was the Mansour District Council office.

We entered the compound through a concrete archway and stepped into the conference room. The council consisted of about 20 well-fed Iraqi men in their 50s and 60s, mostly wearing either short- or long-sleeve dress shirts with the top button open and no ties. They sat at a long, narrow conference table and the PRT members in their pixelated fatigues sat on the periphery.

The council members then discussed the conditions of things like electricity, water, and sewage in their neighborhoods and what needed attention. Whenever someone discussed a problem they could not fix, the committee turned to the American soldiers. The Iraqis asked the soldiers for $50,000 electric generators or more mundane things like office furniture and wheelbarrows. Sitting through the meeting, I got the feeling that the Iraqis viewed the soldiers as a giant ATM that could spit out money and merchandise at will.

The PRTs obliged to the greatest extent possible since the ethos at the time was that if Iraqis had better public services, then the population would support the government and be less inclined to join or support militants. It was the phase of the war when the heavy fighting had ended, and the focus was on "holding and building" or buying security through investments in governance and services.

That had been going on since the outset of the war, but the approach in the early years was much more haphazard. That period generated all the examples of the United States building expensive projects or clinics that were going unused by the Iraqis because they did not fit the community needs. By the time I arrived, the spending was smaller in scale and theoretically based on input from the Iraqis. Not only did I finally get to Iraq after all the intense fighting had ended, but I also missed the era of the epic boondoggles. Instead of seeing medical clinics filled with all sorts of unused equipment, I was watching a U.S. Army colonel confirm to an Iraqi bureaucrat that the requested wheelbarrows were on the way. Heady stuff…

The meeting concluded after all the obligatory glad-handing and photos of the paunchy Iraqi civilians posing with the tall, lean soldiers. We returned to the base and my trailer where I peeled off my body armor and sweat-soaked shirt (it was August and daytime temperatures were in the triple digits). While we were able to take off our armor during the committee meeting, I had been wearing it for a good chunk of the afternoon, and I was not used to how hot and heavy it was. After removing it I felt like I could hop around like an astronaut on the moon.

I showered and hit the DFAC. I sat with some of the PRT members and soldiers with a civil affairs unit. We talked briefly about their mission and work, and a little about my background and work. I found most of the soldiers to be relaxed and comfortable talking openly in front of a journalist. A few kept their distance.

While I had met and known many members of the military before, I had not seen them "in the wild." The soldiers I interacted with covered the spectrum—enlisted, officers, reservists, and National Guard. Most were from "red" America. Some had experienced combat on previous deployments in Iraq and Afghanistan. Others only experienced "building things" missions.

Most were married with kids, including some of the soldiers who weren't old enough to drink. Even though they were deployed in a war zone, they had it pretty easy. They were living on the largest, most developed base in the country and the worst of the war was in the rearview mirror. While some were motivated and invested in the reconstruction mission, others were bored, indifferent, and wanted to go home or go to Afghanistan where maybe they could see action. I empathized with those who were looking for the shit. I was still seeking the danger and the merit badges of covering conflict.

It hadn't yet set in for me that conflict meant death, destruction, and devastation. It would take another year or two before I would internalize the reality that "the shit" wasn't some joy ride, it was life and death and involved tremendous human suffering and cost. At that point though, I was thinking of it as more of a Disney ride.

As I dined with and got to know the troops, I noticed some of the Stockholm Syndrome that came with embedded reporting. By the summer of 2008, there had been extensive discussion about how embedding colored war reporting and made journalists sympathetic to the U.S. military's side of the story.

It was a real thing. I was surrounded by soldiers. They were generally good guys with good intentions. They welcomed me into their world, and they were my hosts and guardians. I respected them for choosing to join the military and put their lives on the line. While I had vehemently opposed the invasion of Iraq (I never drank the Kool-Aid that a lot of the media did in 2002 and 2003, and I felt all the pretexts and justifications were bullshit), I respected the sense of duty of those serving.

I also had a touch of military envy. Even though joining the military never appealed to me growing up—I rebuffed the advances of the West Point recruiter who hounded me in high school—I found that as I got older, I felt a pull toward service. Just as I felt war reporting was the highest calling in journalism, I felt that serving in the military was one of the highest callings of being a citizen. Of course, I don't think that notion ever crossed my mind prior to 9/11.

So, I felt a little like a fanboy being around the troops on that first embed. Over the years, I would grow more cynical and detached and better able to be objective in reporting on wars and the military. But at that time, I thought it was cool to be hanging out with the grunts on a hot and dusty base in Baghdad. Even though I was itching to get out and see action, I was enjoying the adult summer camp-like vibe of life at Camp Liberty.

My next adventure off base was a visit to the Baghdad Chamber of Commerce—again, gripping stuff. I hopped in the back of a Humvee for the first time, which afforded much better visibility outside than the MRAP, but the rear seat had the legroom of a Fiat. Space was further compromised by the incredible amount of electronic gear packed into the vehicle. Some of it looked like WWII surplus and other pieces were state-of-the-art with digital screens packed with data and information. There were boxes and cables and doohickies everywhere emitting so much energy and radiation that I could feel my sperm dying off as we drove along. Given my aversion to having kids, I didn't mind.

The ride proceeded through much busier streets and neighborhoods than on the drive to the district council meeting. There were people out walking and driving vehicles ranging from donkey carts to motorcycle wagons filled with boxes to beat-up little Japanese sedans and pickups. We pulled into a dense area in downtown Baghdad and had to park a couple of blocks from the Chamber office. We walked through a few busy streets with open shops and people going about their business. It felt "normal" except for the fact that we were decked out in body armor.

Most of the side street streets were unpaved and everything was dusty. The most striking feature, though, was the spider's web of electrical wires running everywhere. It was far more chaotic than the Palestinian refugee camp I visited the previous month. For the life of me, I could not figure out how anyone could make any sense of it all, and for that matter, how people had managed to hang so many wires between all the buildings and the generators on each street (without getting zapped).

I sat through a boring meeting where Chamber members and PRT personnel spent half the time complimenting each other and the rest of the time discussing things the chamber wanted from the PRT. It was as far from award-winning war reporting material as you could get.

On the way back to the base, the civil affairs guys agreed to stop and do a street walk through a section of the city so I could get out and stroll around. We piled out of the MRAPs, and the security contingent circled around us looking none too happy that they had to do an impromptu walk in the city to appease a virgin journalist.

We walked along as I interviewed one of the officers about the conditions there. We passed a little auto repair shop and the owner posed for a picture with his two sons. We came across a group of young Iraqis in their early 20s who were out shopping for supplies for a wedding. As we chatted, one of their friends came running up and sprayed party foam all over them. They laughed like they didn't have a care in the world. That seemed like a good sign, although they made the security guys more than a little anxious.

We passed by some open shops selling food, toys, animal-print comforters, and other random crap, mostly from China. We talked with some shop owners who said that things were stabilizing, and life was returning to some sort of normal. One of the officers with me explained that less than a year earlier, the neighborhood was dangerous, like much of the city, and walking the streets wasn't remotely possible. He described how much progress had taken place and how the "war" was largely over in Baghdad.

I thought to myself that was great news and good for everyone concerned—except me. As he talked about the positive developments, I couldn't help but feel like I had missed it all. I had been longing for years to see the fighting and the worst of the worst, to report on a war like my journalistic idols, and there I was walking down a street where shops were open, people were smiling, there were cute stuffed animals hanging from storefronts, and there was not a gunshot to be heard.

Just like my trips to Sudan, Colombia, and Lebanon, I was in the neighborhood of danger, but did not see any shit. I was chasing death and always a few steps behind. Yes, I could impress people back home by saying I had been to all these places. But so what? I hadn't seen anything compared to the things covered by the real journalists. I had no vivid stories to tell. I was still at the little kids' table. Granted, my family was certainly happy that I was getting in and out of dangerous places without a scratch, and I was reporting on valid and relevant, even important, stuff, but it wasn't scratching the itch. I was too self-absorbed to think of the flip side—that the lack of violence was a good thing for the people of Iraq, and it shouldn't be about me.

I was hardly alone in that selfish desire for an exciting story to report. Journalism is as cutthroat and competitive an industry as there is. While there are plenty of noble, public service-minded journalists, there is no shortage of toxic narcissists who will do anything for a story and to get ahead. Sexy stories sell and get attention that you can parlay into promotions and pay raises. I wasn't the pop culture caricature of an ambitious, morally suspect journalist, but I sure as hell wanted stories that would benefit me as much as the audience.

Anyhow, drivers started honking and getting cranky because our walk was stopping traffic, so we piled back into the vehicles and returned to the base. I once again peeled off my sweat-soaked gear and hit the shower.

That was the end of my action-packed embed with the PRT. The next day, I flew from Victory back to LZ Washington where I was picked up and driven to the U.S. embassy to conduct more interviews. The new, ginormous boondoggle, I mean embassy, was in the final stages of construction and would open five months later. So, the United States was still using Saddam's old palace as the embassy.

It was the enormous, gaudy monstrosity with the epic murals of SCUD missiles launching off into the heavens, ornate chandeliers and tiled walls, and hideous golden chairs with worn peach-colored fabric. I of course made it a point to take a dump in one of Saddam's old toilets.

By the way, has anyone ever done a study of why dictators are so obsessed with phallic objects? They all seem to love artwork and decorations depicting missiles and rockets or obelisks reaching up to the skies. You couldn't help but look around Saddam's shit and think the guy was obsessed with or envious of prodigious peckers. Overcompensating much?

After my interviews, I received a quick driving tour of the Green Zone and the bizarre statues and other relics of Saddam's rule—and his fascination with dicks. After, I was deposited back at the press center. I was informed that there were no other PRTs available to take me in and as a result, my embed was done. "You don't have to go home, but you can't stay here" was the message.

I was at a loss since I had been hoping to get to Fallujah or somewhere exciting for a few days and I had no other plans or arrangements. I didn't have any flight plans or even a request in the system to get back out of the country. Plus, my classmate Rudy had rotated out of Iraq just before I arrived, so I had no top cover and I was being rushed out the door.

I threw a Hail Mary and called Jonathan Blakley, the NPR producer in Baghdad. A former coworker had introduced us virtually and we had communicated by email briefly before I set out for Baghdad. I explained my predicament, and he offered to pick me up and let me crash at the NPR bureau for a few days. I told the Army guys I had a ride on the way, and they hovered over me until I was out of their hair. I was pretty sure that CNN and the *New York Times* did not get that kind of treatment, but I was a flea on a dog's ass in the journalism universe.

Jonathan and the NPR driver picked me up and brought me to the bureau, which was NPR's third-to-last bureau location in Baghdad. Situated at the NPR bureau, I tried to stay out of Jonathan and Lulu Garcia-Navarro's hair as I worked on options for both additional reporting in Iraq and my exit strategy. I still had a flight from Kuwait to D.C. booked, but I had no way out of Baghdad. To fly out commercially, I would need an exit visa. One of the local staff for NPR was the resident expert for all things bureaucratic in Baghdad. I gave him my passport and $250, and he took it to the appropriate office. A day later I magically had an exit visa. I didn't need to know the details. That at least gave me one option to get out of the country.

While at the bureau, I determined there was no hope of any additional embed before I needed to get back to D.C. That pretty much put an end to my reporting for the trip.

So, I focused on the social life in Baghdad. *The Washington Post* was throwing a birthday party for one of their photographers, Andrea Bruce, and I got to tag along. The guests were the entire international press corps in the country at the time, as well as a few Iraqi staff for the news organizations, and diplomatic and NGO people.

Once again, I was in imposter/envy mode and trying to act

like I belonged there. I think most people picked up pretty quickly that I didn't.

Like the party I attended in Darfur the previous year, parties in conflict zones are generally excessive due to a need to vent, de-stress, and feel something resembling "normal." That night was true to that form. There was an unhealthy amount of alcohol (and lamb chop) consumption.

I recall playing pool and then accidentally spraying beer on Andrea and Lulu while trying to impress them by opening a beer bottle using a door latch. Later, someone stepped on a broken bottle (I did not break it) with bare feet and lacerated the shit out of his foot, which required a trip to a medical facility. All in all, a typical war zone party.

I ended up spending the night at the *Post*'s house and slept on a mattress on the floor in some sort of guest room with four or five others. It was their equivalent of a drunk tank. I barely slept and felt like ass the next day.

I loafed at the NPR bureau and continued to strategize how to fly back to Kuwait. I reached out to the military press office and determined that I could still try to get on a standby flight. However, I was leaning toward getting a commercial flight to avoid the whole Space-A hassle. The bigger problem was getting to the airport. At the time, there were basically three options: military or diplomatic helicopter flight, private car, or the Rhino.

The Rhino was the armored truck that shuttled people along the infamous airport road, or Route Irish as the military called it. Rhinos traveled in convoys in the middle of the night to get civilians to the airport without being killed by IEDs or attacks—which were still common occurrences. To take the Rhino, you had to show up at a depot in the international zone, sign up, and then sit and wait. The convoy would depart at a different time every night to avoid setting a pattern that militants could track.

The Rhino was my only realistic option.

That night, the NPR bureau hosted a small, under-control birthday party for Jonathan. We had cake and drinks and then sat out in the front yard watching a near-total lunar eclipse. It was a quiet night and an opportunity to bond with a few of the other real journalists based in Baghdad. Of course, it fueled my senses of envy and inadequacy. I was desperate to become a member of the tribe, to live the romantic life of a full-time war correspondent.

The next night, I said my goodbyes at the bureau and got a ride to the Rhino depot. Like the terminal in Kuwait, it was basically a big, ratty bus station. Although, it was a solid building as opposed to a tent. I signed up and then had to sit and wait for several hours for confirmation I would get a seat.

Sometime around 1:30 a.m. the Rhino people came into the waiting area and told us to put on our gear and line up to board. We did as told and queued up outside the hulking, black trucks that looked like larger and beefed-up versions of prisoner transport vehicles. We squeezed into cramped seats. We sat waiting for another 20 to 30 minutes, getting progressively hotter and more uncomfortable.

Eventually, we set off to the airport. We snaked our way out of the Green Zone and onto the highway. The windows were heavily blacked, so it was difficult to see much of anything outside. Plus, we drove with no lights. I vaguely recall seeing vegetation and dirt berms outside and periodically lights in the distance.

I did not enjoy the ride. I felt extremely vulnerable—the most I had felt anywhere in my brief career traveling to dangerous places. I knew that the vehicles were armored to protect us from roadside bombs or RPGs, but we were far from invincible. Attacks on Rhino convoys were less common then compared to the early days of the war, but that was little consolation. Despite the darkness, it still felt like the convoy was screaming "here we are, come and get us!" I spent the entire ride on high alert waiting for something to go boom. Fortunately, nothing did, but I was never so happy to get out of a vehicle once we arrived at the military terminal at Baghdad airport.

A few hours later, I piled into a C-130 with 70 military and contractor personnel. We landed in Kuwait with much less of a thud than the landing in Baghdad, and an air-conditioned bus took us to the camp. From there it was another bus ride to the airport in Kuwait City.

I boarded the flight to D.C. thinking about how I had just completed a trip to Iraq and had not experienced a moment of danger. While I had a journalistically solid and informative story about post-conflict reconstruction, I didn't come home with the experience I had sought. As far as I was concerned, my trip was the equivalent of getting to first base while the cool kids were having sex behind the gym.

Once I got home, I let the cat out of the bag. I had decided not to tell anyone in my family that I was going to Iraq so they would not worry the entire time. I had told them that I was going to Kuwait (which was true). My plan backfired in that I got an earful from everyone who said that they would have rather known up front and worried the whole time rather than potentially receive a bigger shock had something happened while I was in Iraq. Noted. From then on, full transparency about my travels—well, full in terms of where I was going. I would hold back some of the details about what, and who, I did while gallivanting around, at least until I wrote a book...

Chapter Six
Seeing Afghanistan for Myself

January 2009

DULLES AIRPORT, Virginia — On January 7, visa in hand, along with a bunch of new cold and wet weather gear I gleefully picked up at REI in December, I boarded United Flight 976 (aka the "contractor shuttle" due to the large number of military-looking dudes in cargo pants always taking that flight) to Dubai and took my seat in business class. Thanks to my extensive travel in 2008, I had platinum status, and thus began the upgrade era of my life that would last until the end of 2016.

That was one of the paradoxes of the job. I was happy in a sleeping bag in rudimentary tents or huts or in a rundown guest house. However, on the way to and from, or in between adventures, I wanted every luxury I could get—business class seats, hotel suites, airport lounges. Over the years I became a Jedi master of miles and points and how to finesse upgrades.

Anyhow, after the long, turbulent flight, I landed in Dubai none the worse for wear. I checked into the sleek Radisson Royal and completed my usual pilgrimage down Sheikh Zayed road to Trader Vic's Mai Tais and shredded duck.

The next morning, I had my first taste of the Terminal of Lost Souls. At the time, Dubai Airport was one of the glitziest in the world. It was enormous and modern with a plethora of shops and lounges. But that was only terminals 1 and 3.

Terminal 2, aka the Terminal of Lost Souls, was for the discount carriers flying to south and central Asia and parts of Africa—places like Uzbekistan, Bangladesh, Somalia, and Iraq and Afghanistan. The passengers in Terminal 2 were generally poor construction workers, mercenaries, and contractors (and journalists). The laborers would roll into the terminal with what I pejoratively called "Bangladesh Bundles." They were "suitcases" made by wrapping belongings with a blanket or tarp and then tying it all up with a net of rope.

Terminal 2 was shit by any international airport standards. It was one giant warehouse with a few crappy food vendors and no lounge or any comforts. The bathrooms were entered at your own risk. There were a lot of mystery smells.

I boarded the Kam Air flight along with a mix of shady-looking Brits, a few diplomats and aid workers, and an assortment of Afghans in traditional dress. The plane was surprisingly clean and modern, and the flight was much better than I expected.

And so, seven years and four months after 9/11, when Afghanistan first started calling to me, I was flying over the majestic landscape en route to Kabul.

America Abroad was producing a program exploring the Taliban's use of Pakistan's tribal regions as a sanctuary and training ground. The point of the program, and my story, was to show that if the Taliban had a sanctuary the U.S. couldn't touch (at least with ground forces), the war in Afghanistan was doomed.

I applied for an embed in Afghanistan and requested a location in the northeast where the Taliban had rat lines to Pakistan. My goal was to get on the ground where U.S. forces were trying to interdict Taliban movements and shut down their border crossings.

Compared to my story topic in Iraq, which was about reconstruction and therefore did not get me into any action, the Afghanistan story was designed to get me in the shit. Having learned from my experience applying for an embed in Iraq, I wasn't going to screw around with anything soft in Afghanistan.

I was hoping to get to Kunar since it was one of the hottest provinces in the northeast. Unfortunately, I had a fixed time for my trip and had to take what was available.

The embed office responded to my request with two options: Laghman or Nuristan. After consulting with a few people, I selected Laghman, even though it was not on the border with Pakistan. Sources told me that there was a lot of Taliban movement through the province, and I would get what I was looking for there.

People did caution me that since I was going in January, things would be much quieter as the Taliban had largely hunkered down in Pakistan for the winter and there was less movement and less fighting going on at that time of the year. I still held out hope for some bang bang.

The descent into Kabul was unremarkable—it wasn't like flying into Baghdad in a C-130. Things around Kabul had calmed down to the point that anti-peristaltic corkscrew approaches were no longer standard practice.

We deplaned onto a beat-up airport bus to drive to the terminal. After the driver stalled the bus three times and finally managed to engage the clutch (that probably should have been replaced when the Soviets left Afghanistan) he drove approximately 75 yards to the entrance to the terminal—good thing we didn't have to walk…

I cleared immigration and customs and hauled my gear in the smoky, dusty winter mountain air. The altitude in Kabul is slightly higher than Denver, and I was feeling it as I carried 80 pounds of gear the 300 yards to the parking lot to meet my driver.

My initial impression was that Kabul looked like a cross between Moscow and Sudan. The gray, winter weather with scattered trees was the Moscow component, and the rundown, dusty appearance of everything with hordes of vendors selling phone cards and the hustling taxi drivers reminded me of Khartoum. The air quality was a combination of the two. It was a mélange of burnt wood, industrial pollution, and notes of fir trees. The smoke reminded me of Mali and the smell of the Festival in the Desert in Essakane.

I found a man holding a sign for the car service I had contracted. I told him I was Dr. Galazkiewicz. He looked at me like a dog hearing a strange sound.

We hopped in the white Toyota Corolla. It wouldn't be until a few years later when I moved to Afghanistan that I learned the joke about white Toyota Corollas—well, the joke wasn't as much about white Toyota Corollas per se, but that daily threat reporting in Kabul generally said, "There are reports of a possible car bomb attack, be on the lookout for a white Toyota Corolla." The punchline of course was that half the cars on the road in Afghanistan were white Corollas.

My driver and I quickly made our way out to the road north towards Bagram. The airport is on the north side of the city, so I didn't see downtown Kabul on the drive. Instead, I saw what looked more like shanties and settlements.

For the first several miles, the streets were lined with rundown markets and people buying, selling, or begging. We passed several spots where small groups of burka-wrapped women sat in the middle of the street begging for money. I saw a handful of people on crutches missing varying amounts of one leg or the other—one of the unfortunate, but common sights in a country that had been riddled by landmines, bullets, and other projectiles for decades.

As we progressed, the density of development thinned, and there was less street-side activity. We passed through one mildly mountainous stretch with mud houses seemingly stacked on top of each other climbing the hills. My driver explained that much of that area, and Kabul in general, was full of people who had fled other provinces over the years. Whether it was during the rise of the Taliban in the mid '90s or the early years of Operation Enduring Freedom, millions of Afghans had been displaced. Many of the people either didn't want to, or couldn't, return to their homes, and so they descended on Kabul.

It's the same in many places in the world I visited over the years—Bogota, Khartoum, Lima—where people fled violence and poverty in rural areas and crowded into cities, often by building informal settlements. Kabul was severely overcrowded in 2009 and it only got worse in the following years. The air quality was deteriorating due to increased pollution and the roads were clogged with cars and people.

The farther north we drove, the more the terrain widened out, and I could see the snow-covered peaks framing the mud landscape, which was interspersed with crumbling mud walls surrounding mud farm plots, and periodic mud houses. Every few miles we passed a small roadside village with street-front markets—butcher shops with slaughtered and skinned animals hanging out front, "convenience" stores, and other shops. The relatively nicer places were made of mud while the poorer places were rickety wood huts that looked like the Big Bad Wolf could take them out with one puff.

After an hour of driving, we made a right turn in the middle of nowhere to head to Bagram. We drove for a few miles on a beat-up asphalt road that turned onto a dirt road, which was in fact more mud than dirt—have you noticed yet the whole mud motif? We progressed slowly over ruts, some of which looked like they could have swallowed our Toyota.

As we approached the base, two A-10 Warthogs flew over, followed a minute later by an F-15. I thought of it as my own personal escort into the base.

We turned left onto an asphalt road and pulled up to the gate. The gate consisted of concrete barricades on each side and a roll of razor wire that the Afghan security guards hand-carried back and forth to allow vehicles to pass. Outside the gate sat a hodge-podge of different trucks carrying water, supplies, armored vehicles, and goods for the various markets. Some of the trucks looked like they had carried supplies for the Mujahadeen back when they were trying to drive out the Russians. The scene had a certain chaotic feel to it, and hardly the type of security perimeter I was expecting.

A white van pulled out of the gate and over to the patch of

mud where we and other cars were parked. A few kids mulled about trying to sell us nuts, cigarettes, and candy, and they immediately crowded around the driver's side window of the van, hoping for handouts from the sergeant who was there to drive me onto the base. He had nothing for them, and we shooed them away and drove through the gate.

We arrived at the Media Operations Center sometime around 1 p.m., and the crew there jumped into action processing my ID and paperwork, giving me a room at the "Hotel California," (the media bunks) and running through my schedule and movement logistics. They told me that there was a 9:30 flight that evening they hoped to get me on, so I wouldn't even have to spend the night on the base.

That said, I was pissed that they had not booked my flights ahead of time. After my experience in Iraq flying Space-A and the hassles of never being sure if or when you would fly, I had specifically requested that the media folks book my flights to Laghman in advance. They had a week before my arrival to get it done, and for reasons not made clear to me, it had not happened, and therefore I was going Space-A again.

I'll skip the long, gory details of what I went through to get on a flight to Camp Fenty in Jalalabad. Suffice to say it took days, I made countless trips back and forth to passenger terminals, got booked on and bumped off flights, and fretted about how much time I was losing on the ground by waiting for flights.

I finally got on a contractor flight from Bagram to Camp Fenty. The small cargo plane took off and climbed up over the mountains that surround the plain and the base.

I popped on a Zeppelin mix on my iPod and enjoyed the view. It was a transcendent moment as I watched the snow-covered mountains pass below as Robert Plant crooned "That's The Way"—a song penned in the countryside of Wales, another place known for snow-capped hills.

The flight ended too quickly for me—I was immersed in the landscape and the music, and it was a rare poetic moment when everything else just melted away. As I would experience in the coming years, Afghanistan from above was beautiful and peaceful—and vast. On the ground, it was sometimes beautiful and rarely peaceful.

I checked in at Camp Fenty and was shown to my bunk—a small plywood "veal pen" with a cot inside a large tent. I proceeded to kill time while waiting for transportation north to Laghman. I interviewed the brigade commander at Fenty. We had a candid conversation. The takeaway: security was getting worse, there was no chance of locking down the border, and if Pakistan provided haven, the Taliban would be difficult to beat. None of that changed over the next 12 years…

In the late afternoon, a captain wandered by the media office where I was killing time and he mentioned that he knew the Afghan general in charge of the Afghan National Army in the area. The general's office happened to be on the base, across the runway next to the old Nangarhar Airport terminal (that looked like it had been out of service about as long as I had been alive).

The captain, a military interpreter, and I strolled over to see if we could meet with the general. He was outside his compound, and quickly invited us in for tea and a conversation. The general looked like he was about 60, although most Afghans looked older than they were. He was short with a slight paunch and was bald with white stubble for a beard and along the sides of his head.

We sat in his office that smelled like the inside of a wood-burning stove. Coincidentally, at the far end of the office was a wood-burning stove.

He was gracious and happy to share his thoughts about the security situation in eastern Afghanistan and the challenges posed by Pakistan. He repeatedly thanked me and the American forces for freeing the people of Afghanistan. His affection for the United States was mirrored by his disdain for the government of Pakistan, which he said had the capability to clear out the tribal areas and thereby greatly improve the stability and security situation in Afghanistan, but the country was unwilling to do so.

After we spoke, he thanked me profusely and posed earnestly for a picture.

The following afternoon, I was sitting in the public affairs office and the door flew open. An officer looked in and shouted, "hey, reporter!" He told me to suit up and get down to the flight line because the guy in charge of contractor flights was going to try to squeeze me onto a bird. There were some foreign diplomats at the base who were heading back to Bagram, but the contractor guy said there was an open seat, and he was going to ask the crew to make a quick detour to get me to Mehtar Lam in Laghman.

I gathered my gear and camped out by the runway. The stocky Puma helicopter landed, and I watched for a sign from the contractor guy... nothing. I started hearing the Charlie Brown "wah-waaaah" in my head. The contractor walked over and said that I was going to get on the flight—it just had to go refuel first.

So, I waited by the runway feeling self-conscious. As we stood there, two Black Hawks landed, and an entourage got off. It was Brigadier General Mark Milley. I was supposed to interview him two days prior at Bagram, but he canceled on me to hang out with VP-elect Joe Biden who was passing through the neighborhood. Milley was flanked by a CBS reporter, her producer, cameraman, and a few other folks. They walked toward the camp and were met by the commanding colonel and a few other officers.

I stood there watching the CBS reporter and crew getting the red-carpet treatment. I heard that they had come in on very short notice, needed an interview with the general, a room for the night, and then an escort off the base the following day... done. No questions asked.

I stood there with network envy, and to an extent medium envy. When TV cameras showed up, everybody jumped—they manifested special flights, the commanding officers dropped what they were doing. When a lowly (and unknown) public radio guy came to town, it was standby, Space-A, veal pens, and "we'll see what we can do."

Anyhow, they wandered off in a cloud of pixie dust and TV

glitz, and I returned to my job of waiting for the Puma to finish refueling and get me to the next stop. The general and the Black Hawks took off. A C-130 took off. An Apache that had been hovering overhead landed.

Finally, the Puma returned, and contractor guy loaded me on. Next thing I knew, we were in the air. I was waiting for the other shoe to drop. It didn't.

We were probably only a few hundred feet up as we passed over Jalalabad and carved our way through small mountain peaks—many of which towered above us. I soaked in the epic the scenery during the 10-minute flight, and then we touched down in Mehtar Lam. Seriously, all that drama and days spent trying to get a flight to go 30 miles. I could have hired a car to get me there to begin with, but you couldn't just walk in and out of embeds, so I had to eat the time sitting around waiting for mil air.

The base was outside of the town of Mehtar Lam and surrounded by mountains and a tiny amount of development. There was no electricity in any of the houses or buildings outside the camp.

Once at Mehtar Lam, I went through the usual process of base orientation with the information officer and getting a bunk. I ended up with my own B-hut—basically a 15-by-30-foot wooden shed with working electrical outlets and heat. Finally, I felt somewhat situated and ready to get some material on tape.

The next morning, I rolled out of bed and geared up to ride along with the PRT as they inspected paving work on the Alishang Road. It wasn't a combat mission, but at least it was outside the wire.

Road construction was one of the major initiatives of the PRT and the U.S. command in general. It was counterinsurgency 101. The theory was that with paved roads came increased economic development and greater opportunity for the people. Greater economic opportunity would mean less likelihood of people accepting payments from insurgents to shoot at coalition forces or to blow things up. Ideally it also meant greater trust in the government and less sympathy for bad actors, or those who would undermine the state. We all know how that theory played out…

Around 10 a.m. I contorted myself into the back seat of a Humvee. The convoy departed and made its way off the base. We drove along freshly paved road for miles. The road ran along a valley, which sloped down to our left, and to the right were hills and scattered small compounds. In the valley we passed small farm plots with clusters of compounds and scattered remains of walls and compounds. I had visions of Alexander the Great and his troops riding their horses through the fields.

We stopped a couple of times so PRT personnel could get out and speak with Afghans who were operating backhoes and building retaining walls out of large slabs of stone.

The security contingent exited their vehicles first and set up a perimeter around us and then I was let out of the Humvee. I wandered around within the perimeter taking pictures of the valley stretching off between us and the mountains on the other side. I photographed the Afghan workers, who were dressed in a mix of traditional Shalwar Khamees—the traditional pajama-looking male clothing—sweatpants, sweaters, vests, and shawls.

The soldiers inspected the cement the Afghans were using to glue the rock walls together and they weren't happy. The soldiers said the quality was poor—there was too much silt in the mix, and it was not going to dry properly and have enough structural integrity. Young men and boys gathered on a rock pile nearby to watch the goings on. A larger and larger crowd followed along as the soldiers walked the site expressing concerns about the workmanship. The number of times I would see scenes like that in the coming years…

We got back in the vehicles and moved along the dirt road to the next site. We reached another village where the PRT had built the Alishang Boys and Girls School, which was a reasonably solid looking one-story building with dozens of metal desk chairs piled up on the roof. I couldn't get a clear answer what was going on there. One of the many mysteries of the country…

As the soldiers inspected the construction work on the road and some bridges and culverts, a large crowd of men and boys gathered around us. One of the Army translators helped me speak with a couple of the elders about security and Taliban safe havens in Pakistan.

Hold onto your hats, folks, because you're not going to believe it. People were highly critical of Pakistan. I know, right? Who would have imagined Afghans blaming Pakistan for all their problems? But they did. They said Pakistan had the ability to rein-in the Taliban and was refusing to, which meant Pakistan was complicit. They weren't exactly wrong.

The Afghans were friendly and happy to speak with me, and of course thanked the soldiers for building shit for them. They posed for pictures with me looking like a dork in my frumpy body armor and thick-rimmed ballistic goggles. I was so far from badass...

The day proceeded in that fashion. We would drive along, stop, critique the construction work, hear generally nice things from locals, and move on. The only danger we faced the entire time was the possibility of an Afghan taking offense at being criticized for shoddy construction work and trying to start a fight—not unprecedented. Well, there was also possible danger of retaining walls collapsing on us due to the poor construction—not unprecedented.

Still, I enjoyed the day outside the wire in very real Afghanistan. It was a poor, rural area that reflected the Afghanistan outside of the major cities and military bases. The surroundings were rugged, austere, beautiful, and haunting—all the cliches of Afghanistan. It was a good introduction to the landscape, the people, the lack of infrastructure, and the efforts and challenges of building infrastructure.

Even though we weren't seeing any action, my juices were flowing just seeing such a foreign place. It really was another world. Landscape looked like a mix of Scottish Highlands, parts of Arizona, and the moon. The people were equally as rugged and shaped by the sun, wind, and rain that had carved the terrain.

It was also another anthropological experience. I was parachuting in and observing this strange place and people through my western and inherently condescending lens. It was baffling to me to see a society that looked like the 1500s with cars and cell phones. In a world where people had walked on the moon, here was a largely pre-industrial society building houses out of mud and farming using rudimentary techniques that had been passed down through generations. It reminded me of elementary school field trips to Plymouth Plantation or Old Sturbridge Village. Yet, it wasn't a historical recreation, it was living history. It was hard not to feel colonialist observing it all.

The next day was more of the same. Another road trip to the other valley in the area. It was rainier, and really looked and felt like Scotland and the glacier I visited in Iceland with Layla—of course there had to be some reminder of her in Afghanistan.

We arrived at a small village in a nook of the valley nestled under large peaks of time-smoothed rocks. The soldiers sat for tea with elders to hear about conditions in the area and to sell the Afghans on the road construction. Soldiers never missed an opportunity to do counterinsurgency messaging.

The meeting wrapped up and we loaded back into the Humvees. We drove out past a row of men and boys who had gathered to watch when the U.S. troops rolled in. Some waved, some glared.

The next day was a return to transportation hell. I was supposed to head to my ultimate destination for the embed, Combat Outpost Najil. Winter weather was canceling flights. There were no missions. The only excitement was a controlled detonation of a seized cache of weapons and explosives in the afternoon. About a mile from the base a plume of smoke rose, and a few seconds later there was a loud boom.

That day made me remember my grandfather telling me as a kid about his time on a munitions ship in World War II. He always used to say that war was mostly boredom between moments of sheer chaos and panic. That was a boredom day.

The next morning, I was able to get on a convoy going from Mehtar Lam to Najil. I folded into my usual position in the back of a Humvee, and we set off in the rain. We drove up one of the roads I had traveled on one of the PRT missions and then we kept going north. In the middle of one village, one of the Humvees got stuck in the mud road. It felt like a metaphor.

The security forces dismounted and kept watch as soldiers gradually freed the vehicle. I was ordered to stay in the Humvee as it was not entirely friendly territory.

After three hours crammed in the back of a Humvee, we reached Najil, and I could finally unfold my legs.

COP Najil was a small outpost (as anything called a COP was, as opposed to the larger Forward Operating Bases (FOB)) clinging to the side of a small, muddy mountain. The base overlooked the junction of two river valleys and mountains stretched off in all directions. Mountains farther off—at least the ones visible through the thick clouds and fog—had thin tree cover and dustings of snow on their peaks. Closer peaks were barren rock with a few primitive houses growing from their bases like wild mushrooms.

The valleys stretching off into the distance were parts of transit routes the Taliban used to move weapons and fighters back and forth to Pakistan. That was why I ended up at Najil, because it was along transit routes and one of the deepest outposts into Laghman Province, beyond which U.S. forces had little presence or visibility.

Even though it was winter, the valley floor was covered with green grass framed by randomly snaking stone walls, presumably marking off individual farm plots. It was quiet and there was no visible activity around the houses or roads.

The base was exposed and struck me as an easy target. There was a ridge on the other side of the valley facing the base. It looked to be maybe four or five hundred yards off. There were no trees or any natural cover. Even the HESCO barriers (the giant sand-filled bins used to create base perimeters) were of limited use due to the slope of the base on the hill.

Soldiers said that once a week or so, militants would sneak up the opposing ridge and fire on the base. In response, soldiers would line up behind the HESCOs at the front of the base and return fire. At least it sounded like I would finally see some action.

I settled into a bunk in a CHU with a couple dozen soldiers. The kitchen was basically a fire pit, a couple of grills, and a microwave under a lean-to. Unfortunately, a soldier broke a kitchen rule of some kind right before I arrived, and the mayor of the base punished the troops by canceling cooked meals for a week. That meant I'd be enjoying MREs during my stay. The upside was less time spent in the latrine since MREs are reluctant to exit the human body.

Camouflage netting covered the patio area between the kitchen and the main bunker on the base, which served as the TV lounge and meeting area. The latrines were basically privies—open-air huts with a toilet seat nailed to a plywood box, under which were barrels. A muddy little black puppy with a white chest and white stripe down the center of his face huddled around the fire pit.

It was the most primitive base I had visited in Iraq or Afghanistan. It was kind of like a chilly, wet summer camp. Being on small bases conjured memories of sleeping in cabins or tents and playing in the woods as a kid—except at summer camp your dangers were mosquitoes, bees, and possibly a sexual predator counselor, whereas at Najil the dangers were getting shot or blown up.

There was a lone Marine who was at Najil mentoring Afghan forces. He interfaced with an Afghan Army first lieutenant who lived at the COP.

The Afghan officer agreed to speak. We sat on the floor of his tent next to a space heater and of course sipped tea as we chatted.

Not surprisingly, the conversation centered on Pakistan and its duplicity and complicity with the Taliban. Like almost every Afghan I would speak with on that trip, he said everything was Pakistan's fault. Unless and until Pakistan ended its support for the Taliban, the war would continue, they all said. Again, they weren't wrong, and it wasn't secret information, yet the United

States did nothing to change that equation in any meaningful way over the next 12 years.

The next night, shortly after midnight, I joined troops along the HESCO barriers at the front of the base facing the opposing ridge. They had determined that militants were going to attack. I was amped up and ready to chronicle the battle. The temperature was in the low 40s and a steady rain was coming down. That sucked, but it gave me an opportunity to break out all the rain gear I had purchased for the trip. I've always been a gear slut and embeds and war reporting was the perfect excuse to buy kits.

The artillery guys at the top of base fired off three rounds in the direction of the suspected threat. However, one of the rounds was an illuminating mortar—an unfortunate mistake—which hovered over the valley lighting up the base and making it an easier target.

It turned out to be an inconsequential mistake. After 30 minutes of standing out in the rain, the soldiers determined that no one was coming out to play. They explained that the militants who typically attacked the base were "fair-weather" fighters who were not particularly motivated or skilled (they were typically locals paid a few bucks by the Taliban to take shots at the base). So, the chilly rain was a deterrent.

Of course, I was disappointed. I was there to see and report on the war, and I really wanted to get my first firefight under my belt. It felt like trying to lose your virginity—anticipation, excitement, some nervousness, and then frustration when it didn't happen.

The next day, a contingent of troops took a road trip several miles south of the base to check in on a couple of villages and distribute some food and supplies (humanitarian assistance, or HA). It was basically a hearts and minds and intel mission. The goal was to show support for the villages, provide them with some goodies, ask what their needs were, and then gather intelligence about security threats and militant activity.

We pulled into the village of Wantanagu and as soon as we parked, some 75 men and boys swarmed around us. Some of the soldiers and locals were on a first-name basis from previous visits. Soldiers huddled with the elders. The U.S. Marine lieutenant played with some of the young boys and performed a few rudimentary magic tricks for them. It was lighthearted. Still, a platoon of fierce-looking soldiers secured the perimeter around the village.

A soldier explained that there was a good bit of "double dipping" that went on in the villages. There were men who would be friendly with U.S. forces when they came by and they would accept any aid and handouts, but they would also accept money and support from the Taliban in exchange for placing IEDs or shooting at the base. The Taliban would also threaten villagers to attack Americans, so the locals were in a bind.

It was the old "no permanent allies, only permanent interests" thing. Basically, Afghans wanted to survive and feed their families, and they would side with anyone who furthered those interests or would play sides off each other to gain the most benefit. It was more pragmatic than nefarious, although there was no shortage of nefariousness.

What it all meant was that we were surrounded by a large crowd of men, some of whom had probably shot at or planted bombs intended to kill U.S. and Afghan forces. I grew paranoid and scanned the crowd for anyone who looked suspicious.

After an hour and a half in the village, we moved on to a small school. Troops dropped off bags of food and some school supplies as the students posed for photos. From there, we rolled into another small village that was poor and crumbling except for a fancy little irrigation dam built by USAID in 2005.

As we chatted with some of the men and boys about security in the area, I saw several blue and orange "ghosts" gliding through a field a few hundred yards away. They were women, three of whom were wearing the standard blue burka. Two wore bright orange saris, and one of the women had her face exposed as she carried a bale of laundry on her head. The only reason I could see her face was because I had a strong telephoto lens. She most likely assumed she was safe to be uncovered at that distance from the village.

We loaded back into the Humvees and returned to the base. I suffered through an MRE for dinner and stayed up way too late in the bunker watching playoff football (it was one of the few years this century that the Patriots didn't make the postseason) and chatting on the phone with my new girlfriend, Jennifer.

In December, I finally did what I had been putting off for months, I ended things with my rebound girlfriend. The timing was not random. She was home visiting family in Syria, and I took a work trip to Boston. While I was there, I met an old friend for drinks.

Jennifer was a tall, pretty ginger who was part of a group of people I used to mosh with at Axis on Lansdowne Street in the '90s. It was a tribe for a few years of my life.

Jennifer and I went on a few dates in 1996 and hadn't seen each other since. We clicked in December 2008 and quickly started a relationship. The distance between Boston and D.C. and my constant travel meant we only saw each other once or twice a month. Still, it was fun and a refreshing change to be with someone who shared the same cultural literacy—we were from the same Massachusetts Gen X alternative music tribe— and who didn't have any identity baggage.

In 2009 we spent time in Boston, D.C., London, and Dubai. However, the distance was a challenge. And my identity and tribal needs would pull us apart. I found over the course of the year that I needed to be with someone from the tribe who had been to weird and dangerous places and wanted to go to even weirder places.

Anyhow, I took advantage of late-night discounts on Afghan cell rates and chatted with Jennifer in the wee hours a few times while at Najil.

The next day we went on a foot patrol (my first) into the village closest to the base, Qala Najil. A sergeant briefed me on where I was to stay in formation, what to do in the event of an attack, and all that fun stuff. It raised the hope that we would see some action.

I wasn't looking for anything crazy, but a few guys shooting at us that forced us to jump into the ditch by the road and shoot back would have been satisfactory—as long as it wasn't a sewage ditch, we were all safe, the good guys took out the bad guys, and I captured it all on my recorder. Was that too much to ask?

As you might have guessed by now, the patrol was completely uneventful. We strolled in the mud street into the little village that stretched about 200 yards. On one side were metal shipping containers that had been converted into shops. On the other side were two-story mud structures with stores on the first floor and ladders to the offices, storerooms, and sitting rooms on the second floor.

We did the usual routine of chatting with the elders and shop owners about security. Soldiers handed out candy to kids and drank tea with the locals. The troops also talked up the road project and how the road would eventually be paved and how that would make all their lives better.

Locals were friendly and relaxed. That was a good thing in general, but disappointing for a selfish journalist looking for fireworks. At least I heard a few more complaints about Pakistan to add to my story.

I spent a couple more days hanging out at the base waiting for a flight out. Between the weather and the usual unpredictability of flights, that meant I had a lot of downtime. To add insult to injury, there were no attacks on the base the additional days I was sitting around, so I got nothing more than extra constipation from the MREs.

Finally, some contractor flights came through and I was able to get on a bird to Jalalabad. Since I had arrived at Najil by Humvee, I hadn't yet seen the area from the air. It was beautiful—snow-capped peaks; some tree-covered mountains, others barren and haunting; wide, brown plains with green veins around winding rivers; rectangular, tan compounds; and eventually dense housing and development as we approached the city of Jalalabad.

I checked in at the public affairs office on the base, and after hanging out for a few minutes one of the officers told me to get my ass to the landing zone. A colonel I had requested to interview was about to fly out somewhere. They said there was a seat on one of the Black Hawks I could grab, and then I could interview him after the flight. I ran to the flight line and boarded one of the helicopters, and then I realized they didn't even tell me where he was going.

We flew up over a long stretch of snow-covered mountains, and it got damn chilly up there. I started wondering what the ceiling was for Black Hawks and how far over it we were. We landed at Bagram, which was good as that's where I needed to get to anyhow.

I completed my interview with the colonel, and the next day interviewed Brigadier General Milley, who at the time was deputy commander of Regional Command-East (the NATO-led command had divided the country into five regions: North, East, South, West, and Kabul). When I sat down to interview him, he first asked me about my background in the music business in Boston and how I had ended up a journalist. He was notorious for reading the bios of journalists and engaging in lighthearted conversation. We had a brief chat about Massachusetts (where he is from as well) and then got down to discussing the Pakistan border the challenges of securing it and combatting the Taliban who had cross border support.

He was candid and characteristically verbose—as he would be in future encounters I had with him in Afghanistan. In the interview he noted that security had been getting worse and the situation more complex. He said he had confidence that the Afghan military and government would get stronger. It's interesting to look back today at the last line he spoke in that interview:

So over time, I am more hopeful for Afghanistan, more optimistic than anything else and I think it is a realistic assessment to say that if an insurgent, if a terrorist doesn't have the support of the people, then they aren't going to win, and I think that is the case here.

I should have put money on that.

After I completed the interview, one of the public affairs officers drove me back out to the gate where my Afghan Logistics driver was waiting for me. We got to Kabul, and he drove me around so I could do a little sight-seeing and pick up some gifts at one of the markets.

From there, we made our way through the countless checkpoints and security screenings so I could fly out. The process made the TSA seem friendly and efficient.

With that, I was off to Dubai and a night of luxury (massage, alcohol, and gourmet food) before returning to D.C. the next day.

The human brain is barely capable of processing the difference between Afghanistan and Dubai.

In less than three hours, you go from one of the poorest, dustiest, and most fucked up places in the world to one of the richest, glitziest, and most fucked up places in the world. It's like going from the Flintstones to the Jetsons in the blink of an eye. No, that's far too sanitized of an analogy. It's more like experiencing a Neill Blomkamp movie—going from an impoverished dystopia to an opulent dystopia.

I returned to D.C. and started writing my Afghanistan story while preparing for my next trip. Until that point, I wrote my field reports and one of the program's hosts (Ray Suarez or Deborah Amos) would voice the script. But I felt the Afghanistan story required first-person reporting and the listeners needed to hear and feel the reporter on the ground with the U.S. troops.

I wrote the story and made the pitch to the executive producer. From that point on, I would voice my field reports. I was officially an on-air correspondent. Another mission accomplished.

Chapter Seven
No Peace to Keep in the Congo

February 2009

Somewhere in Rural Rwanda — I was lost in photographing the verdant Rwandan countryside when I glanced over and noticed my driver texting. I looked up and saw he was crossing the center line. He was heading straight toward a much larger SUV coming the other direction. I had just enough time to yell "hey!" before impact.

Our fragile Suzuki Vitara slammed into the oncoming Isuzu Trooper. The thunderous impact sent everything in our vehicle flying forward. We were wearing seatbelts, which kept us from launching through the windshield. I smashed my arm on the center console. My camera hit the dashboard, breaking the plastic lens hood. My sunglasses flew thirty feet out the passenger window. We came to a stop, and I paused to do the Terminator internal system scan. My arm was throbbing. Because I saw the accident coming, I was able to brace my feet in the car, but because I was holding my camera, I couldn't grab the door or dashboard to secure my upper body. The seatbelt was the only thing fighting the inertia of my torso, and I had chest pain from the belt cutting into me. I was slightly dazed but didn't seem to have any whiplash or head trauma.

I got out and surveyed the scene. There was a family in the other vehicle. It was a right-hand drive model, which meant the man driving was on the far side of the impact, and his wife in the passenger seat took the brunt of the impact. She was stunned but seemed otherwise OK.

Both vehicles were totaled with their front fenders ripped off, frames bent, axles and suspensions shattered, and debris littered across the street. Fluids bled from both vehicles.

The accident took place in a small village with houses and shops lining both sides of the road. People were out going about their day, and within seconds of the crash, dozens of people had gathered around the scene.

I immediately distanced myself from my driver and let him incur the justifiable wrath of the occupants of the other vehicle and the locals who saw him cause the accident. Temperatures rose, but it didn't look like it was going to go nuclear. I turned my attention to figuring out how I was going to get the hell out of there and continue the remaining 60-mile journey west to Goma in the Congo. It wasn't a place where I could just call a cab or ask one of the locals to give me a ride.

Just as I was starting to panic about being stranded in rural Rwanda, a knight in shining white armor rolled up in the form of a Toyota Land Cruiser. On the side of the Land Cruiser, in big, beautiful blue letters, read "UN."

The driver leaned out the window and spied a slightly dazed white guy amid the chaos and called out to me. I explained what happened. He said he was heading to Goma and offered a ride.

I sprinted over to the shattered Suzuki and grabbed my bags. My driver worked for the Kigali Serena hotel where I had spent the previous night. He overheard me asking the desk clerk about hiring a driver to take me to the Congo. The young man approached me and offered me a deal on the condition that I not say anything to the hotel since he was going to borrow one of their cars without permission. It was fine with me since the price was right.

As I was grabbing my bags from the wrecked Suzuki, I told the driver I was leaving him at the scene and heading off with the UN guy. The young man said he understood and pleaded with me not to say anything to the hotel about what happened. I said I would not, and that he was also not getting paid since he fucked up and almost got us killed. He did not object.

I hopped in the Land Cruiser, and we hauled ass away from the wreckage. It would take close to two hours to travel the rural road to the border. Goma, my destination, is in the eastern province of North Kivu, a mountainous area home to both gorillas and guerrillas.

Just minutes into our journey from the accident site, the 50-something pony-tailed UN guy and I determined we had a close mutual connection. One of my grad school classmates was his boss in a previous peacekeeping mission. You can't make this shit up. Immediately after getting into a car accident in the middle of rural Rwanda, a UN guy passed by, picked me up, and happened to be very close with a friend of mine.

Another upside of the accident and my replacement ride was that when we arrived at the border crossing—which was about a 100-foot stretch of road next to Lake Kivu—he dropped me off at the Rwandan departure shed and drove my bags across. That saved me from bag search lines and any potential hassles over my gear.

I processed out of Rwanda, walked along the road to the security shack for DRC, passed through with flying colors, and then walked up to the arrival shed. I handed over my passport with my DRC visa and was quickly stamped into the Congo. I walked out of the border crossing area and met my new friend. He drove me the 100 or so feet to the entrance to the Ihusi Hotel. As I got out of the Land Cruiser, he gave me some phone numbers for additional contacts with the peacekeeping mission and their medical facility. He advised me to get my arm X-rayed, which was a sensible suggestion that I did not heed (and fortunately did not need to).

With that, he continued to his compound, and I checked into one of the main hotels for journalists and foreigners in Goma. The Ihusi was your typical fragile-state three-star hotel. The room had two double beds, a small desk, working plumbing, barely working internet, and a cute shower curtain with dolphins jumping out of the sea. I grabbed dinner at the hotel's restaurant, which featured mediocre food, but a lovely patio overlooking the scenic lake.

I was in the Congo reporting a story *America Abroad*'s program on the United Nations doctrine of "Responsibility to Protect," which was intended to drive intervention at the first warning signs of a potential Rwanda to prevent a genocide or similar crimes against humanity. R2P had been implemented successfully in Kenya after the contested 2007 election. The Congo was an example of the limits of the doctrine. There, it was too complicated and too late to implement an R2P action amid the violence and chaos in the Congo. Journalistically, it was a stretch to use the Congo as an example in the program, but the Congo was a complicated, dangerous place that not many people visited, and therefore I had to go and add it to my passport stamps.

The next morning, my fixer Ferdinand met me at the hotel, and we went about typical first-day business: getting a SIM card, visiting various government offices to get press credentials and other permissions, and mapping out the days ahead. Ferdinand was around 50 with a slight belly and receding short gray and black hair. He was pleasant and what you would call in today's parlance, low energy.

We rode motorcycle taxis to a small shop so I could get a couple of passport photos for my press card. I had been sloppy in my prep and forgot to pack extra photos. I did, however, bring plenty of cash—I was never going to make the Sudan mistake again.

While I was waiting for the photos, I stepped outside the shop to soak in the scenery of downtown Goma. The streets were packed with pedestrians, small motorcycles, and old model SUVs and small vans. There was some pavement, and a lot of mud with deep ruts. One-story cinderblock buildings lined the streets. The buildings housed the usual assortment of shops selling food, clothing, and electronics. There were pharmacies, auto repair shops, and some restaurants. The bright pastel facades of the buildings popped against the muddy brown streets and the gray overcast sky.

The most vibrant sights on the streets were the exotic sarongs of the women, most of whom were carrying babies in their arms and balancing baskets or bundles on their heads. The men generally wore jeans or dark pants and polos or button-down shirts. They looked drab in contrast to the women.

I took a few pictures of the street scenes, and within seconds a tall, intimidating Black man was in my face. He demanded to know who I was and why I was taking pictures. I asked who he was, and he would not say. He simply demanded information from me. I explained that I was a journalist with a proper visa. He asked to see my DRC-issued press card, which of course I did not yet have. I explained I was getting passport photos and then heading to the media office to get my card.

Well, that wasn't good enough. He angrily demanded that I show him the photos on my camera. I again asked who he was and what authority he had to make that demand, and he did not answer. Given his size and temperament, I wasn't going to fight over it.

I showed the man the few pictures I had taken, and he watched as I deleted them. After I deleted the pictures, the man became friendly and said it would be no problem for me to take all the pictures I wanted once I had the press card. He then welcomed me to Goma, and once again refused to identify who he was and what authority he had (other than being big and local) to accost me.

The encounter triggered a surge anger, fear, frustration, anxiety, and insecurity. I realized I was having a PTS episode from my trip to Sudan a little more than two years prior. I felt shaken by having someone confront me again out of the blue for taking pictures on the street. It was a horrible sensation. I felt infuriated and emasculated.

Once my photos were ready, Ferdinand and I hauled ass to the information office to get my press card. It was a quick and painless process, and I walked out of the office to the street and took a bunch of pictures while in my mind giving my mystery enforcer the finger. An hour later and I was still a little shaky from the adrenaline triggered by the incident.

After exploring the town, we returned to my hotel, and I had dinner by the lake and let the calm setting wash over me. An American woman was dining at a nearby table and after I finished my meal, I struck up a conversation. Susan Schulman was a photographer and videographer from New York who had been living as an expat in London for years. Susan was short with long blonde hair and a deep tan. Like me, she did a lot of parachuting around the world, usually on her own. We determined we were doing non-competing reporting and decided to team up to the extent we could in the interests of security and cost saving.

A couple of days later, we visited the Kibati IDP camp a short drive north of Goma. The camp sprawled across a vast plain of volcanic soil and was surrounded by lush rolling hills. There were some wooden buildings—basically residential cabins and a variety of administrative offices. But most structures in the camp were rudimentary tents. Most were simple arched frames made from tree branches and covered with white plastic sheeting with UN logos. In some cases, families of eight to ten people lived in 6-by-10-foot tents with dirt floors.

The camp had been built two years prior to house people fleeing violence. In the months before my visit, another surge of violence sent more people seeking refuge in camps. The population in Kibati had swelled to 65,000 people. That was why so many of the tents were bare bones—they had been slapped together in a hurry to accommodate the crush of families escaping the recent violence in the area.

UN personnel at the camp explained that Kibati was one of eleven camps in North Kivu and that there were as many as a million IDPs living in conditions like those in Kibati. Pot-bellied children in ragged clothing and covered in mud roamed around playing while their mothers cooked food, made clothes, or worked in the market. There were fewer men than women in the camp, and most of the men didn't appear to be doing much. Some were selling items in the market, but others just seemed to be sitting around or talking with each other as the women tended to their families.

While the conditions in the camp were desperate by any measure, for many of the people there they weren't much worse off than they had been in their villages. They had shelter, food, and necessities. In a lot of the remote villages, people had better shelters, but not much more than they had in the camps. And in the camps, they had security, for the most part. As is often seen in poor, unstable places around the world, people living in camps in the Congo were not too inclined to leave because their needs were met. They feared returning home only to have to flee again when the next round of fighting tore through their villages.

People told stories of how they fled on foot and walked 50 miles or more to get to the camp. Some had been there for two years. Others had arrived less than a month prior when fighting ravaged the area—including Goma. A month before I arrived, it wouldn't have been safe to walk the streets due to ongoing clashes.

The next day I took a road trip to Rutshuru, a village about 50 miles north of Goma. The drive was stunning. The landscape was a wide expanse of thick green vegetation with tree-covered mountains popping up here and there. Some of the mountains were completely covered and consumed by thick, soft clouds. It was *Gorillas in the Mist* territory. We passed a few small villages and some people walking along the road, which was paved about two-thirds of the way to Rutshuru.

We encountered a UN truck full of peacekeepers that had stopped to hand out some food to a group of children. The truck was heading our way, so we decided to follow in the interests of security. Bandits and militias were known to rob people along the road (two days after we drove that road, marauders stopped and robbed two western video journalists in the middle of the day). Granted, I didn't exactly feel that a truck of UN peacekeepers was really going to do much if shit went down, but I figured the truck would ward off the low-level thugs along the way.

As we passed by, children would wave to the UN truck and hold out their hands begging for goodies. Like in the camp, women were out doing chores or tending to crops, and there were few men to be seen. As we neared Rutshuru, the density of villages increased. The typical village was a cluster of primitive houses constructed of small branches covered with mud and topped with thick straw pyramids. The villages made Plymouth Plantation look like a McMansion community.

Our first stop was the MONUC (United Nations Organization Mission in the Democratic Republic of the Congo) compound in Rutshuru to meet with the Indian peacekeeping contingent. Giant coils of razor wire surrounded the small base. White tanks and armored transport trucks sat in one section of the compound and large, clean tent buildings covered the rest of the camp.

We met with the commanders of the force. We sat in a quaint covered patio in the center of the camp and discussed the conditions in the area over tea. I was struck by how it seemed to be a replica of a British camp in India during colonial rule. The posh Brits would be sitting for tea in a comfortable camp or base and discussing the savage and unkempt ways of their Indian subjects.

In the Congo, comparatively upper-crust Indians sat for tea and discussed the primitive ways of the Congolese. The peacekeepers were downright condescending when speaking about the locals. I found it offensive. They made remarks about how the people were uncivilized and violent. They talked down their noses about the lack of development, the inadequate governance and bureaucracy, and the inability of the country and the people to take care of themselves. While some of what they said was true, their tone and attitude was smug and arrogant. It just struck me as colonial transference.

After the briefing, I checked into my tiny room at the nearby church guest quarters. I had a 5-by-8-foot room with a mosquito net-covered twin bed, a wardrobe, a rickety chair, and a sink, which of course doubled as a urinal to save a trip outside to the bathroom—expeditionary living, folks.

After nightfall, I returned to the UN base to join the troops on a night patrol. I donned my dorky body armor. We started out by walking around downtown Rutshuru for a bit to show presence to the locals and "reassure" them that they were secure.

After that, we mounted up on a convoy of white Russian BMPs—infantry fighting vehicles. They basically looked like light-duty tanks and served as armored personnel carriers. The soldier in charge of the patrol instructed me to climb up and sit on top of one of the vehicles next to him. Unlike Mike Dukakis, I made sure there were no pictures of me looking like a doofus on the tank.

Once everyone was in or on a BMP, we moved out into the darkness. The BMPs rattled, buzzed, shook, farted, and spat. The engines sounded like a hoard of overtaxed VW Beetles, and sparks and fire shot out of the exhaust. The mass of metal below me grew hotter and hotter and I became convinced it would burst into flames at any moment.

The convoy drove for about 20 minutes along dirt roads surrounded by thick vegetation. There was a partial moon that provided the only light. I could make out some trees and huts here and there. I could see the glowing caldera of a volcano off in the distance. We came to a stop and dismounted—in the middle of fucking nowhere.

The troops proceeded to march. We followed paths through jungle and palm trees in the faint moonlight. My eyes maxed out their night vision and I could see clearly 20 to 30 feet in each direction. The only manmade sounds in the area were our footsteps as we trudged through the jungle.

We came across some small huts. The leader of the patrol knocked on doors and announced that UN troops were patrolling and checking on security. He asked residents if everything was OK and if they had seen anything unusual or experienced any danger.

Timid voices responded from inside the wood and mud huts to say that they were fine.

It was a tad perverse. Lightly armed UN guys were roaming around the jungle in the dark and waking people up (and in some cases clearly scaring the shit out of them) to ask if they were safe and if they had seen any bad guys.

As we walked along, I couldn't help but feel I was in some surreal outtake from *Apocalypse Now* or *Tropic Thunder*. I was half expecting to see a cameraman glide by on a giant crane. The partial moonlight, the palms trees, the huts, the troops furtively marching through the vegetation: it felt like at any moment artillery and tracers would crack off and we'd have to scramble for cover. Of course, deep down I was hoping for something like that to happen so I would have a more badass story.

We continued trekking through the jungle and knocking on huts and scaring people as the song "Roland the Headless Thompson Gunner" played in my head. At one hut, a man opened a wooden window shutter, and I could see his eyes and bits of his face. He told the troops that he had heard some noise a little earlier and looked out to see two or three young men roaming around. He didn't know who they were and was afraid they were thieves. That was common there as armed men (sometimes government troops) would often roam through villages and steal anything they could.

The man indicated the direction that the men had gone, and we marched off in pursuit.

We marched for a while and emerged from the jungle onto a dirt road where other peacekeepers had already found the young men, questioned them, and sent them on their way. With that, we returned to our Russian death traps and rolled back to the base.

As we motored along, I stared off at the glowing red volcano in the distance and soaked in the moment. I was in the middle of the Congolese jungle, riding on a piece of shit Russian personnel carrier with Indian peacekeepers, staring off at simmering volcanoes in the dark of night after marching through remote villages and scaring the crap out of helpless people at the mercy of marauding militias and criminals. It was a moment. I was all there. I wasn't pining for my ex. I wasn't longing to be somewhere. I was there doing it. I was having an experience entirely my own. It was about as alive as I had ever felt. In that moment, I was in the Star Trek Nexus. I wanted it to last forever.

Alas, we arrived at the base and dismounted. I returned to my guest quarters, showered off the jungle sweat and diesel fumes, and crawled under the mosquito net.

The next morning, we drove farther north to Nyamalima, a village near the border with Uganda. There we joined with another peacekeeping unit on a patrol up a mountain to a remote village.

We hiked through dense jungle and emerged into an open expanse of rolling hills. We crossed a narrow river by walking across a tree-trunk bridge. We hiked uphill for an hour until a village appeared amidst the palm trees. The village was barely more than a dozen houses and a school building. Several dozen men, women, and children wandered about and gathered around the peacekeepers.

One man who looked about 50 explained that they had just returned to the village a few days prior. They had spent a week hiding in the bush. A handful of armed men came to the village, and the residents could not determine whether they were government soldiers or members of one of the many militias or rebel groups, so they fled into the jungle with nothing more than the clothes they wore. They said that the armed men had set up a small camp farther up the hill. After a few days, they left, and the villagers felt it was safe to return.

As the man told this story, his facial expressions and body language conveyed intense fear and helplessness. He explained that the villagers often ran off into the jungle to hide when any stranger came through the village. The locals had no weapons other than a few machetes. There was no government presence, no services, no electricity or running water. They were surviving, and that was it.

I kept focusing on the man's demeanor. I couldn't think of

another time when I had seen a grown man seem so afraid and vulnerable. In Afghanistan or Iraq or other places I had been, I had encountered many people who were living in dangerous conditions. The men all seemed to convey some sense of resilience, toughness, or defiance—they came across as "manly" to some degree, whether it was bluster or not.

The Congolese man was traumatized and made no effort whatsoever to act tough or like he could handle the situation. That has stuck with me to this day. It was the first time I had seen a grown man who presented like a scared and beaten dog who would pick up his children and run at the slightest hint of danger.

Seeing the people in that village brought into focus something I had been starting to clue into in my travels to rough neighborhoods—the psychological impact of sustained danger and trauma. The people there had lived through brutal civil war and then waves of violence from the predatory militias that had been marauding eastern Congo for years. There was no state presence, no security force (that they could trust) where they lived. Their lives were not too far evolved from cavemen in the sense that they lived in the wilderness in primitive shelters and faced constant danger from violent predators—it's just that in their case the predators were humans rather than jungle cats (although there were probably dangerous animals around too).

Those villagers lived under constant existential threat. Similarly, people I had encountered in rural Afghanistan had endured decades of war and violence. That shit eats away at you. You can't endure that kind of constant trauma or threat of trauma without it affecting you.

I was lucky in that I was visiting dangerous places for weeks at a time and could leave for peace and comfort (although I was probably more likely to get shot in D.C. than in some of the places I was traveling to). Still, I was changing from my cumulative time in places like Iraq, Afghanistan, and the Congo. It was dialing up my idle, making me hyper-vigilant. I was constantly scanning for danger and paying much more attention to my surroundings.

Loud noises or people moving quickly around me would make me jump. I felt it getting more difficult to relate to people at home who had not experienced danger. Even though I had not been in a firefight or seen any of the action I had been seeking, spending weeks at a time in settings where violence and danger was possible, if not probable, was altering my brain chemistry.

So, while the fear and helplessness the man exuded was palpable, it didn't surprise me. I could understand where it came from and how it could accumulate to the level it had in him. It sure as shit wasn't a healthy way to live.

After speaking with the villagers, we marched up to the top of the hill and found the camp used by the armed men. There were two palm and straw huts, a bench, and a fire pit. There was no sign of recent activity or anything to indicate who the men were. Even if they had been government troops, they still could have been a threat to the villagers.

We marched back down and through the village again. Dozens of children mobbed me and my camera. I spent 10 minutes photographing them and showing them the pictures on the small display. They laughed and smiled like they didn't have a care in the world. It was such a contrast to the demeanor of the man we spoke with. I wondered at what age they would lose their innocence and become hardened and afraid. I also couldn't help but think about how many children parents were having in a place where people were barely surviving.

That was a cultural thing I could not wrap my head around. At one point Ferdinand told me how his father excoriated him for having fewer than 10 children. Suffice to say that roaming around the Congo did nothing to convince me that Malthus was wrong.

The next day, I returned to Goma and the Ihusi hotel. The drive was once again picturesque and uneventful. It wasn't until I returned to Goma that I learned about the aforementioned journalists being robbed on the road, so I was clueless as to the danger level during the drive.

I only had two days left in the country, so the following

day I completed a couple of interviews and started settling my accounts. Having learned my lesson in Sudan, I had brought plenty of cash with me to the Congo. However, the country threw me another curveball.

While Congolese people and businesses happily accepted the mighty American dollar, they were extremely particular about the vintage of the bills. Most places would only accept 2003 and newer currency. Some places would take 2001, but no one would touch a pre-2001 bill.

That I had not planned for, and it turned out that $800 of my stash was older bills. Ferdinand and I went to several banks to see if we could find one willing to change my money. No luck. None of the bank employees I asked could give me an explanation why no one in the Congo would accept older bills. I should also point out that any bill, regardless of age, that had the slightest tear or damage would also be refused.

While I knew I had a worst-case option, having the office send more money via Western Union, I did not want to walk around the rest of the trip with a pile of "useless" cash. So, we explored one last option—the street.

Ferdinand took me to a block in downtown Goma near the banks where men wandered the street with massive bags of cash. They were moneychangers. I had no idea how legitimate they were, but given the general lack of rule of law in eastern Congo, I figured it was a case of "anything goes."

Ferdinand approached one of the changers. The man was willing to give me newer bills for a 10 percent fee. After some haggling, I got the fee down to 5 percent.

There was one other catch. The man was going to give me $200 in Congolese Francs at a rate of 700 per dollar. It was not a great rate at the time, but I had little leverage to negotiate a better deal. Ferdinand called my hotel to confirm they would take Congolese Francs, since some places would not. They agreed.

We walked down the street to an office where we could conduct the transaction somewhat discreetly. I was looking around to see if anyone was onto us, or more to the point me, and the coast looked clear. We entered the front room of some office (I don't know what it was exactly, but the door was open, and no one was in the room).

I handed over the $800 and the man inspected the bills. He rejected two of the $50s, saying they were too worn. So, I was down to $700. He gave me $500 in newer bills and then 280 500-Franc bills, which were not fun to count. The hassle was the fact that after we completed the transaction, I was carrying three massive stacks of Congolese notes, and I had to distribute them throughout my pockets to avoid being too conspicuous.

I cautiously peeked out the front door of the office to see if anyone was watching and waiting to pounce. I didn't see any possible threats, so we exited and flagged a couple of motorcycles.

Back at the hotel, I handed over the piles of Francs to the clerk along with enough cash to cover my last night. I still had more than enough cash left to pay Ferdinand and pay for a driver to take me back to Kigali for the flight home. We made it without incident.

A few weeks later, I returned to Iraq. I spent the first half of the trip embedded in the Sunni Triangle, the once deadly area south of Baghdad. I saw no death, no danger, as I reported on efforts to train Iraqi security forces. I spent the second half of the trip free-range reporting in Baghdad. I was covering the lack of electricity in the country and efforts to address that persistent problem.

The trip was interesting and informative, and I got a couple of good stories out of it (journalistic and personal). I didn't get any danger points. I did get merit badges for staying at the Hamra hotel (one of the journalist haunts until it was blown up the following year) and interviewing a government official during Easter dinner at the Alawiya Club in Baghdad. I also picked up a painting at the Akkad art gallery in Baghdad, the only original artwork I own.

It was a good trip. I enjoyed it and felt like I knew what I was doing. I was getting the hang of war-zone reporting.

I got a shock a few weeks after I returned. One of the State Department contractors I interviewed who was working on electricity projects was killed. His vehicle hit an IED outside Fallujah. Terry Barnich was a couple of weeks away from wrapping up and returning home to get married.

It was a jolt that made me question the capriciousness of it all. During my trip, I visited a power plant with State Department personnel. We drove to a facility in a rural area north of Baghdad. It just as easily could have been my convoy that hit an IED. I was lucky. Terry wasn't. He was just someone there to help. He was the first person who I had met and knew who was killed in one of the wars. It was no longer an abstraction.

Just like Terry and countless others, I was choosing to go to dangerous places in hopes of making a difference. My mission was to tell the stories of those places so people at home had a better understanding of the human costs of foreign policy decisions. While I had a variety of other motivations for doing what I was doing, at the end of the day, I was a public servant playing my part. We were all putting our lives at risk for a larger purpose. Terry was the first of many friends, colleagues, and acquaintances who would not make it home over the coming years.

As tragic as his death was, it didn't give me any second thoughts about what I was doing and pursuing. I was still chasing the story and the tribe. I wasn't about to turn back.

Chapter Eight
Dodging the Man in Pakistan

August 2009

ISLAMABAD — I awoke at the Chez Moi guest house feeling a tad off. I wasn't sure if it was just the jet lag and lack of sleep from the overly long travel into Pakistan, or if something I ate the day before was not agreeing with me. I had been in the country exactly 24 hours, how the hell could I get food poisoning that quickly?

To be safe, I popped an antibiotic. I can't remember what it was, but I know it wasn't Cipro. The nurse at the travel clinic in D.C. had provided me with a different antibiotic for my trip to Pakistan. She said it wasn't as harsh as Cipro but should do the trick if I encountered any hostile parasites or bacteria.

Over the course of the day, I started to question her choice of drugs. I was getting worse. I hoped that a good night's sleep would solve the problem. It did not.

The next day, I woke up feeling like Long Duk Dong after Jake's party in *Sixteen Candles*. I took more medicine and called my fixer Naveed, an affable man in his 30s, to let him know I would have to reschedule our interviews so I could sleep in and power through the gunk that was in my system (and that was regularly exiting my system at high velocity).

After a few more hours of sleep, I barely had the energy to get out of bed. I was severely dehydrated. I knew I was going to have to bite the bullet and get professional medical help. That was another first, and frankly a merit badge I did not want. In all my trips to date, I had managed to combat food poisoning with Cipro and had otherwise avoided injury or any need to seek medical attention—at least medical attention in theater, there was that trip to ER in D.C. in October 2007 to resolve the food poisoning I brought home from Serbia.

I called Naveed and he picked me up and drove me to a government hospital, which he said was the best in the city. There was one potential problem. There was some sort of doctor and medical worker strike going on in the country and hospitals were minimally staffed.

We entered the hospital, and a man directed us to a large office immediately inside the main entrance. It was an odd room. There was a desk, bookcases, a couple of couches, and a gurney. It did not seem like a reception or intake room. It seemed clean, and the building in general looked modern and well kept, so that was a small measure of comfort.

I sat on a large sofa, barely able to hold myself up, while Naveed made some calls. He knew the administrator of the hospital—something to keep in mind when selecting a fixer, do they have good medical contacts along with all their other contacts?

A woman came into the room and took my information. I had no sense of time at that point, and after a while, a couple of people came into the room and helped me onto a gurney that was against one of the walls. I thought they were going to wheel me into the hospital, but they started setting up an IV right there in the office. They hung a glass bottle full of clear liquid and prepped my arm. I had enough presence of mind to question the safety of getting an IV in Pakistan, but I didn't see much alternative. I figured if I survived, I would never be able to donate blood again.

They hooked me up and let the juices flow. I quickly drained the bottle and a couple of additional syringes they injected into the mix.

About 15 minutes after consuming all the fluids, I sat up and felt remarkably better. They gave me a prescription for additional antibiotics and set me free. Naveed and I walked out to his car, and I couldn't believe how much better I felt than when we arrived. I was hardly ready to rock and roll all night, but I could function. We drove to a pharmacy to pick up the antibiotic cocktail and then returned to my hotel. I took some pills, ate some toast, and crashed.

The next morning, I felt almost as if nothing had happened. It was a damn good thing as I had to spend the day in the car traveling the 200-plus miles southeast to Lahore. We were going there to visit two locations for my story on the lack of and barriers to religious freedom in Pakistan.

One destination was Rabwah, a city home to most of Pakistan's Ahmadi people. Ahmadis consider themselves Muslim, but the first Bhutto regime bowed to Islamist pressures and declared Ahmadis non-Muslim and banned them from referring to themselves as Muslims or calling their places of worship mosques. Hence, they are denied religious freedom in Pakistan.

The other location I was going to visit was Kasur. A month before my arrival, a mob of hundreds of Muslims ransacked a Christian village in Kasur after a specious claim of blasphemy had been leveled at a member of the Christian community.

A western evangelical organization that had been operating in Pakistan surreptitiously spreading Christianity provided me with contacts and two young Pakistani Christians to serve as guides in Kasur. And so, the two of them, Naveed, a driver who did not speak English, and I set out for Rabwah and Lahore along surprisingly clean, modern, and smooth highways. I couldn't help but think that U.S. aid to Pakistan paid for nicer highways than many U.S. states had.

The two Christian men spent the entire trip trying to convert the driver. The driver, who did not seem particularly well educated, listened politely, and appeared to ask many questions. According to Naveed, the driver said he would read some material from the missionaries, but it didn't seem likely that he was going to contemplate converting.

At one point, one of the Christians turned to me and asked about my religious persuasion. I responded, "I am not a person of faith," and gave him a Dirty Harry glare. There was no further attempt to discuss religion with me.

I don't know if being an atheist was an asset in my work or not. I tend to think it was in that religion was ever-present in all my reporting trips and I could stay neutral. I reported from deeply Christian and deeply Islamic places over the years, and since I was loyal to no faith, and in general believe that organized religion has done more harm than good in human history, I treated all faiths and sects equally in my reporting.

While my family essentially forced me to pledge allegiance to Catholicism, once I had completed confirmation (I had my fingers crossed during the rite) and appeased my deeply religious grandparents, I never went back to church—except the usual weddings, funerals, and reporting stories. While some consider me Christian or Catholic because I was baptized and confirmed against my will, I view religion as nothing more than a choice. It is not an ethnicity or race that you are born with and cannot change. I have chosen not to believe in, participate in, or identify as a person of any faith.

That said, I knew that there were situations where I might have to pretend in order to save my life. For example, if kidnapped or detained by any religious extremist group (of any faith), it's generally not a good thing to be an atheist, or heathen. By demonstrating that you are a person of faith (ideally the faith of your captor), it can engender some sympathy. It's not a guarantee, but playing the religion card can be helpful in captive situations.

Fortunately, I was never in a situation where I had to profess any faith or agree to join any faith to save my ass. I avoided any hypocrisy in that regard.

There were certainly times in both Christian and Muslim countries where people urged me to accept their faith. I would listen politely, and bob and weave as needed to be respectful and not commit to anything.

Throughout my life, there has never been a moment when any faith or spiritual practice called to me, I'm just not wired that way. And none of the things I saw, the death, destruction, the suffering, made me contemplate adopting a faith. If anything, quite the opposite. The things I saw further convinced me there could be no god. What god worth worshipping would inflict so much pain and suffering on innocent people and tolerate so much violence and killing in its name? It's all a test to sort out who wins and loses in the next round? Seriously?

We arrived in Rabwah, and I spent an hour touring the Ahmadi village and interviewing members of the community. The Ahmadi people lived in fear and would not let me record their names or anything that could reveal their identities. They had reinforced some of their buildings with sandbags and taken other measures to protect against attacks—at the recommendation of the Pakistani government. Ahmadis had been attacked in the past and the month before my visit, Pakistani security officials foiled an attempted car bomb attack in Rabwah.

As we walked around and talked, Naveed and some of the community leaders started getting antsy that my presence could bring the attention of the Man. The Pakistani government didn't exactly like journalists mucking about and reporting on the fact that Pakistan was a dick to religious minorities. Therefore, by talking to me, the Ahmadis were taking a risk, so we hopped back in the car and continued onto Lahore.

We made our way into the dense and dusty city. It was a stark contrast to the wide, lush, clean, and modern streets of Islamabad, the artificial capital built in the '60s.

We checked into a hotel with moldy showers and stains of indeterminate origin all over the carpets. There was no minibar. We hit a local restaurant for some grilled meats since I was again able to keep down solid food thanks to the armada of antibiotics floating around my bloodstream.

The next morning, the plan was to head to Kasur to talk with residents about the sacking of the village the month before.

However, the two missionary men had news. The day before, while we were driving to Lahore, the same thing happened in another village, Gojra, not too far from Lahore.

A few days prior, a Christian wedding took place in a village near Gojra, and people claimed the wedding procession was tearing up a Quran to make confetti. The notion that a religious minority would do something so flagrantly blasphemous in such a religiously paranoid country with strict blasphemy laws was ridiculous on its face. Civilians grabbed members of the wedding party and brought them to the police. Authorities investigated the claim, determined it was baseless, and released the innocent Christians. That was all it took for extremists to call for a mob to take the law into its own hands.

We set off for Gojra and parked several blocks away from the Christian enclave in the village. As we walked toward the scene of the sacking, anguished people gathered around us telling us about the incident and encouraging me to report to the world what had happened. The air grew more foul and acrid as we progressed through narrow alleys between small brick houses.

We emerged into a wider street packed with dozens of distraught people. They flocked to me. They ushered me from house to house to examine and chronicle the damage.

The streets were littered with smashed televisions and charred clothing. Destroyed houses smoldered. People dragged me through their houses to show me the devastation.

Walls were covered by thick black soot. Furniture was shattered and burnt. Dowries had been looted. Family photos lay under piles of ash and debris. The sun pierced through holes in burned out ceilings. Broken toys and dishes crunched under my feet. I stumbled across floors covered with bricks and tile from collapsed walls and ceilings. Smoke rose from piles of charred debris. The smell... I had never experienced anything like it. It was the smell of people's entire lives—their possessions, their dignity, their sense of humanity—going up in smoke. It was sickening.

People brought me to one house where they said seven people died after being locked inside by the mob. They explained that the episode started with nearby mosques calling over their speakers for pious Muslims to gather and attack the Christian village. People chanted "death to the Christians" and called them agents of America. Thousands of people stormed the village and spent nine hours trashing and burning houses. Victims said that there were villages nearby full of jihadis and extremists. They said that their Muslim neighbors in Gojra were good people who tried to help defend them. One police officer told me that there was nothing they could do. There were too many people in the mob, and many had weapons.

I pressed the officer on why the police didn't take more aggressive action against the mob—not that law enforcement in the United States has had great success in quelling angry mobs bent on vandalizing and looting. The officer said that people fired guns at the police. I asked why the police didn't fire back. He said that would result in a "judicial inquiry." I somewhat incredulously asked why the police would be punished for returning fire, and he said, "Mr. Sean, this is not law of America, this is law of Pakistan."

It was another reminder of the fact that I still couldn't abandon my western sensibilities when parachuting into other places. I judged them by my context, not theirs.

Frankly, events in the last few years have shown that in America, mob violence is pretty much impossible to stop even when you have trained and equipped law enforcement and fairly clear rules of engagement.

Officials and experts I spoke with in Pakistan emphasized that there, the state and the rule of law was too weak to prevent religious-based violence. Blasphemy accusations were almost always specious and often just a pretext for terrorism against minorities. While Pakistan had fostered Islamist groups over the years and used them to the country's perceived benefit in Afghanistan and Kashmir, it had blown back on the country. Jihadist groups proliferated and could not be controlled by their former masters in the military and intelligence services. That led to attacks like the one in Gojra.

Around every corner was more destruction. Villagers said at least 70 houses had been destroyed. Their church was burned and destroyed—a sickly ironic act of blasphemy.

In one street the villagers had erected a long awning of red fabric. Underneath were seven wooden coffins with glass panes through which you could see the faces of the deceased. Hundreds of people gathered around the coffins crying and wailing.

As I surveyed the scene, I felt the vulture dynamic. This is a thing in journalism. There are the local TV news crews that flock to people who lost a relative to murder or tragedy or who lost their homes to a disaster. People are in shock and pain and reporters are shoving cameras and microphones in their faces to extract gut-wrenching, emotional comments that will lead the broadcast and win awards.

Similarly, in war and hostile environment reporting, journalists seek out the most painful and devastating scenes and pry vivid accounts from victims. The goal is to produce compelling, impactful, and powerful journalism.

Within the field of vulture journalism there is a spectrum. There are those like Dick Thornburg in *Die Hard* who are sociopathic, narcissistic, predatory reporters who want pain and suffering to capture audiences, win awards, and advance their careers. They don't give a shit about the distressed people in front of them. Some of them will cross lines like staging photographs, coaching interviewees, or inventing details and conversations. They will further traumatize interviewees by pushing their buttons to get more vivid material. From my experience, those personalities are most common among TV journalists because of the nature of the medium. That said, I have known plenty of radio and print reporters who made my skin crawl.

At the other end of the spectrum are bleeding heart journalists who want to save every life they encounter. They are often crusaders and advocates who sometimes lose objectivity and should probably be working for aid groups or the UN.

I skewed a little off-center toward the sociopathic end of the spectrum, although I was hardly a Thornburg. I am not a Type-A personality, more of a Type-B+, like most of my grades in high school (we won't discuss my college grades). I had empathy and gained more the longer I did the job. I felt an obligation to the people I reported on to inform the world about their plight. Raising awareness was how I could help them.

That said, I also wanted my work to benefit me and my career. As I mentioned in an earlier chapter, while they might not admit it, almost every journalist thinks that way to some degree. That was the case at that moment in Gojra where I was still relatively early in my international reporting career and trying to build my personal brand.

I was the only western journalist there. I had the story to myself. I was trying to balance my responsibility as the conduit for the people there to voice their plight to the international community with my selfish desire to produce a story that could take my career to the next level. Fortunately, those two things weren't necessarily in conflict—the better my story, the more it could help the people of Gojra, or if not them it could help prevent another Gojra, and it could help me advance my career.

That to me was the essence of the bargain of vulture journalism. Do right by the people on the ground, make the world aware of their situation so that governments, NGOs, the UN, whoever, would take action to address the underlying dynamics that led to their suffering. In the process, get recognized and rewarded for doing important work that makes a difference, a win-win.

Over the years, I had many suffering people around the world ask me to help them. Some asked me directly for money. Others asked me to talk to government officials on their behalf. I always told them the same thing, that my reporting would call attention to their plight and that was the public service that I provided. I was not a savior or a humanitarian there to help them in person. I was a conduit. I was there to call balls and strikes. I would make the world aware of them and their problems so that the world could decide on what action to take.

Plus, how do you decide which individuals to help? You can't help every person you meet on the job who is in a bad place. So, you have to focus on the big picture and hope to drive change at a policy level rather than an individual level.

In the case of Gojra, I had a problem in that I worked for a monthly program and did not have an easy way get the breaking story out to a wide audience. Had I been more experienced and entrepreneurial, I would have called major news organizations as I was standing in Gojra to pitch the story. But I wasn't accustomed to thinking and working that way.

Instead, that night after I returned to Islamabad, I wrote a blog post about it. Fortunately, it caught the eye of former colleagues at WBUR in Boston who reached out to interview me about the attack. (The Gojra attack was central to my long-form story for *America Abroad* that came out a month later, so I gave the episode as much coverage as I could.)

That got the attention of the Pakistani government. The next day I received a blocked call to my Pakistani cell. It was a man from "Special Branch." He told me that he was aware of my visit to Rabwah and to Gojra. He said he wanted to meet to discuss my reporting and my plans to travel to Swat—the restive valley in the west of the country that Pakistani forces had recently recaptured from the Pakistani Taliban. He stated that it was very dangerous to travel to Swat. The government could not guarantee my safety and did not want me to travel there. Let's face it, they didn't care about my safety and just wanted to avoid any potential bad press resulting from me uncovering malign activity or getting killed in the process.

The man said he wanted to meet me at my hotel the following morning to discuss everything in person. He asked me where I was staying, which I thought was odd. "Don't you know?" I replied.

"You managed to get my phone number; don't you know where I am staying?" I asked.

He said he did not and that he would call me the next morning to get directions.

I did not hear from him again. I don't know whether he felt he said everything he wanted to—to dissuade me from going to Swat and to generally put a chill on my reporting—or whether he simply decided I was too small of a fish to waste any more time harassing.

Either way, I was psyched and proud of myself for making enough noise to get a call from Pakistani intelligence. That to me was a sign I had done some big boy reporting. Yes, it was dumb luck that I happened to be in the right place at the right time to capture the aftermath of a horrific event, but there is a shit ton of dumb luck in journalism. Anyhow, I had earned another merit badge with the intimidating call from an intelligence agent.

What I don't know to this day is whether my reporting on the Gojra attack made a difference. I doubt a single perpetrator of the attack faced any consequences. The U.S. government continued to be played by Pakistan who took aid from Washington and turned around and supported the Taliban who was killing U.S. troops in Afghanistan. Best case is that maybe my reporting caused some private groups to help the people of Gojra rebuild.

That was one of the perils and frustrations of parachute journalism. I was in the country for 10 days and then on to my next story. I have not been back since—not that the welcome mat is likely to be rolled out for me given the things I've said about the country. Had I been a Pakistan-based reporter, I could have gone back to Gojra months or years later to follow up on the story.

I spent the next three days in Islamabad interviewing current and former officials—generals, senators, academic leaders. They were all gracious and generally very candid. In each interview, there seemed to be a moment where the interviewee would make some bizarre statement or accusation. The conversation would be perfectly reasonable and rational, and then suddenly someone would say something like, "and of course we know America is tainting our water supply as part of its campaign to steal our nuclear material."

I'm being hyperbolic, but not by much. Just about everyone I met at some point offered a random conspiracy theory about America's interests in the region and how it was ultimately working to undermine Pakistan to the benefit of India or some such thing.

That was all before Comet Pizza and other conspiracy madness had swept through America, so I was not accustomed to hearing conspiracy theories left and right like I did in Pakistan. As I said, even the most rational and educated Pakistanis were prone to making unfounded allegations about American activity and intentions.

During my pre-trip research, some experts had warned me that Pakistan was damaged goods and people were prone to paranoia and conspiracy theories. It was an outgrowth of the existential angst Pakistan has experienced since it was carved out of British India in 1947. Pakistan has faced constant territorial disputes and lived in constant fear that its neighbors are seeking to divide and conquer the country.

Anyhow, based on the warning from the Special Branch guy and the fact that the logistics were too difficult to manage—and the consequences too high if I got caught—I decided against trying to sneak to Swat. Likely, I would have been turned away at a checkpoint along the way for not having permission.

Instead, I decided to head to Peshawar and visit IDP camps to talk to people who had fled violence in the tribal areas. I did not have permission to do that either, but that was much easier to get away with. There were no checkpoints on the route from Islamabad to Peshawar, and it was possible to visit a camp under the radar.

Naveed and I set out along the clean and modern highways on the 115-mile drive to the west. A few hours later, we pulled into the dense, bustling, and of course dusty city of Peshawar. Ornately decorated busses and "jingle trucks" dwarfed the tiny Suzuki cars and pickup trucks darting about the streets. Electrical wires dangled from every building and utility pole. Men in white or tan *shalwar khameeses* and women wearing floral shawls walked the streets.

The contrast between Islamabad and Peshawar is like the difference between the National Mall in D.C. and West Baltimore. Peshawar was dense, dirty, and gritty. The electrical wires and the plethora of signs on all the buildings created a painful visual cacophony. Add to that the actual noise of traffic, horns, vendors, construction, mosques, and the city was pure sensory overload.

We had to drive around and visit several hotels before we could find rooms in a habitable establishment that was also safe for a random American guy. I wouldn't say I felt unsafe or in danger per se, but I didn't feel particularly welcome, and things did tend to go boom in Peshawar. Of course, that was part of why I was there.

We finally found a reasonable hotel, dropped our bags, and drove to an IDP camp. The camp was next to the site of a former refugee camp that had housed countless Afghans dating back to the days of the Soviet invasion. Also next to the camp was a sprawling cemetery that was the resting place of Afghans and Pakistanis.

Between the cemetery and the road into the camp was a small shallow pond of filthy brown water. Six children around seven or eight years old were splashing around washing clothes in the nasty water. They smiled and laughed and waved at me as we drove by. Once again, children living in horrible conditions—an IDP camp with tent shelters—were just being happy kids and making the most of what was available to them. As I so often did when seeing scenes like that, I just wondered when they would reach a turning point.

We pulled into the camp and immediately a group of men and children gathered around us. We hadn't contacted anyone ahead of time, and I had no idea who was in charge and whether we were going to run into any trouble. Most of the tents and dividers between sections of the camp were UNHCR tarps, but we did not see any UN-types milling about. I asked the crowd if anyone was a leader or "mayor" of the camp, and they said that each section had a leader, but there wasn't anyone who oversaw the whole place.

So, I figured I would take my chances and talk to people and hope no one raised a fuss. Most of the people in the camp had fled the Bajaur Agency in the Federally Administered Tribal Areas about a year prior. They said they fled when the Pakistani government started a campaign of airstrikes against the Pakistani Taliban.

They were angry—first the Taliban moved into their turf, then the government started bombing them, and they were caught in the middle. They said they could not support either side as the other would then target them. Ultimately, most of the residents ended up in the camp in Peshawar in horrible conditions with no electricity or running water, and they were holed up in tents or at best simple brick or mud structures with tent roofs. They lacked food, medical care, and other basic services. The summer heat was cooking them, they said. Children played in filthy drainage trenches to cool off.

As we walked along talking to frustrated camp residents, more and more men and children flocked around us. After 30 minutes, the scene started getting tense as more and more men gathered and voiced their anger over their plight. The energy was turning. While the United States was not the cause of the violence in their home area, they felt the United States was not doing enough to help them. Plus, some felt that things had gotten worse in Pakistan due to U.S. activity and involvement in the region since 9/11.

Naveed said bluntly that it was time to go. Given that we didn't have official permission to be there and the security situation in Peshawar was dicey, I realized I had called enough attention to myself and should get out before anything went sideways. We got in the car and returned to the hotel.

The next morning, I did some quick souvenir shopping in the city and then Naveed took me to the airport. I hadn't booked a flight out of Pakistan at the time I booked my flight in as I wasn't sure which city I would fly out of and exactly when. The day before we drove to Peshawar, I booked a flight from Peshawar to Sharjah, UAE, on Air Arabiya airlines—a discount Emirati carrier I had flown a couple of times in 2006 when I was working in Dubai for the summer. Arabiya is the Spirit Airlines of the region, and that comparison is apt not just because of the discount service, but because Arabiya is a religious carrier that does not serve alcohol and starts every flight with a prayer.

Arabiya only flew into Sharjah, the conservative emirate about a 40-minute drive from Dubai, but it was the only flight available out of Peshawar to UAE, so I had to take what I could get.

Naveed dropped me off and we said our goodbyes. I thanked him profusely as he pretty much saved my life by getting me medical care when I was in bad fucking shape.

I entered the small, ratty airport and got in the first screening line. I was the only white dude. After 20 minutes I made it to the check-in counter. I got in the security line that snaked around a corner and up a set of stairs. I stood in line for a few minutes until I noticed a security guy waving in my direction from the front of the line. I gave him the "who me?" gesture and he nodded and waved for me to come forward. I wasn't sure if it was a good or bad thing as I walked past all the cranky people in the long line.

The man told me to follow him, and he ushered me through the security check and passport control and walked me to the gate. He instructed me to sit, and I did. He then left and I figured that he was just making sure the white guy was not going to miss his flight.

The gate agent instructed us to start boarding and signaled to me to get my ass on the plane. I walked out of the gate door to a staircase outside. I descended to the tarmac and followed the yellow line to the plane.

As I approached the steps to the 737, I noticed a guy in some sort of military uniform standing near the front of the plane. He was fixed on me as I walked up the steps. Just before I entered the plane, he started dialing his phone. Clearly, he was reporting back to Special Branch that the American reporter had boarded the plane and was heading out of the country.

I felt badass.

Chapter Nine
Things Go Boom in Afghanistan

October 2009

KHOST, Afghanistan — The Black Hawk flight from Bagram to Forward Operating Base Salerno in Khost province took about 30 minutes. We flew over American southwest-like mountains, valleys stepped with farm plots, a large lake, and then tree-covered mountains as we got closer to the base.

Upon arrival I checked into the media center, which was a weird appendage on a corner of the base. There was a wooden office and then a couple of large tents, each with inner plywood walls creating four "rooms" in each tent. The center and tents felt exposed on the corner of the base. There were nearby peaks that seemed like good places for bad people to shoot from. Plus, it was a long walk to the showers and a really long walk to the dining hall.

I was stuck killing the day at the media center as there were no missions going out and really nothing else happening. It was another stark example of the boredom of war for the "fobbits" (soldiers who spent their deployments almost exclusively on large bases and who never went outside the wire).

My efforts at chilling were interrupted by the thunderous booms of outgoing shells. The Howitzers at Salerno were close to the media center. They shook the building, and you could feel the percussion in your chest. Interestingly, many of the shells were not hitting targets in Afghanistan. Rather, they were aimed at Taliban sanctuaries in Pakistan. It was one of those not-so-secret secrets of the war.

I Ambiened myself to sleep and woke up at 6:30 a.m. to the melodious sound of birds. It was disconcertingly calm and peaceful—more so than any base I had visited. I guess it was a Sunday morning thing. I had breakfast and then went to the terminal to check in for my flight to Gardez in neighboring Paktia province.

As I was twiddling my thumbs outside the terminal, a tall, attractive female specialist with an exotic accent came outside and asked if anyone was going to Gardez. I said, "I'm your huckleberry." She stared at me like a dog hearing a strange sound. I told her I was going to Gardez, and she said she could get me on a cargo resupply flight that was sitting on the runway. She told me to grab my bags and head over to a row of Gators.

She drove me over to a Chinook that was loading in a few soldiers. Along the two-minute drive we chatted—OK, she chatted, and I flirted. She was from Ukraine and had come to the United States two years before and had been in the Army for a year. She said she was initially afraid of deploying to Afghanistan, but she had been there a few months and it was better than she expected. I asked her where she lived in the States and she said, "I don't know." She said she hadn't planted any roots and the Army was her home.

That was as much info as I was able to get in the moment it took to reach the Chinook. Of course, that sample of information only made my journalist brain want to know more about why she had moved to the United States, why she joined the Army, where she was going with it, and if she was single and liked rakish American journalists.

I thanked her for the ride and walked up the rear ramp into a Chinook. It was my first Chinook, so I was able to add that to the expanding list of military aircraft I had experienced. I watched out the open hatch as beautiful, rugged mountain terrain passed below us.

After about 25 minutes, we landed at Gardez. A young soldier gave me a briefing and orientation, including a quick tour of the small base. It sat out in the open in a wide plain with mountains a mile or so away. Atop one of the distant peaks was the remainder of a fortress dating back to the time of Alexander the Great. There was an old Afghan cemetery in base. The center of the base was an old Qalat—a mud fortress. The troops had set up offices inside. Scattered around the base was the usual assortment of containers, tents, and B-Huts.

I won the embed lottery and was assigned VIP housing. I had my own cozy trailer with a private bath in a secluded section of the base. It certainly made masturbating downrange easier. I was moving up in the war correspondent world.

The next morning, I joined the PRT for a mission to inspect some of the U.S.-funded construction projects in the area. I was reporting two stories on the trip: one on the security situation in provinces bordering Pakistan, and the other on development and reconstruction efforts, which was why I was going on a PRT mission.

We loaded into MRAPs, which was another change from my previous visit and a sign of things getting worse. Humvees were rarely used anymore because they couldn't withstand the increasingly powerful IEDs used by the Taliban.

The convoy of four MRAPs rolled onto the rough, dusty roads. Although road paving was one of the top priorities of the PRT, there was precious little pavement in the area.

We stopped at a small school under construction, and I followed along as Captain David Masuck, the PRT's chief engineer, led the inspections. He was tall with wire-framed glasses and a short mustache. He came across as mild mannered and candid as he explained that the construction work at the Balladeh school had not been up to par—some of the mortar, stone, and masonry work had not met the standards of the contract. In addition, he said that a couple of weeks before, locals had found an IED that had been planted in the school.

That was not uncommon. Insurgents had been targeting

development projects. Since the goal of those projects was to build the local population's trust and confidence in the Afghan government, it was a strategic imperative for insurgents to prevent development work.

I followed the captain inside the structure, which was a jungle of long, thin tree limbs holding up the unfinished roof. Bricks, mortar, and other debris were scattered all over the place. The captain walked around making muted disapproval and frustration sounds like Kif from *Futurama*. I mean, even I could tell the work was complete shit.

There were no workers present at Balladeh and therefore no one the captain could reprimand. After walking through the school, the team piled back into the MRAPs. We rolled on past stunning Mojave-like landscape to visit another school under construction.

It was a similar scene—poor quality construction that needed to be redone. There were a couple of Afghan workers there. One confessed that he was a cousin of the Afghan contractor in charge of the job, and the other guy was his friend. It was clear they did not have the requisite experience, and no one was overseeing them.

Captain Masuck said that was typical and the Afghan contractors regularly tried to see what they could get away with. I couldn't help but think of the scene at the end of *Back to the Future* when Biff was waxing George McFly's car. Biff said he was just finishing the second coat, and when George said, "Now Biff, don't you con me," Biff confessed that he was just starting the second coat. I couldn't help but think that often the Afghans were getting away with a single coat.

In between stops, I sat quietly in the back of the MRAP absorbing two things—unhealthy amounts of dust being sucked inside the vehicle, and surreal conversations among young soldiers and an Afghan interpreter.

The interpreter was getting married in a few days, and two soldiers who both looked to be 19 or 20 were giving the slightly older Afghan relationship and wedding night advice. I sat somewhat dumfounded as these two soldiers, they were still kids in my eyes, explained to the Afghan man things like the importance of lubrication and what to expect when his wife lost her virginity. The kids were dead serious and frankly giving solid advice as to how the guy should please his wife. They were looking out for their interpreter, who was listening earnestly. That might have been the most useful thing the U.S. Army did in Afghanistan that day.

It made me wonder how many Afghan women had ever been pleasured. The interpreter clearly had never had any kind of physical or sex education and knew nothing about female anatomy. He knew the basics—insert peg into hole and repeat—but until he got a lesson from the American soldiers, that was the extent of his knowledge. If only I could have interviewed the interpreter after the wedding to find out if he followed the advice and how it went.

Then, the soldiers mentioned a recent IED strike on one of their MRAPs. That quickly pulled me out of the relaxed reporter headspace I was in soaking up the conversation and brought things back to reality. We were outside the wire in a war zone and in an area where security ebbed and flowed. There was constant danger.

That night I slept like shit. I had anxiety dreams. I wasn't sure what to make of it. I hadn't really seen or experienced anything dangerous, but I think I was starting to tune into the general stress level of being in a place where something could go boom at any moment. I wasn't having any second thoughts or regrets about running around in war zones, but it was finally sinking in that I wasn't at an adult version of summer camp.

The next morning, I caught a flight to Combat Outpost Herrera, a small base about 10 miles from the Pakistani border. The base was about the area of half a football field and sat on top of a small hill overlooking a village. A mix of partially tree-covered and completely bare mountains rose about a mile away in each direction from the base. I threw my gear into a B-Hut with about 14 bunk beds in it. No more VIP housing.

I ended up at Herrera because the embed folks thought it seemed like the ideal place for my story on security challenges in

Afghanistan and how the Pakistan border was nothing but a line on the map to insurgents. I was working on an updated version of my January story about the rat lines insurgents used to cross back and forth and bring weapons into Afghanistan. In fact, the troops at Herrera recovered a large cache of weapons a couple of months before I arrived. In a fluke of timing, a Fox News crew was at the base when it happened. They were at the base for two weeks and got lucky—at least lucky in the terms of the news business. I was only going to be at Herrera for a few days, so I had a much smaller window during which to get lucky.

The base had seen a fair amount of action. Soldiers said they had been attacked on a regular basis and insurgents had been coming close enough to the base to attack with small arms. While that was bad for the troops, it was good news to me.

Nothing happened the rest of the day. The next day nothing happened. Seriously, not a fucking thing. I sat around the base watching soldiers try to keep themselves occupied playing video games, working out, or watching TV. Complete boredom—for them and me.

The next day was more of the same, until something finally went boom. There was an explosion in the vicinity of the base. The base alarm went off and I scrambled for the bunker along with a few civil affairs soldiers. The security forces ran to their posts around the perimeter. There was no further activity and after a few minutes of huddling in the cramped space, we got the all-clear.

It was the first time something hostile happened while I was on an embed. Granted, it was just a mortar that landed outside the base, and it didn't trigger a firefight or anything dramatic, but it was enemy activity. It gave me some hope that I might finally see some action and gain an understanding of the realities of combat.

That evening, the troops on the base had a cookout. They were loose and having fun squirting gasoline on the coals in the oil-drum grills to stoke the fires. It struck me how most of them really were just kids. Many were not old enough to drink. Most of them were probably 10 or 11 when 9/11 happened.

When I was 19, like most of the soldiers at Herrera, I was going to fraternity parties, playing guitar, chasing girls, and in general being a class clown. I can't begin to imagine how that version of me would have processed and handled heading off to an alien land to fight an enemy of weird guys with long beards wearing sheets and sandals and longing to be martyrs. I mean, I get that when it's your job you do your job. Still, when I looked at those young faces, I couldn't help but think that I did not have the emotional maturity at that age to do what they were doing. I wondered how many of them had the maturity and faculty to process what they were doing.

The next day was more nothingness. With the boredom was coming more anxiety. Every minute I was not on a patrol or covering some action was one minute less I had to capture compelling story material before I turned into a pumpkin and had to return to Washington. Even though I might only need two or three good days out in the field to get enough material, the days were passing, and I was sitting on a base with a bunch of soldiers going to the gym, doing laundry, and fixing latrines (to be clear, the soldiers were fixing them—I had not been pressed into duty to earn the Friday night steak and lobster dinner).

The next morning, I was supposed to go on a mission to inspect an Afghan border post. However, the mission was canceled. The starter motor in one of the MRAPs conked out. Fucking hell.

I sulked off to the TV room to kill time. As I was shooting the shit with a couple of soldiers in the plywood structure, there was a slight boom and rumble. It felt like someone stomping on the roof or stepping off a chair onto the floor. It didn't seem like an explosion. We looked at each other and pondered whether we needed to react.

Then, the alert came over the base PA system. Off to the bunkers we went.

I huddled in the bunker as soldiers casually donned their gear and dispersed to fighting positions around the base. They seemed rather low key about the whole thing, which made me think it was not an attack, but was perhaps an IED or some other explosion outside the base that was no threat.

After about 10 minutes, we got the stand down order. According to soldiers, the explosion happened about 500 yards from the base. They speculated it could have been someone stepping on an old mine or unsuccessfully planting an IED, but most likely it was a mortar or rocket that was poorly aimed—intentionally or otherwise.

As I emerged from the bunker, I got word that the border mission was back on. They had found a replacement vehicle. Happy Peanuts dance.

The mission briefing started around 12:15 (about four hours behind schedule), and I was glad there was no quiz, because I couldn't remember half the shit the sergeant said about the various defensive procedures and rules of engagement. It was like watching the sky-diving lesson in the movie *Fandango.*

What stuck with me was the fact that there had been attacks along the route in the past. That had the dual effect of getting me excited about the prospect of contact and worried about the prospect of contact.

We loaded into the MRAPs and drove off the base. It took close to an hour-and-a-half to cover roughly nine miles. The "road" was as rough and winding. On the upside, it probably cleared out any potential kidney stones. While MRAPs might be able to survive attacks, the tradeoff was that the 25-thousand-pound beasts of armored burden lumbered along slowly and awkwardly on mountain terrain.

The worst part of the drive was a private first class in my MRAP who would not shut the fuck up. I mean, I don't think he stopped talking long enough to inhale. He was Donkey from *Shrek.* He griped about one thing after another. I tuned most of it out as background noise.

However, there was one thing he said that stuck with me—it was the summation of all his venting and said a lot about the mission in Afghanistan. "In Iraq, I was a soldier," he said. "In

Afghanistan, all I do is play video games and build shit." That was the perspective 8 years into a 20-year campaign…

After winding through a few small villages and climbing up to 9,000 feet, we arrived at Border Check Point 12. A pine-covered peak rose behind the post and snow-covered mountains towered above in the distance. It was gorgeous landscape like the mountains around Yosemite.

I huffed up the 50-foot hill from where we parked to the small, white-walled post. I wasn't in bad shape, but clad in body armor, layers of warm clothes, and carrying my electronic gear at 9,000 feet, I thought my heart was going to pull an *Alien* chestburster. I was so winded I could barely ask questions of the less-than-fit-looking, middle-aged Afghan base commander. He said that security was good, and they had no problems with insurgents crossing the border. I couldn't make any assessments about his credibility, but I had been told by several U.S. soldiers that militants did move weapons across the border and likely not all that far from the outpost.

So, either the Afghan commander wanted to paint a rosy picture, or his troops were simply not seeing what was going on. They were equally plausible.

The U.S. troops walked around and jotted down notes about the winterization needs of the rudimentary post as I spoke with the Afghan commander. No more than 15 minutes after we arrived, we loaded up to return to Herrera. I couldn't believe I spent days waiting to get out on a mission, and that was it. While I joke about how my embeds to that point had been complete teases, at that moment I was starting to think I was either cursed or incompetent. How was it that I so consistently failed to see war in a war zone?

I loaded into the MRAP and sulked the entire ride back to the base. While the mission fell short of what I was hoping for, it did provide some insight. I was able to see how vast and rugged the border area was. With peaks jutting up to 14,000 feet, rugged terrain, and areas of dense forest, it put in perspective the challenge of trying to seal off the border. The infrastructure and resources, and boots, necessary to prevent militants from trafficking across was not just beyond what the Afghans could ever accomplish, it was beyond what the United States could. That was a point made to me during my January embed—the United States couldn't control the border with Mexico, how could it seal off the Afghanistan-Pakistan border?

A couple of days later I flew back to Salerno. The public affairs people there hadn't received warning that I was returning, so they had nothing planned for me and no prospective missions. I ended up killing time with the media team and roaming the base looking for the Ukrainian specialist. I did not see her again. "No Action" was becoming the bumper sticker for my embeds.

Like most bases, Camp Salerno had an Afghan-run bazaar. It consisted of a couple dozen metal containers that had been converted into shops. Local Afghans sold everything from rugs to bootlegged DVDs (I never understood how that passed muster on military bases).

Relations between the shopkeepers and the soldiers and civilians on the base were friendly, and Afghans often invited soldiers to lunch and cooked for them. I joined a group of soldiers for tea outside one of the shops. The shop owner, Saeed, was a slight man in his late 20s and the de facto mayor of the bazaar. As we sipped sweet tea on the small wooden patio in front of his shop, he said that he faced threats for working with the Americans, but there was no other job that paid him enough to support his family. He was frustrated by the corruption of the Afghan government, and he felt that security was getting worse.

As we were discussing the 2009 presidential election, the results of which were still in dispute, there was a loud boom. It sounded like the sound of the outbound mortars I heard at the base the previous week. Then, there was a quick whistling sound.

In that instant, my brain said that something wasn't right about that sound and I felt my body tensing. And then, BOOM!

I caught the impact out of the corner of my eye. A black cloud of smoke rose from behind a building about 75 yards away.

Some two-dozen people scrambled to the bunker in the center of the bazaar. As we huddled, I overheard a variety of comments—most of them about nothing had landed that close before. Some people were rattled, others laughed it off.

We sheltered in the bunker for several minutes as the base siren blasted and armored trucks hurried to the site of the impact. Given the sound, vibration, and visible smoke of the impact it seemed like there must have been substantial damage—especially since the rocket hit a dense spot in the base.

After a few minutes, people began to relax and wander over to the shop to fetch our cups of tea. For the next 15 minutes, we stood in the bunker, sipping tea and sharing war stories.

As helicopters took off to conduct surveillance of the area, people began to ease out of the bunker and return to their business. About 10 minutes later, the "all clear" announcement came over the PA.

I spoke with a few of the Afghan shopkeepers. They all said it was the most frightening moment of their time at the base.

Then, I walked to the scene of the impact to investigate. What I found was shocking—in terms of how lucky everyone in the area was.

A tree broke the fall of the shell. The projectile hit the tree, detonated, and then sprayed a comet tail of shrapnel all over the area. A canvas tent sat about 20 feet from the tree. Seven people were sitting inside at the time of the impact. Chunks of shrapnel sliced the tent and cut through the interior plywood like it was wet bread.

I walked through the tent as soldiers were cleaning and inspecting the damage. There were holes everywhere—ceiling, floors, chairs, lights, computer monitors. The soldiers' body armor was perched on stands in the tent, and several of the vests sustained tears from the flying chunks of metal.

Amazingly, shrapnel hit only one of the seven soldiers. And it was such a mild injury, he didn't even notice it until a few moments after the blast. He walked off to the medical tent under his own power to have the metal removed from his ass (literally).

Surrounding buildings had several-inch deep impact craters in their brick and cement walls. So, the blast had more than enough power and force to kill everyone in the tent, and yet there was only one small flesh wound.

It was like the scene in *Pulp Fiction* when the kid runs out of the bathroom and unloads a revolver at Vincent and Jules. The wall was full of holes, yet they stood there unscathed and amazed. That's basically what happened in the tent.

Had the tree not been there, or if the rocket had not hit one of the heavy branches, the rocket would have landed in the tent and probably killed everyone. If you want any proof that war is a game of inches, well, that was it.

That night, I struggled to sleep as howitzers blasted off shells and helicopters fired tracer rounds into the hillside next to the base. Apparently, they did it for the fuck of it, not because they were shooting at a hostile target. The earlier blast replayed in my head. Given the size of Salerno, or any base in the country, and the size of the mortars or rockets that militants fired at the bases, you really had to be unlucky to get hit. Yet, people did get hit. You had to have it in the back of your mind that anything could happen at any moment. It was another reality check that war wasn't like a game of tag—there was no safe zone.

The next day I joined the Agribusiness Development Team (ADT) on a mission to a village to inspect another construction project. We loaded into MRAPs and motored off to the village of Tani. After driving through a valley, we drove up a dirt road to a flat, wide rocky expanse surrounded by small bushes and mud farmhouses. We exited the vehicles amid a crowd of dozens of men and boys wearing *shalwar khamees* and sandals. There was not a woman to be seen.

The village was one of the most remote and "primitive" places I had visited in Afghanistan. There was no electricity. Houses looked almost as ancient and worn as the hills. The ground was dirt and rock with unkempt and dusty shrubs and small trees scattered about. It looked like it could have been years since the last time the area saw water. Living there looked to me to be the very definition of a hard life.

After the ADT inspected the substandard (by Afghan standards) construction work, they set up a couple of tables so they could pay the 100 Afghan workers. The long, slow process took almost two hours.

As we were loading back into the MRAPs to head back to Salerno, a loud explosion rang out. The security forces instructed the rest of us to shelter in the MRAPs while they investigated.

Adrenaline kicked in and my mind was racing as I was sitting in the back of the MRAP. While I wanted a firefight and some serious bang bang, I was also hoping that the explosion was the extent of the danger, and we could get out safely. It was an example of the growing paradox inside me. I wanted to experience and chronicle war, but I really wanted to stay alive. My post-Layla death wish had been subsiding over time.

After a few minutes, the security forces said they had determined the source of the blast and there was no further threat. An Afghan on a motorcycle had hit the tripwire for an IED that was planted in the road into the village. The motorcyclist survived the blast.

The IED was not meant for him.

There was one road in and out of Tani. That meant we had to leave the same way we entered the village. While the ADT was doing its thing, someone planted the IED for the convoy to hit on the way out of the village. It was a ballsy move as the stretch of road was out in the open and potentially visible from where we were on the hill above.

There were disconcerting implications to the whole thing. It was possible that on our way into the village we passed by some bad guys who saw an opportunity to plant the IED. It was also possible someone in the village tipped off bad guys. Either way, it meant insurgents were camped out in the area and possibly mixed in with the local population. The soldiers might have just paid someone for working on the check dam who had called someone to plant the IED. That was the war in a nutshell.

Had the motorcyclist not hit the IED, our convoy would have. The troops looked at the blast crater as we drove out of the village. They said the explosive was more powerful than what they had been seeing to that point. Presumably, the lead MRAP in the convoy would have hit it and been disabled and there would have been casualties. Often, militants would attack with small arms once a convoy had been disabled by an IED. We were lucky.

We made it back to Salerno with no further incident. The rocket the day before and the IED near-miss pierced a bubble for me. I think a lot of journalists, myself included, had false senses of security during embeds. By virtue of being surrounded by the best troops and military hardware in the world, it was easy to think that you were safe. I think subconsciously I felt like it was a TV war sometimes—it was a highly detailed recreation but there was no real danger. In my case, that sentiment was probably fueled by the fact that nothing scary had happened during embeds up to that point. I had not faced any danger—at least not that I was aware of. Even the blasts at Herrera happened so quickly that the threat was over before I was aware there was a threat.

The rocket blast on Salerno and the IED crater in Tani brought home that it was real, it was war. It made me question what it was that I had been seeking. Until that point all I wanted was to be in the shit, to witness and experience the kind of combat that had taken place in Fallujah and Ramadi, or in places like the Korengal Valley in Afghanistan. I felt that I was not a real journalist until I had been through that. I was jealous of the vivid stories other journalists had from their time in serious combat.

However, I think my perception was that even in a firefight, I would somehow be in a protected bubble as a non-combatant. I would be an observer, and yes there would be danger, but I would not be a target. It was naïve and probably came from watching footage of those battles where the cameraman was "removed" from the soldiers. It reinforced the illusion of the journalists being somehow safe.

That day was the first time I started to think deeply about what I was doing and why I was doing it. I couldn't answer the question in my head as to whether I was chasing firefights because I felt it was critical to cover and report on them, because of normal competitive juices, or because of what I wanted people to think about me for "having the courage" to cover them. I started to realize it might have been more the latter—I needed to prove something to myself and everyone else. I wanted the respect of others for doing badass journalism. Some of it was a case of buying into notions of masculinity, that real men did combat journalism.

Furthermore, I hadn't been considering that people died or suffered life-altering injuries during firefights. I had been ignoring the human cost.

Over the years, I would learn how wrong and misguided I was to believe that experiencing bang bang was the pinnacle of war reporting. I'm generalizing to a degree, but typically male journalists would flock to the front lines to cover the bombs, bullets, and blood. Female correspondents would capture some of it, but then move around and find deeper, more compelling stories that humanized the conflict and had more impact. Granted, there were plenty of alpha females out there, particularly TV reporters (a blonde Australian comes to mind), who wanted to be on camera with bullets whizzing past their heads. Their reports always seemed to be more about how badass they were for being in the thick of the action. Many were narcissistic, ambitious, and in some cases I would say damaged.

In 2014 I was part of a group embed in Helmand and there was a beautiful female correspondent based in the U.S. who had traveled to Afghanistan to cover the closing of Camp Leatherneck. I overheard her say, "I'm only happy when I'm being shot at." In 2009, I might have felt the same or at least empathized. But in 2014, after years of covering conflict, I thought that was about the most defective thing I had heard in a war zone.

Point is, there were plenty of women out there who were adrenaline junkies seeking journalistic glory, but more often it was the men who were like that. That was certainly my mindset in late 2009. However, a couple of close calls made me start to question that. It didn't stop me from continuing to go to dangerous places and head toward front lines, but it made me more aware that I was playing with fire. It also made me wonder if I would have had any appetite for it if I had a partner who was the center of my universe the way Layla had been. None of the women I had dated after her was enough to pull me from the battlefield.

My embed came to an end and I caught a flight to Kabul on a U.S. embassy helicopter. A young Afghan in a Toyota Corolla picked me up and took me to the Kabul Intercontinental Hotel (which was built in 1969 under the chain, which severed its affiliation after the Soviet invasion), where I would spend a few nights while going free range in the city.

The hotel sat on top of a hill and basically screamed, "shoot at me." And people did. The worst attack happened in 2018 and resulted in more than 40 fatalities. It was far from the safest hotel in Kabul, but it was reasonably priced, and I didn't know better at the time.

I spent the next few days roaming around the city visiting USAID projects, interviewing NGO personnel, and doing a little tourism. One of the interviews I conducted was with Ashley Jackson, then with Oxfam and now one of the leading experts on development in Afghanistan. We met at the Flower Street Café, which was on Taimani Street #2 (not on Flower Street). The NPR bureau where I would live from 2012 through 2014 was on Taimani 1, and I would end up spending a lot of time at Flower Street drinking tea and eating huevos rancheros.

That October 2009 afternoon chatting with Ashley was my first taste of the free-range expat life in Kabul. The small garden of the café was lovely and peaceful with street cats begging for snacks. It was a surprising touch of comfort and normalcy that I wasn't expecting to find in the city.

That night, I dove further into the expat life in Kabul and went out for drinks at Lounge. It was one of a handful of bars hiding behind giant metal gates and barbed wire in the city. The scene there was more like what I expected—the Star Wars Cantina bar.

In the courtyard were burly British security contractors shouting and slurring at each other while leaning against high-top tables covered with empty Tuborg cans. Inside was a large bar, and on the brick wall behind it were shelves holding bottles of misfit booze—Sloe Gin, oddly colored schnapps, mystery whiskeys, and other castaways deemed undrinkable in more civilized locales.

I camped out at the bar drinking beer and chatting with (OK, hitting on) the young American woman making drinks. She was a videographer who was tending bar to pay the bills. She was a more extreme version of half the people in LA working in restaurants to support their aspiring film careers.

In the shadows of the room, I saw what looked like transactional interactions between white men and Asian women. I was pretty certain that I recognized a USAID guy cuddling with a Thai woman in a banquette. I soaked it all in for a couple of hours. Eventually, I determined I was not going to hook up with anyone, so I called a car.

I flew out the next day. Unfortunately, the Afghan airport security screeners pulled me aside and confiscated the spent AK shell casings I had picked up as war trophies and tried to smuggle home. I was somewhat impressed that they spotted them in the X-ray of my checked bag.

I arrived at my hotel in Dubai, showered and shaved and went to the 1847 Men's Spa at the Emirates Towers for a massage. I discovered the spa when I worked nearby in the summer of 2006, and I popped in for a massage whenever I had time on layovers. For the record, the spa is completely above board and is a high-end place with no Bill Kraft business, not that there's anything wrong with that (although, if you have his money, why are you getting a handy in a strip mall salon?). My regular masseuse ground down the knots from the various uncomfortable embed beds.

I returned to D.C. and had difficulty readjusting. I had been no-ticing with each successive trip to a war zone or a place like the Congo that I was feeling on edge and "outsider-ish" when I got back to D.C. I was still in danger mode and my Spidey-sense was tingling. I couldn't just throttle back to normal and be at ease in the city or around friends and coworkers.

One morning after I returned, I was having anxiety dreams. Then, a car bomb went off outside my condo. That's what it sounded and felt like.

I shot up out of bed and stood pulsing with adrenaline. I looked outside the window and saw no smoke or debris. What I did see was the beginning of a thunderstorm. What I thought was a car bomb was an epic clap of thunder. Even though I deter-mined the cause and that there was no danger, it took at least an hour to calm down from the shock.

Although I had not been in what I defined as the shit, my years of chasing it and being in the more general shit was rewir-ing my brain. I was perceiving and processing danger differently than friends and coworkers. I was also carrying around more and more pain, suffering, and loss that I was observing and absorbing during my field trips.

There was a Dorian Grey thing happening. I was keeping up appearances and would tell people everything was fine, but that painting locked away in my emotional closet was getting darker and uglier.

That phenomenon was increasing my need for tribe. I needed to be in and among fellow war correspondents who knew the deal. I had no one in my life with whom I felt comfortable talking about what I was feeling.

So, I had to process things in silence on my own. The only upside was that I was developing a better understanding of my grandfather. He had served in the Navy in World War II. He used to tell a few funny (invented) stories about his life on a munitions ship in the Pacific, but he never talked about the real shit. I always wanted him to tell me the true war stories, but he refused. He simply did not want to go there. I didn't understand it. It was disappointing.

However, as I experienced more horrors, and saw the realities of conflict and its aftermath, I could relate to my grandfather's headspace. The one difference was that I reported on some of what I saw, so I did tell stories. The thing is, my reporting told what I saw and heard, not what I felt. People often asked, "what was it like?" in a particular place or situation. My responses were clinical and descriptive. They were not personal. I didn't want to have to dig down. I didn't want to look at the painting in the closet.

In November 2009, I received a reward for my hard work and struggles. I spent two weeks in Peru on a fellowship through the now-defunct International Reporting project.

A dozen of us experienced a guided junket through Lima, Cuzco, Machu Picchu, and the Peruvian Amazon. We gorged on ceviche, alpaca, and pisco sours in between sessions with civil society groups, government officials, and environmental organizations.

It was a phenomenal experience, and a refreshing change to go on a reporting trip with other people. It was also important validation for me. I was on a fellowship with journalists from the Associated Press, Reuters, *Washington Post*, the *Christian Science Monitor*, and I had been selected based on the merits of my reporting in the two years since I had joined *America Abroad*. I felt that maybe I did belong at the big kids' table.

I had reported from Serbia, Kosovo, Russia, Sudan, Egypt, Taiwan, Colombia, South Korea, Iraq, Lebanon, Syria, Morocco, Afghanistan, Congo, Northern Ireland, and Pakistan. Even though they were all parachuting trips and I never felt on par with any of the expat journalists based in those places, it was a solid rap sheet for my first two years of international reporting.

Aside from the adventures and experiences I was having on the ground, all that travel was paying another dividend: air miles.

The Peru trip was on American Airlines since that was what the fellowship arranged. However, all the rest of my flights had been on United or Star Alliance partners. As a result, at the beginning of December 2009, I was about 20k miles short of reaching United 1K status.

I decided to go for it. I scoured the United travel map for a round trip (that I could afford) that would get me 20k miles. Vietnam fit the bill. I flew off on a five-day junket to Vietnam and Cambodia to see the sights, visit night markets, drink beer, eat street food, and other stuff, because what happens in Saigon…

I returned to D.C. with the miles I needed to earn 1K status. For the next six years, I would not sit in economy class on a United international flight, and I probably upgraded 60 percent of the time on domestic flights.

The weekend after my epic mile run, I attended a holiday party at a friend's place in D.C. At the party was a petite brunette in a blue dress who had that Latin or Middle Eastern look that always does me in. She had a glimmer in her eye and a sly smile that screamed, "I'm fun trouble."

I approached, we talked, and I learned she was from Iraq. That gave me pause as I really did not want to be stigmatized as having a fetish for Arab women.

By the end of the night, those concerns had faded. Anna (not her real name) was funny, passionate (she and a friend of mine had an animated argument about the invasion of Iraq that I had to referee), and by virtue of being foreign was intriguing to me. We began dating.

I entered that relationship on somewhat firm emotional ground. Layla was largely out of my system (although subconsciously I was still comparing other women to her), and so I was open to the possibility of something serious with someone new. However, no relationship was going to fill my need to be a full-time foreign correspondent, ideally in a war zone. The quest for tribe would continue to be my animating passion.

Chapter Ten
Lunch in Sana'a

February 2010

SANA'A, Yemen — When I exited passport control in Sana'a at 1:30 a.m., a somewhat smarmy-looking, balding and musta-chioed man in his 30s was waiting for me. He confirmed he was the minder assigned to me by the Ministry of Information. He told me to get my checked bag while he spoke with the customs officer. I saw him show a piece of paper to the agent. I also saw him give the "grandfather handshake" to the agent, so it wasn't clear whether the paperwork was necessary.

Yasser and I hopped into a typical yellow-and-white taxi to head into the city and to my hotel. The ancient dented and rusted Peugeot wagon looked like it had been through a few wars in the decades it had spent on the streets of Sana'a.

The drive into the city at that hour was eerie. The orange-hue of the sulphur streetlights was about the only sign of electricity for the first half of the drive. The buildings were dark, shuttered, and decrepit. It certainly fit the image of a fragile state beset by a raft of socio-economic hardships.

Gradually, we started to pass through streets with little food stands open for business at 2 a.m. We passed a few cars and a hand-ful of people out on the streets. We passed through one checkpoint, and the Kalashnikov-clad police officer let us pass after heavily scru-tinizing all our paperwork. There was no money exchanged.

The first two-thirds of the drive gave me a sense that the city was a wasteland. It felt mildly post-apocalyptic. There was a touch of *Escape from New York* to it. I briefly contemplated slapping on an eyepatch.

However, as we got closer to the hotel, things perked up. There were more cars, more people, and more street front restaurants open. The buildings looked habitable, and by the time I got to the hotel (around 2:30 a.m.) I was starting to feel like the city was alive and like other cities in the region.

I checked into the Mercure hotel without incident and drugged myself to sleep.

I was in Sana'a to report on the general fragility of the country that had made it a terrorist haven. If you recall, on Christmas Day 2009, a terrorist failed to ignite the explosives in his underwear, thus sparing the passengers on Northwest Airlines flight 253 from Amsterdam to Detroit. Nigerian Umar Farouk Abdulmutallab had received his training in skivvy pyrotechnics in Yemen. That sparked a global moment of awareness that Yemen existed (people had long forgotten about the 2000 bombing of the USS Cole), and the United States and others went into a panic to come up with ways to triage the situation. The media flocked to Yemen to report on why it was such a basket case, why terrorists had set up shop, and what, if anything, could be done about it.

I of course wanted a piece of the action. No way I was going to pass up a chance to travel to a strange, fragile land and explore the roots of terrorism. So, I pitched a show on Yemen and got my ass there.

The next morning (very late morning when I finally woke up), Yasser, the government stooge, met me at the hotel to discuss my plans. He said that he would spend his time making calls for me, preparing "permissions," and would serve as my translator.

At the end of the meeting, he sheepishly started discussing payment for his services. He said that his job was to work in the ministry from 10 a.m. to 2 p.m. (standard civil service working hours in the country), but if he made calls for me after hours, or went to interviews, or traveled with me, I had to pay him $50 a day plus transportation and lodging expenses.

Even though it was normal institutional corruption for government minders to charge fees, I felt like it was bullshit. I told him I was not going to pay for his services when his government forced him on me to begin with. Plus, the guy's English wasn't very good, and he generally creeped me out.

He protested, but I held firm that I was not going to do business. He left in a huff and said I was on my own. That was fine since I had made arrangements with a proper fixer anyhow.

I wandered out to find a shop where I could buy a SIM card. The streets were full of cars and people. Shops were open. Car horns honked constantly, and pedestrians darted in and out of traffic like a game of *Frogger*. It felt like Cairo or Damascus—crowded, alive, and dancing to a chaotic rhythm.

I found a downtrodden shop that sold SIM cards and bootlegged DVDs. The floor inside undulated as you walked across, and the whole building looked like it was held together with rusty nails and chewing gum. But they had plenty of SIM cards. I made my purchase and returned to the hotel.

I was supposed to wait 30 minutes for the SIM card to activate. An hour later, the card still wasn't working. I returned to the shop.

The two men there spoke English as well as I spoke Arabic—meaning about 25 words, and most of them about female anatomy. But I was able to communicate that the card wasn't working. They made some calls, entered some codes in my phone, and magically I was all set.

I thanked them and was about to leave when one made a gesture to a cooler in the back of the tiny shop. I assumed he was asking if I wanted tea, and even though I didn't, you do not turn down hospitality in the Arab world. I gestured in the affirmative.

He proceeded to place a square plastic tarp on the floor, and the other man went to the front of the shop and locked the doors.

That was the moment when the nervous or paranoid (or fans of *Dexter*) might start to panic that the guys were al-Qaeda and going to slice me up on the tarp. I briefly contemplated that possibility and then decided based on their demeanor that I was not likely to be exsanguinated.

They produced a lunch spread of chicken, rice, bread, and yogurt sauce. I was expecting tea, not a freaking Yemeni buffet. Nobody expects a Yemeni buffet.

I joined them on the floor, and they signaled for me to dive in, with bare hands. I have never liked eating anything other than bready things with my hands, let alone chicken and rice. There was no avoiding it in that situation, and I dug in.

As I ate, I thought about how huge of a deal it was. The average Yemeni could barely afford food. The meal probably cost several times the limited profit the young men made on the SIM card that I bought. In that moment I was thinking as an American—I was putting a monetary value on everything.

For them it wasn't about money, it was a cultural imperative to be welcoming and hospitable to a stranger from a strange land. And so there I sat. Twelve hours after arriving in the country, I was having a home cooked lunch on the floor of a random cell phone shop with two men I didn't know and couldn't speak with. It was as authentic as you could get.

After we finished, I thanked them, we shook greasy hands, and I left. They asked nothing of me, and I walked out the door knowing I would never see them again. Yet, I would have a memory and story to tell for years to come, and they would be able to say they shared lunch with an American man, quite possibly the only one who had ever entered their shop. If I'm in that neighborhood again, I would most certainly stop in to say hello.

I returned to my hotel room to wash my hands. I was distracted by the distinct sound of a ruckus. Let me describe the ruckus.

Out the window I saw a mass of people marching down the street singing songs and carrying signs (ok, they weren't so much singing songs as chanting, but still). It was a demonstration of some sort.

Journalists are drawn to demonstrations like family values-preaching white male politicians to an affair with a young man or underage woman, so I grabbed my gear and ran outside. The crowd stopped in the middle of the street outside my hotel and people began delivering speeches over a shrill battery-operated PA system.

The overwhelmingly male crowd continued down the road, and finally turned off down a small side street. The crowed made its way into the outside patio of a small building. It was the Yemen Journalists Syndicate—a rights organization.

People took turns making speeches for 20 minutes. The event ended and people began to file out of the courtyard. I approached the woman in charge. She was Tawakul Karman, the president of Women Journalists Without Chains (who would go on to be one of the leaders of the Arab Spring movement in Yemen in 2011 and win the Nobel Peace Prize). She said it was a weekly protest for press freedom and to call for the release of imprisoned journalists.

There was just enough freedom in Yemen that people could stage a weekly march through city to call attention to the lack of press freedom in the country (Yemen ranked 167 out of 175 on the 2009 Reporters Without Borders Press Freedom Index). Yet, the government had journalists in custody, and there were outstanding allegations by rights groups and journalism watchdogs that the government of Yemen was behind the disappearance of journalists.

Around that time the government admitted it had Muhammad al-Maqaleh in custody. Al-Maqaleh wrote for an opposition publication and criticized the government's conduct in the military campaign against Houthi rebels in Yemen. He mysteriously disappeared in September 2009 after he began covering the offensive, and until the week before I arrived in Yemen, the government had denied that it had taken him into custody.

Like in many authoritarian countries, Yemen allowed a certain degree of freedom of the press to cover benign topics, but criticizing the government was a red line—at least for local journalists.

As a foreigner, I often had to jump through hoops to get approval to enter or report in a foreign country, but once I was in the door, I could get away with reporting on sensitive or controversial topics to a far greater degree than local journalists could. That's not a surprising dynamic when you think about it. Countries that do bad things want to control the domestic narrative as tightly as possible, but they tend to be less concerned with controlling the international narrative—well, maybe not less concerned, but certainly less able. The only way they can completely control it is to forbid foreign journalists from entering, or only allow them in on government-run and controlled press junkets—the North Korea approach.

Yemen did not go that far, but they made it difficult to the point that there were few foreign journalists at a time in the country, and the only ones who were based there full-time when I visited were flying a bit below the radar. Typically, they entered the country on student visas to study Arabic and then worked as freelancers for international news organizations. That was a common tactic in Syria as well.

While authoritarian countries sometimes detain foreign journalists, they generally avoid that because of the backlash. Detaining a journalist from the *New York Times* or CNN is going to cause a shit storm. However, detaining a local journalist often goes unnoticed.

So, while it can certainly be dangerous for international journalists to report in places like Yemen, Syria, or Egypt, they are rarely targeted by those governments. Yes, in 2013 Egypt jailed a group of Al Jazeera journalists, and the Syrian regime intentionally killed Marie Colvin and Remi Ochlik in 2012, but those were exceptions.

Bottom line, I was always cognizant of my privilege as a foreign reporter, particularly as a white American reporter, when operating in countries where the local press faced constant threats.

Plus, I had another advantage. Because I worked for a monthly documentary program, I usually did not file any stories while I was on the ground. Therefore, most of the controversial reporting I did was published or released after I had left the country in question. There were some exceptions like in Pakistan when I reported in real time about the mob attack on the Christian village and attracted the attention of the Man. I was also doing short reporting trips of one to three weeks, so governments didn't have much need to detain or deport me. Like the case of Sudan, they just played prevent defense and tried to run out the clock on my stay.

After the demonstration, I met my fixer for lunch to discuss my goals for my stay. Nasser was around 40 and one of the few clean-shaven men I encountered in the country. He was one of the most prominent Yemeni journalists and fixers and was in high demand during that window when people cared about Yemen.

Nasser convinced me to change hotels. The Mercure was off the beaten path and there were few people of significance either staying at or passing through the hotel. I needed to be in the center of the city at one of the major hotels for the international community. That would make it easier for me to get around and would mean I would likely bump into important people in the hotel. Another journalism hack—stay where important people loiter, assuming you have the budget.

With that, I moved to the Sheba Hotel, an upscale establishment close to the Old City. The move immediately paid off when I discovered that the hotel was full of NGO staff and other international officials I could stalk for information and interviews.

Once settled in there, Nasser and I went about our business. We roamed around the city interviewing and sightseeing. We visited Wadi Dahr Park and the Dar al-Hajar, or rock palace. Like the buildings of the Old City in Sana'a, the rock palace looked like a giant square-roofed gingerbread house on top of a large rock. Throughout the park, which looked like the same geology as Bandelier in New Mexico, brown box-shaped houses with frosting-like white trim rose from the prehistoric ground. From a distance, it almost looked like a miniature model created for a movie. I had not seen anything like the houses and buildings in the park, or the Old City, before and have not since.

The next day we wandered through the Old City's narrow winding streets lined with shops selling everything from spices to suitcases. The city dates back more than two-thousand years, and while the thousands of tower houses have been restored, they retain their ancient aesthetic of square stone/brick towers with large, arched windows, and elaborate cream trim. Picture Venice without the canals, and the buildings are all made of gingerbread.

Walking through the Old City was like something out of an episode of *Stargate*—it seemed like an alien world. During the day it was electric with activity among the ancient buildings—throngs of people in the streets and the bustle of vendors and customers. At night, it was hauntingly beautiful with the gingerbread facades glowing in the Sulphur lights and interior lights illuminating the giant, arched stained glass windows. It was easy to drift into a mystical headspace wandering the city in the dark, only to be jarred out of it by a crowd of young men shouting and cheering around one of the outdoor foosball tables that were scattered around the streets of the city.

The following day, Nasser invited me to join him at a qat chew at his house. I had some reservations about chewing since I get jittery from too much coffee and qat has stimulant properties. However, there was no way I was going to skip the opportunity to witness a formal chew, and if that meant indulging, well, that was a journalistic sacrifice I was going to have to make.

Qat is a plant common to Yemen and the horn of Africa. It has long thin stems and leaves that resemble mint. There is enormous debate about its narcotic qualities. Some say it is nothing more than a caffeine variant. Others claim it has hallucinogenic properties like mushrooms or LSD. For the record, I say it's the former.

One thing was clear, though—qat is addictive. Seriously, Yemen is hooked on the shit. Over the last few decades, the country turned from growing food crops to growing qat. A country once known for produce became so food insecure (even before the Arab Spring unleashed a civil war) that it imports most what people eat. To make matters worse, qat is an extremely water-intensive crop, meaning the country is blowing its limited water supply on a drug—and a lame one at that.

Practically all Yemeni men chew qat and many women do as well. People work during the day and chew in the afternoon and evenings. Many poor Yemenis spend their days scavenging for work so they can buy qat in the afternoon.

The formal qat chew at Nasser's house began around 4 p.m. Men carrying cellophane bags and bottles of water slowly gathered in an upstairs room. The floor of the rectangular room was covered with an ornate carpet (covered with protective plastic) and cushions lined the perimeter creating comfy bench seating. It was basically a Yemeni man cave.

The men settled into the ritual pose—leaning on a foam bolster on the left elbow. They made small talk as they began to pull stems out of their plastic bags. Then inspected the leaves—throwing firm ones on the floor and stuffing the tender ones into their mouths.

They briefly chewed the leaves and then moved them into one of their cheeks. The process progressed until they were all sitting with Louis Tiant bulges in their cheeks, and the juices absorbed into their systems.

Then, when the stimulant had taken hold, they dug into deep conversation. They discussed politics, security, and other current affairs. When a tribal leader held a chew, villagers would present him with their needs and concerns. That was the romantic ideal of a qat chew—a roomful of men buzzing on the plant and discussing business, making deals, getting things done.

The typical scene, at least in public, was rather different. From lunchtime on, most of the men you saw in public were chewing qat. Men would be selling socks and sunglasses on the street with wads of qat in their cheeks. Taxi drivers had bags in between their legs and stuffed leaves into their mouths as they zipped through the streets.

Anyhow, I copied what the men at Nasser's chew did and stuffed my cheek. I started to feel like I was drinking strong coffee. I was feeling alert, borderline hyper, and maybe ever so slightly high. I am not a drug person and never liked pot. I simply never understood the appeal. Qat was a kind of energy buzz that felt good, but not euphoric. It was certainly nothing I could see being addicted to.

The group of us at the chew talked for hours. I really don't think the drug had much impact on the conversation. Get a group of guys together in a room for an evening and they will talk all night about sports, politics, women (not a lot of talk about women at a Yemeni qat chew), and anything else. So, while qat was the impetus for the gathering and there was a whole ritual process of picking and chewing the leaves, I didn't feel like it was any be all or end all and the conversation could have been the same without the plant.

At the end of the night, stems, discarded leaves, and empty water bottles littered the floor. I took a taxi back to my hotel and took an Ambien to counteract the qat and go to sleep.

The next night I engaged in a more familiar recreational activity. I ventured out with some of the expats. There were only a few places in Sana'a outside of embassies that served alcohol. One was the Movenpick Hotel. Another was the Russia Club.

To be transparent—I went to the club twice, once in the middle of my trip and on my last night. Since it was 12 years ago, and there was alcohol involved, I can't remember every detail of each visit and what specific events took place in each of the visits. So, I'm just going to merge it all and run through what I remember.

The Russia Club was on a hilltop not far from the U.S. embassy. There was a small parking lot off a main road and a tall black iron fence around the small establishment. You'd walk up to the gate manned by ginormous and intimidating security goons. If you passed muster, they'd let you inside.

The club itself was quite small—maybe 15' by 25'. There was a bar along one wall, a half dozen or so tables with chairs along the sides of the room, and I believe dartboards or other bar games on the far wall. I remember it not being too dark inside. I think there were some TVs, and maybe a few Russian flags? The place was a dive.

The music was fucking loud and annoying. Way too loud for the size of the room. There were no more than a dozen other people there (foreigners only). We had a lot of drinks. There was some bad dancing. It was difficult to hear. I think there might have been an attractive female bartender I flirted with. There were also attractive young NGO women there I probably tried to hook up with. I recall our table covered in empty glasses and bottles. One of the nights there were some Marines from the U.S. embassy there. They got drunk and stupid. They ended up in a fight in the parking lot with the security goons. The Marines lost.

That's about all I remember: dive bar, Russian goons, loud music, too much alcohol, not hooking up, and Marines getting beat up. Now that I think about it, that could have been a night out in just about any city in the world.

I spent much of the next day musing about tribes. As a parachuter, I still didn't have a tribe. I was a guest, but I was not a member. The time I spent in Washington in between reporting trips was mostly working on writing the stories from my trips and producing the monthly programs as well as researching future programs. I wasn't immersed in a tribe in Washington. I worked for a small organization and while there were a few kindred spirits there, we were not a tribe the way expat journalists are.

The tribe in Yemen was unique. It was one of the smallest expat communities I had encountered. Due to the difficulty of getting into Yemen and the living conditions there (and the limited appetite for news from Yemen), there was only a handful of journalists living there full-time. That made the group inherently closer than in some of the other places I had visited.

I was envious of that group on multiple levels. First and foremost, they were living full-time in a foreign country, something I was longing to do. Second, they were all essentially freelance, meaning they had gone for it on their own, which took a greater measure of courage and adventurousness than being a staff journalist in a foreign country. They were the kind of people who made me feel inadequate. I was working for an organization that paid me to drop into places for a week or two at a time and then return to the comforts of D.C. I had a salary, benefits, and in theory an organization that had my back, even though I knew the organization had really no idea what to do in an emergency and I had to look out for myself.

The crew in Yemen were simply out there going for it. They figured out the angles to get into the country and stay there. They had to hustle for work. Several had regular stringer gigs, but from what I recall, they weren't staff reporters with any security that comes with such a position. There was also a certain simplicity to their lives—they were just out there living and working and not overthinking everything the way that I did. They were a tribe in a fascinating place living their lives. Seeing them reinforced my sense of urgency to join their club. One way or another, I was going to make a home in some far-flung basket-case of a country like Yemen or Afghanistan.

The next day, I set off for Aden. I had coordinated with UNICEF to spend a couple of days with them seeing some of their programs in the south. Like an embed in Iraq or Afghanistan, roaming around with UNICEF was a vehicle for me to get to talk to young people in the south and see the dynamics that created a pool of potential terrorist recruits.

I arrived at the airport in Sana'a for my flight to Aden. I did not tell my ex-minder, nor did I request permission.

There was a baggage X-ray at the entrance to the airport before the check-in counters. The security people weren't happy to see my audio recorder and they pulled me aside. They asked what it was and what I was doing. I told them I was a reporter and going to Aden to meet with UNICEF (all true). I explained that I was carrying the equipment that I was authorized to bring into the country two weeks before (also true), but that didn't satisfy them.

They took my recorder and passport and walked off. A few minutes later, a man approached me and handed me a cell phone. A man from the Ministry of Information was on the line and asked if I had permission to go to Aden. I said that I did (not true), and then he asked if I had a piece of paper stating so. I told him I didn't but that I had a journalist visa and was not going to Aden to meet with anyone in government (once again true).

After the conversation, the airport security agent disappeared again for about 10 minutes. I assumed I was boned. Then, one of the agents returned with my recorder, handed it to me, and apologized for the delay and inconvenience. A moment later another man returned with my passport and apologized as well.

I checked in without incident and flew to Aden. When I was walking out from baggage claim, a man approached me and asked if I was "the American journalist." I told him I was "an" American journalist. He asked what I was doing, and I explained that I was meeting with UNICEF (true). He then asked if my name was "Daniel." I said no (Daniel is my middle name and listed on my passport). He then said I could go. During the whole exchange, I kept saying in my head "I'm not the journalist you're looking for…"

I thought I was in the clear, but a moment later, an imposing man in a military uniform approached. I felt like Ferris Bueller staring at Ed Rooney at the back door. He asked if I was an American journalist and if I was meeting with UNICEF. I said yes to both. He then asked if my name was Daniel, and some last name that might have been a complete butchering of mine, but I couldn't tell. I said no. He then shook my hand, smiled, and said, "welcome to Aden." I didn't know it if was a trick. I didn't stick around to find out.

I walked out of the terminal and didn't see my ride waiting. I hopped into the first cab I saw and told the driver to step on it—he didn't understand that, but it was the perfect opportunity to tell a taxi driver to step on it, so I couldn't resist. I needed to get away from the airport before they figured out that I was the droid they were looking for. I could see out the window as the taxi pulled away that the two men were still looking around the arrival area for Daniel (me).

I checked into my hotel and received a call from a friend of my Aden fixer (who didn't speak English) alerting me that I had an interview in three hours. That left me with time to kill. I did the only thing I could think of, take a taxi to the center of town and walk around.

The driver dropped me off in what seemed like the center of action. I got out and decided to pull out my camera and take my chances. Flashbacks of Sudan ran through my head.

In Yemen, the situation couldn't have been farther to the other extreme. Men, cheeks bulging with qat, would whistle from across the street and yell "sura," and make picture-taking gestures. I would snap a few pictures and they would thank me—nothing else. They didn't ask to see the picture or for a copy. They didn't ask for money. Some asked where I was from, and when I responded they would give a thumbs up or say something to the effect of "America good," and welcome me to Yemen. For all the reported anti-Americanism in the country, I certainly didn't encounter any in Aden.

People smiled at me, said "How are you?" as I walked by, and generally seemed friendly and curious. It caught me a little off guard based on my experiences in other countries in the region. Not to imply that people in other Arab countries aren't friendly, but a white guy walking around with a camera didn't attract such cordial attention in Beirut, Damascus, or Cairo.

I continued walking around the dense and downtrodden city center. Webs of electric wires hung above me. Myriad signs protruded from the buildings, beckoning you to visit the various shops and businesses. Most of the signs were exclusively in Arabic, but some, such as the "Modern Hair Saloon" and the "Al-Zaituna Tourist Restaurant" had signs in English as well. Newer Toyotas and thoroughly battered and beaten taxis roamed the streets evading the aimless pedestrians. I was the only white guy I saw, and only non-Yemeni as far as I could tell.

I stumbled across the qat market. It was about 3:30 p.m., and the place was in full swing. There must have been 40 different stalls, and most were manned and selling the preferred pastime of Yemen. As I wandered around taking pictures, men would pose, and make small talk.

A vendor called me to his stand. He introduced himself as Omar, and said he was from Nairobi. His mother was Yemeni, and he moved to Yemen in 1969.

We chatted for about 20 minutes. Omar, who also went by "Obama" due to being Kenyan (from the same village as the former president's family) and having a faint resemblance to 44, had three jobs. He spent his mornings driving a taxi, afternoons selling qat, and evenings making silver jewelry. He said that like most Yemenis, he needed to work multiple jobs to support his children.

From the qat market I headed to the fish market and Sira Fortress overlooking the city before returning to my hotel to clean up for my interviews. Unfortunately, they did not go as planned. The only translator available spoke such poor English that I could not understand her. We tried interviewing two different civil society leaders, and I had to shut it down. I canceled the interviews for the next day.

With the following afternoon to kill, I called my buddy Omar the qat vendor. I asked him if he could take me on a tour of Aden. Within five minutes, he was at my hotel in his micro-van taxi.

We spent close to three hours driving around, seeing sights, and talking about politics, economics, and anything else about Aden and Yemen I could think to ask. It was a bit of a blessing because I got a more real perspective than I would have from any political muckety-muck. Omar detailed all the socio-economic problems in Aden as we drove along—poor education, not enough jobs, the north-south political schism, the qat addiction and on and on. It was depressing and easy to see why terrorists had plenty of potential recruits.

Omar dropped me off at a fish restaurant and he headed off

to sell qat. I entered the restaurant and sat at one of the only open tables. I ordered grilled fish. As I sat alone at the eight-person table, a group of four men in their early 20s sat down next to me. Their two giant platters of lamb and rice arrived before my fish. They gestured to me to join them. I picked up a spoon (they ate with their hands) and dug in.

The lamb was so succulent and tender I could cut it with the flimsy plastic spoon, and the men kept encouraging me to eat their food. My plate arrived and it was the most overcooked and disappointing piece of fish I'd ever eaten—so much for fresh seafood right next to the ocean. The men next to me piled hunks of lamb onto my plate and reluctantly let me surrender once I was full of the tender meat and my dry fish.

They spoke no English, but they were exceedingly friendly and generous—they refused my offer to pay for my share of the food. They finished and left. They piled into a new, yellow Volkswagen Beetle. A waiter explained in broken English that one of the men was a soccer player in Yemen and the Beetle was his car. Unfortunately, I couldn't find out his name and team, but it sounded like I had been dining with one of Yemen's few celebrities.

The next day, UNICEF folks picked me up at my hotel and we spent the day visiting their projects and programs. UNICEF sought to help young Yemenis build life and job skills, and to have leisure options other than qat and high-risk sex. Due to the prohibition against premarital sex and the difficulty of earning enough to get married, Yemeni men turned to prostitution and male-on-male sex (since homosexuality is also forbidden, the term "gay sex" was replaced with a clinical term). Yemen had one of the highest rates of HIV in the world when I visited.

I accompanied UNICEF personnel to peer education and training programs where Yemeni teens received training in HIV awareness and prevention and communication methods so they could then go out and inform and educate their peers. We visited training sessions and some after school programs where peer trainees were working with student groups.

It looked like good work, but a drop in the bucket. That was evident when we stopped at a street corner in one of the rundown neighborhoods of Aden. A few young boys were out playing foosball at one of the random tables on the street. As I started talking to them about their lives and why they were out on the streets during school hours, a crowd of dozens of young males swarmed around us. They were jostling with each other to get in front of my microphone and camera. They were eager to discuss how much things sucked: schools were terrible, there were no jobs, families had too many children that they could not support. The young men had no jobs and said they slept until the mid-afternoon when they went out looking for some labor work for a few hours so they could get money to buy qat. They said the government needed to fix things, but the government was corrupt and useless.

Things started getting a bit edgy. Older teens and young adults flocked to us. The UNICEF people started to feel we were in danger of a small riot breaking out. One of their drivers was particularly anxious and signaled for us to get the hell out of there. We piled into the cars and drove out of the neighborhood as more young men gathered. I didn't sense any specific danger, but the UNICEF people said things were on the verge of going sideways, and I trusted their situational awareness better than mine in that setting.

From there we drove to a shantytown. It was a maze of little alleyways between rudimentary houses and buildings made from corrugated metal and discarded plywood. Children ran around barefoot playing in the trash-strewn dirt allies. Like in Pakistan, the Congo, and other tough places I had visited, the children laughed and smiled and posed for pictures despite living in horrid conditions that you would think would suck any joy out of the air. Always the amazing thing about young kids—they can make any setting fun. The kids there seemed to enjoy mugging it up for the strange white guy's camera. I couldn't help but think about how dire their futures were and wonder how many would end up joining militant or terrorist groups. While the UNICEF people were doing heroic work, it looked to me to be swimming against the tide. Situations like that just made me ponder apocalyptic solutions like pressing the remote control from *The Good Place* to reboot humanity.

After seeing some of the poorest of the poor in Aden, I returned to my hotel and scraped it off. I put on nice clothes and took a taxi to the Sheraton Hotel to have dinner and visit its infamous night club. The night club was a medium-large space with a long, curving bar and a small stage and dance floor.

The decor looked like a cross between a Trader Vic's, a restaurant in Santa Fe, and a Wisconsin Elks club. There were about 40 tables and only 4 were occupied when I arrived. There was one definite hooker, a few Saudi men, and a couple of other women, fully covered.

I took a seat at the bar and ordered a beer. Typical dance-club techno music blasted. The club gradually filled up. Covered women would enter and head straight to the bathroom. They would emerge barely dressed, some looking like their clothing was painted on. The bar got busier, and I stayed in my seat soaking it all in. As the night wore on, women covered in abayas would walk past me at the bar and rub their hands across my back. They asked me to buy them drinks. I thought about it. Some tried hard to chat me up. Others gave up quickly when I signaled my lack of interest.

Were the covered women just bar employees there to encourage more drink buying? Were they prostitutes? What was the going rate? I was intrigued and somewhat tempted but thought better of it. Heading off to a hotel room with an abaya-clad woman from a bar in Aden, scene of the USS Cole bombing, what could go wrong?

I focused on people watching. Several scantily clad women danced. Saudi men drank and danced. Periodically, one of the Saudi men would fling money at the women.

I surreptitiously recorded some video of the Saudi men engaging in their debauchery. After a couple of beers, I had all I could stomach and returned to my hotel to rinse off the sleaze.

The next day I returned to Sana'a. I made one last trip to the

Old City and the Russia Club. The following day I was off to the airport. Since I was leaving the country, the airport security folks went easy on me.

I had a layover in Dubai that afforded me enough time to grab dinner with friends. Just like after my trips to Afghanistan the year before, the reentry into Dubai was jarring and surreal.

While it was pleasant to take an air-conditioned taxi to an air-conditioned restaurant and enjoy a fine meal with a nice glass of wine after three weeks of dust, distress, and dysfunction, it felt kind of wrong. It was like I was thumbing my nose at the struggling people of Yemen I had spent three weeks getting to know.

I had to keep in mind the journalistic bargain. I was in Yemen to observe and report, to provide a fair and accurate accounting of life and conditions so the American audience could understand and make informed policy decisions. If I provided that service and treated the people of Yemen with dignity in my reporting, I had no reason to feel guilty or apologize for my privilege.

There's no question that if someone offered me a choice at that moment between spending a year in Yemen or a year in Dubai, I would have chosen Yemen in a heartbeat. To this day, Yemen is one of my favorite places I have visited. It was gritty, real, weird, picturesque, and the people kind and generous—although, we're talking the Yemen of early 2010. The Yemen of today is far worse off and unlikely to ever return to conditions of 2010, let alone improve beyond that. Still, sign me up to go back.

A lot took place during the remainder of the year, let me explain. No, there is too much. In my best Inigo Montoya voice, let me sum up. I traveled to Iraq, Hungary, Jordan, Egypt, Morocco, and South Sudan.

OK, that's too concise. I'll unpack a bit.

In April I made my third trip to Iraq. I was starting to know my way around the place. I embedded in Kirkuk to report on the ongoing dispute over whether the city should be under the control of the central government in Baghdad or the Kurdish Regional Government. It was another non-combat embed, but it provided a fascinating window into the sectarian struggles in Iraq, some of which would lead to the rise of ISIS in 2014.

In June, I embarked on a couple of trips to gather material for a three-part special series on Arab youth that I had conceived (and that would win a major award the following year, thank you).

I started in Amman, which was exactly as people had described to me: clean, pleasant, and a bit boring. Amman struck me as essentially a giant college town—nice, quiet, and bursting with cafes and shops. It was sleepy and completely lacking in edge or grit, aside from the prostitutes in the basement bar in my hotel, but they were pretty mild-mannered, although interesting to talk to. One had been a seamstress in Russia and came to the Middle East to turn tricks to earn enough money to return to Mother Russia and buy a flat. She offered me a deal because I wasn't Arab, and I considered helping her with her cause, but read ahead and you'll see I had another object of my affection.

There were no danger points to be earned in Amman (at least West Amman where the upscale and international crowd lived). That said, a big part of the reason it was sleepy was the quiet efficiency of its security apparatus that kept things in check, in no small part thanks to U.S. support since Jordan is a key U.S. ally in the region.

The most interesting part of the trip (for me at least) was running into a long-lost infatuation in Trader Vic's. In the summer of 2006 when I was working in Dubai, I frequented the multiple Trader Vic's there and visited the restaurants in Oman and Bahrain on weekend trips. In 2013, I made it to the Trader Vic's in Doha. Those restaurants were a boozy bubble in a turbulent region. A couple of Mai Tais and some shredded duck and I'd forget what was going on outside the restaurant.

Most nights of the week, Cuban musicians perform in the Trader Vic's restaurants in the Middle East. In my 2006 work stay in Dubai, I visited Bahrain for a weekend and was transfixed by the flute player in the band at Trader Vic's there. She was one of the most naturally and effortlessly pretty women I had seen.

Her brown eyes glimmered and matched the hue of her long, straight hair and brown satin dress. She radiated as she performed. During a set break, I approached and flirted using my rusty, but adequate Spanish. She was lovely and friendly. She gave me her number.

Unfortunately, she was not feeling well the next day and unable to meet for lunch. I did see her one more time at Trader Vic's before I returned to Dubai. I flirted some more, but that was as far as things went. I was enchanted by her and thought of her often as one that got away, even though nothing had even happened.

Fast forward to June 3, 2010, and I was sitting at the bar in Trader Vic's in Amman drinking a Mai Tai. At the other end of the room was a Cuban band. There was a flute player. From my seat and in the dim light, I couldn't tell if it were she.

They took a break and the flute player walked by the bar. I said her name, and she stopped and looked at me with a quizzical expression. I told her we had met in Bahrain and talked a couple of times and that I had asked her to lunch. She could not piece it together. I could tell she was skeptical and probably assumed I was just playing an angle to hit on her, which given how stunning she was happened constantly.

I pulled out my phone and scrolled through the contacts until her name and number came up. I showed it to her, and she recognized her old Bahraini number. She lit up in surprise. We talked the rest of the night. I couldn't believe the serendipity of it. She was the last woman I had a crush on before I entered my life-altering relationship with Layla.

My Cuban crush and I ended up dating during my week in Amman. Even though we would not see each other again, that time gave me something I needed. She had been dancing around in the back of my mind ever since I met her four years earlier. To be able to spend time together and realize the fantasy allowed me to clear out one more piece of romantic baggage I had been hauling around. There was a peace and closure that came with no longer wondering "what would have happened" if we had gotten together in Bahrain. She was sweet and delightful, but I realized we were not compatible, if for no other reason than the fact that we were from vastly different tribes.

I completed my reporting and flew from Amman to Cairo, and Egypt quickly dampened the afterglow. I reported a story about the harassment, pressures, and sexual double standards young Egyptian (really all Arab) women faced, and how they were struggling to change cultural norms that treated women like property.

The following month I traveled to Morocco to report on the lack of political participation by youth and how young Moroccans were unable to afford marriage. Therefore, the average age at marriage was steadily increasing, and that had some serious consequences.

While reporting the story, my fixer Merieme (we bonded over our antipathy toward marriage and kids) and I visited a catering business to discuss the cost of weddings. The young men working there were loading stuff into a van for a wedding party that night. They invited us to tag along to see the process of setting up the hall.

We climbed into the back of the blue Mercedes van with the doors propped partially open. Forty-five minutes later (after ingesting a lot of exhaust fumes) we emerged at a wedding hall about the size of a basketball court with tables set for 250 guests. Family members started to arrive. Merieme introduced us and asked if any of the family members would be willing to speak.

The father of the groom agreed. After we spoke about the soaring cost of weddings, he demanded that we stick around for the party. Merieme and I politely tried to decline. He was having none of it. We were his guests, end of story. Those are the rules there.

The man escorted us to two empty seats at a table not far from the head table. There were an assortment of aunts and uncles at our table, and we politely sat and chatted with guests who kept asking if we were a couple and when we would wed (we laughed awkwardly as we tried to diffuse the inquiries without revealing that we both hated weddings).

Servers brought out multiple courses of food, and we dined and smiled awkwardly. Finally, around 2:30 a.m., the dining ended, and the music and dancing started. We explained to the father we had an early morning meeting the next day, and he reluctantly let us leave.

After the Morocco trip I was stuck in D.C. for a few months. I spent much of the time applying for full-time foreign correspondent positions. I was eager to leave *America Abroad* Media as the organization was moving into government-funded public diplomacy work and I did not want to work for an organization that was producing both an independent radio program and overseas propaganda.

While I enjoyed the minor-level of celebrity and recognition from being on the air once a month, I was ready to move up to the big leagues and work for an organization and/or program that people around the world knew. America Abroad aired on NPR stations, but it was not an NPR program and reached only a fraction of the NPR audience. Invariably, I would introduce myself as working for a public radio program, and people would say, "Oh, you work for NPR!" and I would have to explain that was not the case.

Plus, I was over the whole parachuting thing and needed to be immersed in a country and an expat tribe. I felt that moving overseas would solve my relationship conundrum since I was still in the catch-and-release dynamic with Anna—I didn't feel she was the right person for me to commit to, but instead of letting go, I kept trying to convince myself she was the right person, and I could make it work. I kept putting the burden on myself to make something work that I knew deep down wasn't the right fit. That never goes well.

In November 2010 I got back on the road with a trip to South

Sudan to report on the preparations for the territory's independence referendum in January 2011. I felt alive again to be back on the road and in a difficult environment. South Sudan was raw. It was poor, undeveloped, and tough to get around—I was in my element. At one point I had to pay a cargo plane operator $300 to get a seat on one of his small planes because I couldn't get a commercial flight to Malakal, a small city about 400 miles north of Juba. It turned out the cargo flight was going to Malakal to pick up the body of a slain police officer, and when I got off the plane I had to stand on the tarmac until the 75 officers completed their ceremony and loaded the casket onto the plane. Awkward! It was another case of doing whatever you had to do to get from one place to another for a story, and it's another of the bizarre memories from my time in the field.

Looking back on 2010, I spent most of it in the moment. I was no longer longing for Layla. While I still wanted a partner who made me feel the way I did with her, I was getting much of that satisfaction from my work. While it was work in the traditional sense, it was also a life, a structure.

As of the end of 2010, I was enjoying the journey and feeling that I was getting closer to the destination—the tribe. I was hitting my stride: I was far more comfortable operating and improvising in strange lands, and my reporting was improving in substance and style. People were noticing. Other programs were reaching out to me to report for them while I was on the road. I was starting to believe in myself, and I felt the "dream job" was not that far off. I was making crap money and was outgrowing my organization, but 2010 ended in a good place—and with more than enough miles to maintain my 1K status.

Chapter Eleven
Late to the Party in Cairo

February 2011

CAIRO — I arrived in Egypt on February 28 and met up with photojournalist Susan Schulman who I had met in the Congo. We had stayed in touch and had been looking for an opportunity to work together (strictly platonically). I was reporting on Iranian influence in the Middle East (and grabbing material on the ongoing Arab Spring) and our plan was to visit Cairo, Baghdad, and Beirut. However, as soon as we got to Cairo, we learned that Iraqi visas were not going to happen. We decided instead that we would go to Bahrain, which was also in the midst of uprisings, and we could get into the country without visas. I could still get material on Iran's influence in the region by going to Bahrain, although the story there was far less sexy than in Iraq.

In the meantime, things in Egypt were in a lull after the epic protests and clashes that had taken place in January and February and led Hosni Mubarak to step down after a 30-year reign. We were late to the party, showing up when the hosts were sweeping away the debris from the festivities and the guests (the real correspondents) had moved on to the next rave.

That was taking place next door in Libya, where things were hopping as rebels were pushing west after taking over Benghazi. There was simply no way I could be that close to such a major story (and active conflict) and not go for it. Journalists had been transiting in and out of Libya from Egypt, so there was a well-established body of knowledge and contacts to tap into.

We reached out to some other journalists and received the contact information of a Libyan man who was based in Cairo and had put together a bit of an underground railroad for journalists to report in Libya. We got in touch with him, and he provided the details and contacts we needed.

In the meantime, we went about gathering all the material we could in Cairo.

Mubarak had stepped down, the military had secured the city, and people were out on the streets celebrating the change—for the most part. Vendors were selling T-shirts, flags, posters, and other mementos of the revolution. Groups of people walked around cheering and waving flags. Cars honked their horns—well, that's the norm in Cairo year-round, so that didn't mean anything. Young men flocked to us to pose for pictures and to shout into my microphone.

Tanks and troops guarded government buildings, some of which had been burned and ransacked. People waved to the soldiers or walked over to the tanks to pose for pictures and shake hands with soldiers.

It wasn't all fun and games. There was still plenty of protesting going on in the city. Tahrir Square had been the hub of protest in Cairo for about five weeks. And while it had ramped down from its peak before Mubarak stepped down, the tempo had picked up again in the square. Protesters were not satisfied with the pace of change. Frankly, it was a bit ridiculous on their part to expect instant transformation to a rights-based democracy. That said, they were right in arguing that the government needed surgery and chemotherapy to rid it of any remaining cancerous cells of the Mubarak regime. So, they remained in the square trying to keep the heat on.

The island in the middle of the square (which was in fact a roundabout) was covered with tents and vendors. Hundreds of people milled about both sightseeing and protesting. I couldn't compare to the scene before Mubarak fell, but the square had become a mix of demonstration and a carnival. Young men and women with bullhorns led chants while young men walked through the crowd offering to paint Egyptian flags on people's cheeks. Vendors sold keychains and protest memorabilia while young people next to them debated the level of ideological rigidity needed in the protest movement. The revolution will be commercialized.

There were carts where you could buy eggs, popcorn, tea, sausages, and pastries. Tents were scattered about the ground, and you had to watch to avoid tripping over stakes. Throw in a little rain and some Joe Cocker, and you'd have a mini-Woodstock.

Yet, the protests were hardly contained to the square. Easily hundreds of young students marched through the streets surrounding the square. They were focused on a single issue: education. Their grievances were best summed up by a poster one young man carried. The picture showed students wearing green shirts and blue pants walking into a structure labeled "Our Education System," and out the other side walked donkeys wearing green shirts and blue pants. Just in case people didn't get the metaphor, the demonstrators (who were exclusively male) were quick to articulate that the educational system in Egypt was broken and needed to be reformed from top to bottom.

Less than a mile away, on the other side of Tahrir Square, a group of about two dozen men in their fifties and sixties stood on a street corner chanting. A tank sat about 20 feet away and young soldiers watched with moderate interest.

The men worked for the Arab Foreign Trade Co. and said that 12 years ago the government privatized the company. They said that since then, they had seen their wages, pensions, health care, and all other benefits decline. The men said they wanted the office returned to the public sector where they felt they would be better off financially. They were not pro-Mubarak by any stretch and were not calling for his return; they simply wanted to be public-sector, rather than private-sector employees—a stinging indictment of the private-sector economy in Egypt.

The third protest in the neighborhood was taking place in front of the Ministry of Awkaf (religious endowments and charity). A group of several dozen imams wearing red hats with wide white bands (that looked like a summer version of a Santa hat) chanted angrily and waved signs.

They wanted the minister to make reforms in the administration of religious practices in the country. They met with the new minister the previous week, and he said that he would meet all their demands. But the imams said that their demands had not been met.

The only thing was, I couldn't quite determine what their demands were. Despite their spokesman's attempts to articulate their grievances, it was not clear what they were. He said something about them wanting the right to wear certain clothing signifying their religious training, and something else about separating religion and security. Perhaps it made more sense in Arabic, but ultimately, I could not understand what the problems were that they wanted to government to address.

Cue the ominous foreshadowing music.

As I stood watching the protest, someone tugged at my arm. I turned and saw a man in his late teens or early twenties with a long black beard. He reminded me a bit of Crazy Harry from the *Muppet Show*. "Islam is coming," he said. He flashed a sly look and repeated himself. "You understand?" he asked. I gave a quick nod and turned my attention back to the crowd.

Then, just seconds later, another young man came up to me and asked my religion. I declined to answer, and he immediately began to tell me that Islam "is the best religion" and that he wished for me to convert.

As I was in the process of leaving the scene, another older man approached and said he wanted all people to see that Islam was the one true religion. He urged me to find a particular book that gives Koranic explanations to scientific "miracles" such as the Big Bang. I thanked him for his advice and packed my gear and left.

Those three men were a microcosm of what would (predictably) play out in Egypt over the next year. Due to Mubarak's evisceration of any secular political parties and the jailing of individuals who could have galvanized the electorate against him, Mubarak had laid the conditions for Islamists to come to power. They were the only organized entity in the country outside the government and military, and it didn't take a PhD in Arab Studies to know that the Muslim Brotherhood was going to be the immediate winner of the Arab Spring sweepstakes in Egypt.

The next day, we met with one of the young activists who had been front and center in the uprising against Mubarak. We met by the square.

"Let's go somewhere else," she said. "I need a beer."

And with that, we followed her through a dark alley near Tahrir Square to a little restaurant. We sat down and ordered Stellas—one of Egypt's domestic beers, not to be confused with the Belgian brew.

"I'm in a bad mood," she said. "For the last day I have been in a bad mood."

She said that she was worried that they were losing the revolution. Her fear was that the regime had not truly changed, and that the movement would run out of steam in the face of a resilient old guard.

On February 11, it seemed victory was in hand for the January 25th movement. They had succeeded in ousting one of the longest-serving rulers in the world. They celebrated and packed up their tents. They cleaned up Tahrir Square and swept the streets. They put their trust in the army, which had long been the only credible institution in the country.

However, she said that on February 22, it started to change. Ahmed Shafiq, the new prime minister, was not what they bargained for. The youth movement felt he was a corrupt relic of the old regime and he had appointed people who were Mubarak loyalists whom the activists did not trust.

So, they started to return to the square with a new set of demands: Shafiq must step down along with the rest of his appointees; Mubarak had to be tried and all his assets returned to the people; other regime figures had to be prosecuted; political prisoners had to be released; and the government had to dissolve the security system.

Hundreds had returned to Tahrir Square to voice those demands. The leaders of the movement had established a system of rule of law in the square. There was a string fence around the circle that was far more symbolic than substantive, but it was designed to force people to enter through gates. People checked IDs and searched people for weapons or contraband.

Volunteers were policing the crowd and making sure that anyone who was drunk, selling drugs, or in any way trying to agitate was removed from the scene. They didn't want anything to tarnish the integrity of the protest, and they didn't want interlopers to stir up trouble.

And there was an air of tension and suspicion. While there were many friendly people who would see a strange face among them and say "hello" and "welcome to Egypt," others were saying hello as part of a vetting process. They wanted to know who you were and why you were there. One man was suspicious of my claim that I was a radio reporter. "If you are in radio, why do you need a camera?" he asked. He seemed unconvinced by my explanation that I took photos for the Web as well. Several people asked to see my press ID.

They said that they were trying to keep a peaceful and relaxed atmosphere, but they were nervous with so many new people wandering through the crowd. Periodically, there would be a rush of people surging through the crowd to push out a troublemaker. They had caught people dealing drugs in the crowd and dragged them to the security forces nearby. There had been others who started agitating and pushing people around who were ushered out. While the network of organizers was doing what they could to keep peace and order, there was still a sense that things could easily boil over.

People were quick to point out that there was a different mix in the square then compared to the first 18 days of the movement. As the woman we spoke to said, and others echoed, there were more strangers in the crowd.

They were not part of the original movement, and they were a cause for concern. Some were simply poor and homeless people who had been drawn to the scene. Others were suspected of being Mubarak thugs who were looking to disrupt the scene. There were accusations that Israeli spies were lurking in the crowd. And then there were those who were coming out to try to convince the protesters to leave and allow the city to get back to some sort of normalcy.

I really had no context or perspective and struggled to make sense of it all. I had not covered a regime change playing out in real time before. The stakes were enormous. Those on the losing end of the revolution could easily decide they had nothing more to lose and go nuclear. So, it was rational for the activists to be wary and on edge. I couldn't appreciate at the time how potentially volatile things were.

With the story in Egypt in a bit of a holding pattern, we focused our energy on Libya logistics. There was no quick and easy way to get into Benghazi, which was the provisional capital of the opposition movement in eastern Libya. There were no flights as the airport there had been shut down due to the fighting. We were advised to either hire a car to drive us the 470 miles or so from Cairo to the Libyan border, and then hire another car there to take us the 310 miles to Benghazi, or take the train from Cairo to Alexandria, catch a connecting train to Marsa Matrouh in western Egypt, and then hire a car from there to Saloum—the last stop in Egypt before hitting Libya. We chose the latter. When we informed the Libyan contact of our plan, he said he would have one of his people meet us at the Libyan border to drive us to Benghazi, which at least solved that piece of the puzzle.

Chapter Twelve
Stealth Trip to Libya

March 2011

CAIRO — On the morning of March 3, Susan and I boarded a train in Cairo. Taking a train in Egypt at that time was every bit the shit show you would expect. The station was a filthy mess that looked like a bomb had gone off. The train was also a filthy mess easily 30 years past its useful life. People crammed into the spaces between cars to chain smoke. Passengers slept in the overhead luggage racks. The bathrooms... to quote Warren Zevon's "Poor Poor Pitiful Me," I don't want to talk about it.

The train lurched along slowly and emitted sounds and smells that made us wonder if we would make it to Alexandria at all, and if so, what diseases we would contract in the process. Nearly four hours later, we arrived in Alexandria to our delight and surprise. We burned through much of our hand sanitizer stash along the way.

Like the time I hopped a seat on a cargo plane in South Sudan or the countless sketchy taxis I took over the years, the train in Egypt was another example of the "whatever it takes" approach needed in foreign reporting. Modern planes and cars can be a rare luxury in conflict zones or fragile states, and you have to be creative sometimes to get around. If you're not willing to hop in a leaky, unstable canoe, a Russian helicopter years past its overhaul date, or a rusted-out military vehicle with a bunch of soldiers who don't speak English and haven't showered in a week to get to the story you're chasing, you're not going to get far in the trade.

Unfortunately, we were given suspect information about the connecting train, and arrived in Alexandria to find that there was no train for the rest of the day. So, we hopped a taxi to the bus station where we figured we'd get a bus to Marsa Matrouh and spend the night before continuing to Libya the next morning.

As soon as we exited the taxi at the bus station, a group of young men flocked to us and asked us if we needed a ride. After some back and forth, we cut a deal with a driver to take us to the Libyan border (with an overnight stop in Marsa Matrouh). Osama, a curly-haired man of about 30, had a mischievous, yet more-or-less trustworthy, smile. He had a newer Hyundai Elantra in excellent condition, so it seemed within reason to break the rule about getting into cars with strangers.

We sped off from Alexandria in the maroon Elantra averaging 95 mph. The road ran along the coast, but for the most part stayed just enough inland that the scenery was desert wasteland, scattered towns, and periodic industrial facilities. We arrived in the port city of Marsa Matrouh—sort of like a Biloxi or Port Arthur of Egypt—in good order and secured rooms at one of the nicest hotels in the city, which charitably could have been given one star. We found a nearby restaurant and dined on some three-star kebabs and turned in early.

Osama picked us up at the hotel at 4:30 a.m. and we set off in the dark for Saloum—a dusty, undeveloped port town best seen from a moving car. After passing through the town, the road headed up a small desert peak. A few switchbacks later and there was a moderately scenic Mediterranean vista. We continued through an arch-covered security checkpoint and then from there it was a few hundred yards to the border.

At first, it appeared desolate. The parking area to the right of the first building seemed quiet and empty. A few feet further, a scene of chaos came into view.

There were hundreds of people standing outside in the cold

morning air. They wore jackets, hats, scarves, and many were wrapped in blankets with colorful prints. Some walked around, others huddled together for warmth. Piles of luggage and belongings spread in every direction. There was a row of 30 or so buses all pointed in the direction of Egypt, but very few were loading on passengers.

According to Egyptian border officials, people had been arriving from Libya at a rate of 6,000 per day. Yet, it was clear that they were not leaving the border area at that rate.

Some had the proper paperwork to transit into Egypt but lacked the resources to pay for transportation out of the makeshift refugee camp. They were waiting for friends, family, or their governments to provide transportation home.

Others had no passports or proper documentation. That was a function of the large-scale illegal immigration in Libya. The International Organization for Migration claimed that there were about 1.5 million foreign nationals in Libya, and hundreds of thousands were there without proper documentation. And without papers, they couldn't easily transit through Egypt to go home (although many were hoping to head to Europe).

In addition to the ones who came into the country without appropriate credentials were countless who had them confiscated by employers in Libya. A group of men from Ghana said they had been at the border for days and they didn't have passports because they were taken by the construction company that employed them.

They looked tired and frumpy. They wore layers of clothes—hoodies and zip-up jackets that looked like they came off the clearance rack at Burlington Coat Factory. The men rocked back and forth to keep warm in the chilly morning air.

Many said they had hoped to work in Libya for a while to earn enough money to transit to Italy where they could earn even more. The men grew more agitated as they vented about their experiences in Libya. They spoke louder and faster and I could see the anger in their eyes. More men gathered around as they heard the heated conversation. They started talking over each other trying to get their stories to my microphone. I stayed quiet and let them vent.

They claimed that they had been robbed. Their houses had been looted during the fighting. Friends of theirs had been attacked and beaten, their money and luggage stolen. They said that everyone in Benghazi had an AK-47 and that rebels were attacking and robbing Ghanaians and other Africans.

The Ghanaian men said that they were praying for their fellow countrymen who were still in Benghazi, and they wanted the international community to save them. They complained that their government hadn't helped them. There was little to no food available at the border, and they were sleeping outside in the cold.

We heard similar stories as we walked among the crowd. People said they were exploited in Libya and were stranded with no money. Inside the departure hall, the floor was covered with what looked like an entire village from Bangladesh. Some were sleeping under their fleece blankets, others playing cards and passing the time. They seemed calm. Some smiled at us.

Under a stairway in the building, a Ghanaian woman huddled holding her terrified infant son in a light-blue fleece blanket. She had spent seven years doing domestic work in Libya while her husband worked as a laborer. She was the only woman I saw at the border. Officials shooed us away before she answered questions about the fate of her husband and where she hoped to go.

The whole scene was hard to process. My brain toggled between journalist and human like someone turning a radio dial back and forth. I was fascinated and wanted to take in all the facts and details and find tear-jerking stories that would jump out of the radio. Yet, I was surprised to see such a mass of people stranded at a border station wearing and carrying everything they owned.

While the scene was overwhelming and challenging to process as a privileged, white westerner, it was something I was growing accustomed to. By that point I had seen abject poverty, suffering, and desperation in the jungles of Colombia, IDP camps in the

Congo and Sudan, villages in Afghanistan, and slums in Peru, Morocco, and Yemen. I could compartmentalize and focus on my job—capture the pain and relay it to the rest of the world.

The more time I spent doing the job, the less shocked I was when I came across scenes of suffering, but it was all accumulating inside me. I grew angrier at the perpetrators of conflict, injustice, and suffering. Part of me wanted to fight for change, to somehow fix all the conflicts and problems, to help the helpless. Part of me wanted to become a vigilante—to seek out and kill the perpetrators of cruelty and abuse, of sexual violence, of the slaughter of innocent people. Part of me wanted to give up on humanity. I grew more Hobbesian. People are selfish and those with means and power will do anything to maintain their status and force those without to make unimaginable choices (like selling their children) to survive.

I pulled my mind back from those thoughts and returned my focus back to finishing up reporting the scene at the border and figuring out our next move. We had called the driver who was supposed to pick us up at the border and he did not answer. We called Libyan contacts and then the Libyan businessman in Cairo. It turned out that since we had arrived early on a Friday morning—the day off in Muslim countries—the driver would not be able to pick us up until much later in the day. We could not afford to lose the limited time we had sitting at the border, so we negotiated with Osama to take us all the way to Benghazi. He was reluctant. We upped our offer to $250 to take us to Benghazi and that did the trick. With that, we pressed onward across the border.

The first Libyan we encountered was a tall man in his 30s wearing dark sunglasses, a hooded camouflage jacket, and sporting an AK-47. He was the guard at the first gate along the border crossing into Libya. He asked to see our passports. We really had no idea what to expect from him—he looked like he was nothing but serious business.

The moment he saw that we were two American journalists, he was all smiles. He welcomed us to Libya and then invited us to step out and take pictures. He posed in front of a wall where someone had written "We Want Fredom [sic]." He hopped on top of a military pickup truck and stood beaming as he clutched his AK. He was gracious and warm, and he set the tone for our interaction with rebels and opposition members in Libya.

The border crossing into Libya consisted of that "guard" and two older men sitting at a little table under an archway who were smoking and writing down the names and passport numbers of those traveling into Libya. They welcomed us, scrawled our information in a ledger, and posed for photos. With that, we were on the road to Benghazi.

About an hour into the six-to-seven-hour journey to Benghazi, Osama started getting antsy. He pulled over and stopped a passing taxi. He tried to unload us into the taxi, but fortunately the other driver wanted nothing to do with heading all the way to Benghazi. Osama reluctantly continued through the expansive desert.

An hour later, we stopped for coffee at a little roadside cafe in the desert and ran into a couple of Dutch journalists on their way back to Cairo. Their driver was from Benghazi, and we quickly agreed on a car and driver swap. The Dutch guys paid their driver (more than we were paying Osama) and we paid Osama. The deal also worked out well for us as we had a driver who knew Libya and the location of our hotel. He didn't speak English, but he was fast. Since we were about the only car on the road on remote highways, I had no qualms about him flooring it, although Susan was not a fan of fast driving and periodically yelled "shway" (slowly in Arabic) from the backseat. Months later when I was in Tripoli working for NPR, I would come to understand that Libyans were the most batshit insane drivers in the world. Seriously, they drove at ludicrous speeds regardless of the traffic and road conditions.

We pulled into Benghazi in the mid-afternoon. We checked into our appropriately gaudy and tacky room at the al-Wahat hotel. The real reporters with expense accounts of course stayed at the fancy Tibesti Hotel, along with members of the transitional government and other important people.

We dropped our bags and caught a ride with a couple of Finnish reporters to the media center to obtain press credentials from the rebels. The media center was across the street from a corniche along the sea. Cars were packed up to eight across flooding into the port area. People were coming out to celebrate the liberation of Benghazi and the ongoing successes of the revolution. Thousands of people gathered outside the media center, in the street, and along the corniche. They climbed on abandoned tanks and strolled along as celebratory gunfire and explosions rang out. Celebrants waved pre-Gaddafi flags. Children had flags painted on their faces.

We went up to the roof of the media center building to soak it all in. History was unfolding before our eyes. People had risen and were casting off one of the world's most reviled dictators. To bear witness to something like that, well, that was my job and why I got in the game. However, it was surreal to see it happening in real time. It was more powerful than watching the South Sudanese registering to vote for their independence, which at the time I thought was one of the biggest moments I had witnessed.

While in the past Libyans were reluctant to speak out or say anything critical of the Gaddafi regime, that had all gone out the window. Libyans were aching to talk to western media. Men and boys would approach us and ask to tell us stories. They would yell "Sura, sura" and ask you to take photos of everything, including them.

One man followed me through the media center for 20 minutes as I was completing my registration process and recording and photographing the sounds and sights. The man could barely contain himself. Once he saw that I was finished recording, he asked if he could tell me a story.

He wanted me to explore the controversial case of the Bulgarian nurses (and a Palestinian doctor) who were convicted of injecting 400 Libyan babies with HIV in a Benghazi hospital.

In 1998, the Libyan government charged the "Benghazi six" with the crime and their case played out over the next 9 years in Libyan courts. They were sentenced to life but transferred to Bulgarian custody and pardoned by the Bulgarian president.

The Libyan gentleman claimed that it was Gaddafi all along who infected the children and that the western media needed to investigate it so the world could put it on Gaddafi's tab of terrorist offenses and crimes against humanity.

The man said that he could never say anything about it before because he would be arrested at best and killed at worst. He kept talking about how now there was freedom of speech in Libya, and he wanted to talk. I was hoping he was going to hand me some game-changing evidence that would lead to a killer scoop, but he just kept telling me that the media needed to report that Gaddafi had been responsible for the HIV epidemic. To date, there is no concrete explanation for the outbreak.

While I was disappointed that he didn't have new and sala-cious details, I realized that wasn't the story. The story was that he felt it was finally safe to speak out loud and denounce Gaddafi. It was as if the Libyan people were turning away from the shadows on the cave wall and walking out into the light. It was humbling to witness people exercising what Americans take for granted: freedom of speech.

That was the case the whole weekend. People were relishing the ability to talk for the first time in their lives. They would launch into anti-Gaddafi diatribes and list off his crimes against the world and the Libyan people. They would often say some-thing to the effect of, "I could never say this before, but..."

Upon meeting anyone, they would instantly ask, "CNN, BBC, Jazeera?" They were hoping that we would be from a global, recognizable media outlet where they felt anything they said would be broadcast to the entire world and then the world would stand behind them. While there was some understandable naïveté about the power and reach of media and what would come of the world seeing and hearing stories of decades of repression and suffering, they were also quite savvy in their efforts to convey mes-sages through the media.

They focused on stories about relatives arrested or killed by the regime. They highlighted visceral tales of torture and suffering. They went straight to the red meat that the media love.

They also repeated narratives that had been questioned since the revolution started. Almost everyone had a tale about Gaddafi mercenaries, and most people offered what they thought was proof: pictures of dead Africans that they had received on their cell phones. They talked of "black men" with guns killing civilians. They pointed to the passports that had been seized in takeovers of some of the military establishments in the area.

At one point during the weekend, we visited the court building in Benghazi where rebels were holding dozens of sub-Saharan Africans they claimed were mercenaries. Rebels would not let us interview or photograph the prisoners, but they presented their "evidence." They dumped a bag full of foreign passports onto a desk and pointed at them with a certainty as if saying "the prosecution rests."

The passports were from Chad, Sudan, Congo, and other nearby countries. Was it plausible that some were mercenaries? Yes. Did the rebels offer any concrete proof beyond a sexy and decades-old narrative of Gaddafi recruiting Tuaregs from Mali to kill innocent civilians? No.

That was one of the challenges of sorting out fact and fiction in Libya. There was a war going on over both territory and narratives. People were speaking freely for the first time in their lives, and sometimes they had more passion than facts.

Rumor and speculation were rampant. Journalistically speaking, unless you witnessed something, you had to be skeptical of narratives presented and be more cautious than usual about tracking down additional sources and verifying stories.

We were standing on the roof of the media center in Benghazi when we heard several loud explosions. We ran back inside to take cover. Fortunately, it turned out to be people setting off fish bombs in celebration. For years, Libyans had used homemade bombs to stun and catch fish, and those bomb-making skills were coming in handy during the conflict. While it was reassuring to know the explosions were not hostile, it was still unsettling when they went off.

After receiving our media credentials, we went out into the street to continue being mobbed by "free Libyans." People swarmed to our cameras and recorders like D.C. interns to an open bar at a think tank event. Amid the chaos, we found the two young volunteer fixers assigned to us by the Libyan businessman in Cairo.

Like everyone else we met to that point in Libya, they were kind, generous, and endearing. They came across as a Libyan version of Bill and Ted. Their attire had a quirky 80s pop look to it, and they were a tad goofy, but sweet. We drove off with them to get SIM cards and then returned to the hotel to have dinner and work before crashing for the night.

Saturday morning, Bill and Ted arrived and said that a training center had been attacked by Gaddafi loyalists the night before as people were out celebrating in Benghazi. That was big news considering that the rebels had taken Benghazi more than a week before and the front line was a couple hundred miles away. Our fixers said that 23 people died when an explosive went off at a camp where rebel forces were training to go fight.

We visited Benghazi Medical Center in search of survivors and information. Staff and volunteers told us they had received survivors and bodies. Several young men wearing rebel ID cards joined us and escorted us down the hall. They didn't ask us to check in or show ID of any kind—our handmade press badges from the volunteer-staffed media center in Benghazi were enough to get us access to anything we wanted.

We piled into a room where a man with a tube in his nose was lying in bed. Doctors told us he was at the scene, but unfortunately, he was not able to talk.

Hospital staff called us to the morgue to see bodies. There

were six complete bodies (all but two were grotesquely disfigured), and then a table with human pieces still to be identified. Whatever had happened, it was clearly powerful, violent, and gruesome.

That was my first-time seeing casualties of war in the very literal flesh, and it was unpleasant to say the least. Nothing can prepare you for seeing mangled bodies and parts like that. It reinforces how fragile the human body is and how many threats and dangers there are.

As we photographed the remains, Susan explained techniques for conveying the fact that they were dead without being pornographic about it. Photograph the shoes or hands lying on the torso and avoid the mangled and bloated faces. I photographed the faces and body parts anyhow, just to have them. Although I'm not sure to what end. It turns my stomach anytime I scroll past them in my photo library. But like my ethic of recording everything as you never knew when a seemingly random piece of audio would be useful in a story, I felt I needed to photograph everything as well.

As we were examining the remains, a young man came to identify one of the bodies. It was his brother. He broke down in tears as a couple of friends held him up. Some of the people with him said his brother had been working with the rebels at the scene of the incident.

We set off to the scene of the blast. We drove for about 20 minutes, past the airport and well outside the city. We pulled off a side road and came across a slew of parked cars and rebels running a security checkpoint. We flashed our press badges and the rebels yelled "Sahafeen" (reporters) and waved us through the traffic. After about a mile, we came around a bend and there it was.

Down a slope from the road was smoldering wreckage of buildings, burned out cars, charred land for hundreds of yards, and debris scattered an unfathomable distance. We pulled over and got out to walk around the site. A battered and barely recognizable black Chevy Malibu sat on the hillside looking over the twisted metal beams and panels of what had been several buildings.

About 200 to 300 yards up the hill from the center of the blast site, trees were lying on their sides with their roots freshly exposed. It was no little car bomb. The enormity of the wreckage explained the mangled condition of the bodies and body parts at the hospital morgue. Anyone within a couple of hundred yards would have been lucky to walk away.

As we walked around the site in amazement of how much debris had been spread so far, we heard a strange, low-pitched rumble in the distance. For a second it sounded like something about to blow up, but then it sounded like an aircraft approaching. That set off a panic and people started yelling and scrambling to their cars to flee. We did so as well and drove off (well, minus the yelling). We did not see any evidence of aircraft or hear any further sound, but in a chaotic environment like that, there was no point pushing our luck.

On the way back to the city, we passed a huge crowd of cars and saw a gathering of people off the side of the road. We also heard blasts of gunfire—but it was from men firing their rifles into the air, not shooting at anyone.

It was the funeral of men killed by the blast. We parked and once again, as soon as people saw that we were journalists, they rushed us into the cemetery. They pushed us through the crowd of hundreds, and quite possibly a thousand or more. They brought us up to a long trench in the ground where men were hunched over pouring cement onto the coffins.

They used their bare hands to spread the cement. When they saw our cameras and recorders, they broke into brutally loud and emotional chanting. Men fired their AKs into the air. It ramped up to a fevered, and rather disconcerting pitch.

From the funeral, we made our way back into town, and to Jellah Hospital, where several survivors were being treated. One man in the ICU said he was working in the warehouse as a volunteer security guard (all rebels were technically volunteers since there was no state paying them). As he lay in bed with metal rods and brackets holding his fractured right thigh and shin in place, he said that he saw smoke and started to run from the building. He obviously got far enough away to survive the blast.

By the end of the day, we had determined that the initial claims that Gaddafi loyalists had attacked and destroyed a rebel camp were false. We pieced together that a fire had started in a former regime military complex captured by the rebels. It was most likely caused by a careless smoker. The fire started a chain reaction of explosions as all the weapons and munitions in the warehouses ignited. It culminated in an epic blast that created the wreckage we toured.

It was abundantly clear that people wanted us to convey a message to the world that Gaddafi had been behind the "attack" and that potentially hundreds of innocent people died. They wanted us to see the bodies, the wreckage, the burials, and the grieving family members. They wanted the world to see victims of Gaddafi brutality. Most believed that was the narrative.

As we found, there were many facts behind the explosion, but in war and revolution, the facts are not only casualties, as the saying goes—sometimes they just don't matter to people. A narrative that started out as a deliberate attack on a rebel training center in the middle of Benghazi, ended up as a suspicious (and most likely accidental) series of explosions at an ammunition storage depot in a remote area on the far outskirts of the city. Regardless of the narrative, the one fact was that many people died, and many were still missing.

That night, it started to dawn on me that I was covering a war. I still had the notion in my head that war reporting was front line stuff and bang bang, so I didn't completely grasp that I was in fact in the shit. Libya was in an active state of civil war. Benghazi had been liberated just a week or so prior. The rebels were scrambling to keep the city functioning and bolster the war effort that was moving along the coast.

A little more than a week later, Gaddafi forces would attack Benghazi again, only to be fought off. So, it was all in flux and there was real danger all around. I was doing war journalism, whether I fully realized it or not. For the most part, I was focused on the moment, the work, the importance of capturing as much material as possible rather than reflecting on it or contemplating what merit badges I was earning. Even though I was still working for a small organization and camped out at a low-rent hotel while CNN and the *New York Times* were across town at the fancy place, I was there doing the job.

The next morning, we set out to the south of Benghazi to see what was happening closer to the front line. Rebels had taken Ras Lanuf and were moving on toward Bin Jawad. That meant the front line was more than 200 miles from Benghazi and out of range for us for a day trip.

We passed several rebel checkpoints along the coastal highway. Fighters would peer in the window of the car, see two Americans, and smile. "Welcome to Libya," they would all say as they waved us on giving a thumbs up or a victory sign.

Without fail, imposing men with nasty looking weapons would smile and say hello and welcome. Those who could speak English would chat and thank us for being there. They would call Gaddafi a variety of names and talk about the gruesome things he had done to the people of Libya.

We ran across groups of young rebels driving in pickup trucks with large weapons in the back: .50 caliber machine guns, anti-aircraft guns, mortars. Often, they would get amped up and fire off a few rounds in the air. Sometimes, men fired off weapons just to try to get a start out of us. It worked, especially when one man decided to fire an anti-aircraft gun while we were 10 feet away and had our backs turned to him. The rebels looked at us and laughed like school kids after we damn-near crapped our pants.

We reached Ajdabiya, about 90 miles south of Benghazi. We saw a hospital and stopped. Doctors and nurses welcomed us. They gave us a quick tour and read out on conditions there.

The medical staff included a team of Egyptian doctors. One of the doctors was a tall, attractive woman in her 30s with straight black hair. Her English was excellent, which allowed me to interview her and flirt shamelessly. She was based at a medical school in Lebanon and had returned to Egypt during the revolution to add moral and medical support. When things quieted down there, she and the other doctors traveled to Libya. I got her contacts, and we discussed prospects of meeting up in Lebanon sometime. Of course, it had to be Lebanon.

The doctors said that a hospital in Ras Lanuf (near the front line) was handling the critical care and then patients would transit to the hospital in Ajdabiya for secondary care. There were a few rebels in the hospital recovering from significant wounds, and there were also several children who had been injured by the conflict.

One child was in critical condition with a bullet wound to the head. The child's father held up an X-ray showing the large bullet still in the child's skull. The man said his son was playing outside their house in Ras Lanuf and suddenly fell limp.

Then, we heard a siren. An ambulance and several cars came racing up to the entrance of the hospital. Rebels said that Gaddafi forces had ambushed them at Bin Jawad. They carried in a large man in his 50s with a gunshot wound to his chest. They brought him into a large exam room that was serving as the ER in the hospital, which was not at all equipped to handle trauma cases.

More than a dozen doctors and nurses scurried around the makeshift ER. A doctor pulled back the dressing on the man's chest, revealing a small hole. "A bullet in his chest, inlet and exit." A doctor called out, "air in this lung and blood in this lung."

The medics stabilized the man and moved him into a ward to make room for the next patient. Over the course of the next couple of hours, patients streamed in every 10 to 15 minutes. Most had non-life-threatening wounds and had been well patched up close to the front line before being transported to Ajdabiya.

One of the patients was a French journalist who had been shot in the right calf, which had been expertly bandaged in the field. He was in pain but otherwise fine. He didn't speak English but gave us a thumbs up.

Then another rebel arrived. He looked to be in his 40s and had a wound on the right side of his torso. Medics helped him from an ambulance into a wheelchair at which point I could see the man holding a lit cigarette in his left hand and there was an IV line in his forearm. I couldn't help but chuckle at the sight—nothing could pry a cigarette from a Libyan's hands.

The surge of patients gradually slowed, and the medical staff sat exhausted in the ER. Both the Libyan and Egyptian doctors said it was something they had never experienced before—gunshot wounds and injuries from explosions and shrapnel. They said they were doing the best they could with the facilities and the local staff they had. Medical students and even Libyan Boy Scouts were helping, along with other volunteers. The doctors said that people meant well, but mostly they just got in the way.

The doctors also said that in addition to being overwhelmed by the combat injuries, they were also freaked out by the fighting itself. Just a few days before, Ajdabiya had been the front line as rebels pushed out from Benghazi. Gunfire and explosions kept the doctors awake through the night. They said that they had been shot at a few times.

As they were catching their breath, word came from down the hall that the young boy had died from the gunshot wound to his head. It was the first conflict victim that the doctors had lost. The Egyptian doctors said that they had initially come to Libya with a plan to stay for 10 days, but they realized they would be needed longer.

As we exited the hospital, dozens of rebels and locals milled around out front, smoking and blowing off steam. It really struck me how the rebels came in all shapes, sizes, ages, and appearances. Some were teenagers who often looked a little too eager to be running around with powerful weapons. Others were clearly seasoned army soldiers who had defected in the face of orders to kill their countrymen. Some wore their official uniforms, while others sported jeans, polos, and casual jackets.

They had an electricity and enthusiasm about them. At the same time, there was a certain naïvety. Some had military backgrounds and seemed to grasp the magnitude of the situation. Others seemed to me like they were caught up in the spirit of the moment as if playing a video game.

There was also a heavy dose of religious fatalism. When people would shoot off their guns, it was routinely followed by chants of "Allah Akbar!" Many young men said that they were following God's will, and that they were prepared to die for Allah and freedom.

That was a striking difference between these rebels and American troops I'd seen in Iraq and Afghanistan. With U.S. troops, there was (almost) always an appreciation of the gravity of combat (yes, there were a few dingbats here and there who also seemed to be treating it like a game, but that was rare). I can't remember meeting an American soldier who was eager to die or talked about martyrdom.

During our brief visit to Libya, more and more young Libyan men volunteered to join the fight. Many were going as soldiers, while others were going to provide any kind of logistical support they could. They would hop on trucks carrying nothing more than a backpack and smile. They'd wave at cheering bystanders as the trucks pulled off down the road.

In one sense it was amazing to see so many people joining the cause of liberation, but it also seemed like there might be a surprise waiting for some. Up until the previous weekend, the rebels had made steady progress and were gaining more and more ground and confidence. They were pushing the front lines closer to the strategically vital city of Sirte, but as they got closer, things started getting uglier. Gaddafi forces stepped up their counter offensive.

If wars could be won on enthusiasm alone, there was no question that the rebels would quickly take out Gaddafi. Yet, recent days had shown it would take more than heart.

Still, the rebels made it clear that it was their fight, and they did not want any foreign troops on the ground. There were a few rather sanguine rebels who admitted that they weren't sure they could win the war without that help, but they were pressing on, nonetheless.

Many said that they could use some airstrikes and a no-fly zone to protect them from Gaddafi's Air Force. I realized that rebels were viewing us as a method of communicating with foreign powers—they repeatedly said that they did not want foreign troops, but they hoped NATO or the United States would provide air support. They got their wish.

We made our way back to Benghazi and our fixers dropped us off at our hotel. As we were departing for Cairo the next morning, we thanked them and offered money, which they refused. They said it was their duty to their country to help us. Then, they dropped a bombshell on us. They said that they were going to join the rebels and head off toward Sirte. They said that it was a historic moment for their country, and they needed to be a part of it.

On one level, I could relate as I had felt the same urge after 9/11—as a journalist I had to get in the game and "head off to war." There I was almost 10 years later still chasing and getting close to, but not quite into, the thick of battle.

So, while I felt Bill and Ted were a little cavalier in their attitude about going off to war (and they didn't remotely look like warriors), I could hardly criticize them. I was still looking for a front line where I could finally earn my stripes and assume some place in history with the correspondents I admired and envied over the years. Of course, at that moment they were all at the front lines covering the action while in my mind I was dicking around behind the scenes.

Later, I would learn that in war, sometimes (if not most of the time) the best stories are found well behind the front lines. The competitive juices drive the media to the bang bang. Yet, the front line is often full of sizzle, but not always a lot of steak. The meat of the story is often found in the wreckage left behind when the fighting moves on. In fact, the stories I later filed about the hospitals in Libya were some of the powerful warzone reporting I had done and were submitted for award consideration.

At that point, though, I was still suffering from bang bang envy and wanted war stories like the legends had from their time on the front lines around the world.

Anyhow, I have no idea what ever happened to Bill and Ted. I don't know if they ever made it to the front and if they did, whether they survived.

The trip back out of Libya was somewhat more organized. We hired a driver from Benghazi who was recommended by another journalist. He got the job done with a minimal amount of drama. The only problem was the fact that he couldn't sleep the night before, so we had to make a few extra coffee stops.

Along the way, we called Osama and asked him to meet us at the border and take us to Cairo. He agreed and met us on time at Saloum. About eight hours later, we were back in Cairo.

We spent the next day in the city where things were quiet. The army was still out on the streets and tents stood in Tahrir, but there were few people. The story had gone quiet in Egypt.

Had it been up to me, I would have gone right back to Libya. That was the story, and there were other outlets and programs hungry for reporting from there. But I had to serve my organization first, and that meant moving onto Bahrain to gather more material for my primary story on the trip—Iran's growing influence in the Arab world.

I had mixed feelings about Bahrain as it was a fallback option since it wasn't possible to head to Iraq as I had originally planned. It seemed anticlimactic after Libya. Bahrain had experienced some upheaval and protests in the weeks before, but it had not gone nuclear the way other countries had. That would change shortly after we arrived.

Chapter Thirteen
Bedlam in Bahrain

March 2011

MANAMA, Bahrain — On March 13, shit started going sideways in Bahrain. It began with demonstrators blocking sections of the highway through downtown before rush hour. Police massed on the overpass next to the Pearl roundabout (the basecamp for the protest movement) and tried to push back protesters. That led to escalating clashes. Who started it was of course in the eye of the beholder. Regardless of who provoked, it set off a daylong chain reaction.

Massive demonstrations had been taking place the previous two days and the government decided enough was enough. It was taking the gloves off. We could hear tear gas and other munitions being fired the moment we walked out of our hotel a few blocks from the roundabout. We walked toward the Pearl and came upon an open area about the size of a football field adjacent to the main highway through the neighborhood.

A couple hundred young men were scattered across the field yelling at security forces who stood along the raised highway in front of protesters. Security forces periodically fired into the field and men would run toward us carrying those incapacitated by tear gas or wounded by rubber bullets.

Security forces upped the tempo of their volleys, and the white clouds of tear gas grew. That further enraged protesters who were massing in greater numbers. They shouted and some threw rocks at the security forces who were well out of range.

Women massed behind the men. They screamed at the security forces and decried the increasingly volatile scene. Men filled shopping carts with the spent canisters and munitions being fired at them. It was clear the day was only going to get worse.

We left the field and followed crowds of people flooding into the roundabout. It was standing room only. Medical tents were full of people covered in welts from rubber bullets or delirious from tear gas. Clerics and other people were crowded onto the stage. People were shouting and chanting. We climbed up onto a media riser about 40 feet from the stage in the center of the roundabout. There was a sea of people extending in every direction. They chanted along with the clerics on the stage.

Some men started charging up the embankment to the highway. Police closed on the protesters on the highway and fired at them. Then, they started firing tear gas rounds into the crowd in the roundabout. Several rounds landed near the riser and gas wafted in our direction. I got a couple of good whiffs, and that was enough. We jumped off the riser and pushed through the crowd to get some distance from the security forces.

The roundabout turned into a complete cluster. Men and women were yelling and screaming. People rushed fallen protesters to the medical tents. Those with more severe injuries were loaded into cars or trucks and rushed out through the panicked crowd in the streets. People were dousing their faces with baking soda solutions or any liquids they could get their hands on. People were pressing onions to their faces. Medical volunteers were administering oxygen to collapsed men. The medical tents were overflowing. It had the look and feel of a war zone.

My adrenaline was pumping on two levels. First was the legitimate chaos and danger around. It was my first time in the thick of a for-real clash between protesters and security forces. People were getting knocked out by tear gas and seriously wounded by projectiles. Protesters were running and screaming. My eyes were

watering and my throat and sinuses
the thick of it. We had not packed
no masks or ballistic goggles. We ha
amid the chaos.

While Libya was at war and we had
did) hoping to see combat, Bahrain had been
test movement, and I didn't expect to end up in
we did. It evolved organically without me thinking
chasing it there. It was kind of like losing my virginity
years fantasizing about it and chasing it, and then suddenly
party it was happening with someone I barely knew when I w
expecting it.

So, there we were in the middle of some real shit where people
were ready to die and there was a legit possibility that security
forces could come unhinged. We were getting gassed and running
for cover.

The second source of the adrenaline rush was the journalism.
It was a story. There were few other western reporters there as
Bahrain simply hadn't been as sexy of a story as Egypt and Libya.
So, we kind of had a monopoly on a situation that was spiraling out
of control and could get really ugly. Certainly, if that happened,
the rest of the vultures would descend on Bahrain, but for the
time being, I had several outlets requesting reporting from me,
and I was going to run with it.

Eventually, with noon prayers came calm. The police moved
out of the area, and protesters regrouped. For the time being, the
protesters had control of the roundabout area and the highway
next to it.

The whole scene was chaotic and dangerous to the point that
I was not consciously thinking about how "cool" it was or the
danger points I was accumulating. I had to focus on staying safe
and getting the story and later, once I was safely back in the hotel,
I could navel gaze and ponder the merit badges I had earned.

Again, it wasn't Fallujah or Korengal, but it was a legit tear
gas and rubber bullets clash with the potential to escalate into live

like the rocket attacks I had experienced in Afghanistan
ompted sprints to a bunker, that clash in Bahrain was a sus-
episode of violence and chaos. We had to balance the two
al imperatives in that moment—maintain our wits and situ-
nal awareness to stay safe and keep focused on capturing the
ry. That is the essence of conflict reporting. If you are blindly
ocused on the story, you tend to end up kidnapped, wounded,
or dead. Obviously, if you simply run for safety, you can end up
missing the story.

That day was when I fully came to realize and appreciate the
world that I was in, that I had chosen. Like the military and first
responders, it was my job to run to and stay in the conflict. I don't
think most people appreciate how counterintuitive that is—it
defies the human instinct to survive.

The good thing for me was that I didn't come out of that
clash feeling like it was fun—it was work. There are some lunatic
journalists (and demonstrators) out there who "enjoy" shit like
that and come out of firefights feeling and acting like they just got
off a roller coaster.

I was definitely in "holy shit" mode and recognized that it
was seriously dangerous, and I had to do what I needed to walk
away in one piece, but it was my job to capture the story. If I and
others didn't bear witness as referees, then the narrative was up for
grabs. So, that day was another defining step on my journey as a
war correspondent. While part of me was feeling a little badass, I
was also starting to feel a certain acceptance and humility. My job
was to cover hairy shit, and at the end of the day it wasn't about
me and how cool I was, or the danger points I was earning. It was
about doing the work and reporting on important, complicated
stories that a relatively small pool of journalists was willing and
able to cover.

We had arrived in Bahrain on the evening of March 9. Susan and
I were lucky we arrived when we did. Bahrain was still letting in

reporters, but they would shut the door a few days later when the situation in the country went sideways.

During the taxi ride to the Elite Suites hotel, I could see the city of Manama had developed substantially since my first visit five years before. More land had been reclaimed from the sea and developed. There were new, exotic skyscrapers, new malls, and more infrastructure in general.

We visited the Dana Mall, which looked like the set of *Weird Science*. Calvin Klein, Versace, and "Veronica's Secret" stores filled the small, but upscale mall. There was an indoor theme park for kids with the ubiquitous ball pit, stands selling gold jewelry and state-of-the-art cell phones, luxury cars for raffle, and Nick Park animations on the big screen in the food court.

The crowd was small, but well-heeled and mostly traditional. Men wore *dishdashas*, women *abayas*. They clutched exotic handbags and wore expensive shoes.

The scene at the mall seemed worlds away from the images of the disenfranchised segments of the population who had been out on the streets protesting for the previous month. And in any figurative sense, it was a world away. While some of the people in the mall might have had democratic aspirations or the desire for reforms, they certainly didn't show any signs of economic hardship or frustration over their lot in life.

After the mall, I took a taxi to Trader Vic's. As much as it was a ritual to throw back a few Mai Tais whenever I was in proximity to a Trader Vic's, I also wanted to see what the vibe was given the chaos in the country.

The restaurant was the quietest I had ever seen a Trader Vic's anywhere in the world. There were a handful of people quietly eating and drinking. There was no band. The energy was dark. While it was still somewhat of a bubble, it was clear that the regular crowd was either bunkering in their hotels and apartments or had fled the city. I had one drink and returned to the hotel to crash.

The next morning, we saw the other extreme—the Pearl roundabout. Walking into the circle was like entering a cross between a street fair and a political rally. Booths lined the outer circumference. In the center of the roundabout was a stage for speakers, presenters, or for clerics leading prayers. In front was a collection of blankets and tarps covering the ground for people to sit and pray. On the stage were seven black coffin-like boxes and photos commemorating the seven people killed when police stormed the roundabout the previous month.

People were selling food, handing out literature, and even selling local art. Human rights groups had set up tents. Families of those killed in the protests had posters and booths or sitting areas where they invited people to join them for tea and talk about what was happening.

Everyone there had something to say and something to demand. They were almost exclusively Shia, the underclass in Bahrain despite being the majority. Each person there was quick to run down his or her talking points (not to demean the seriousness of their situation and demands, but after a while it was sounding repetitive and rehearsed). They said the movement wasn't about money, it was about freedom, democracy, and equality. They simply "wanted their rights" they would say.

Shia were generally excluded from many jobs in the country. They couldn't join the army. In fact, according to many sources, the army was largely staffed with Jordanians, Syrians, and Pakistanis who were offered citizenship in exchange for their service. The Shia people said that was a deliberate ploy by the government to bolster the numbers of Sunnis in the country. They said that the government was afraid having Shia in the service in general.

The people at the Pearl were going to great lengths to try to dispel any notion of it being a sectarian conflict. They said it was a regime and people conflict, a "have and have not" conflict. More than once I heard someone say that "my neighbors are Sunnis," or "my closest friends are Sunni," or "my husband is Sunni." They were quick to point out though, that they were referring to Bahraini Sunnis, not those from Pakistan or Syria.

In general, the scene at the Pearl was calm and orderly, yet clearly passionate. As was the case in Libya, whenever we pulled out a camera or recording device, people would flock around us to tell stories, make demands, and ask us as journalists to tell the world that they were peacefully demonstrating for their rights.

Unlike the uprisings in Egypt, Libya, and Tunisia where the United States voiced some measure of support for the protesters, the people of Bahrain were on their own. They had two things against them—Iran and the 5th Fleet. While Iran was not a major player in Bahrain, it expressed solidarity with the Shia community. That allowed the regime to claim that Iran was behind the uprising and therefore it had to put down the protests. The United States wasn't about to wade into the situation due to its cozy relationship with a government that hosted the United States Navy in the Middle East.

Protesters had one other major obstacle: Saudi Arabia. The two kingdoms are connected by a 16-mile causeway, and there is a sizable Shia population living in eastern Saudi Arabia. Not surprisingly, they are not treated as equals in Saudi, and get cranky from time to time. The last thing Saudi Arabia wanted, or wants to this day, was the demonstration effect of a successful Shia-led uprising in Bahrain that forced the regime to make significant concessions, or worst case, collapse. Therefore, Saudi Arabia was going to do whatever it had to prevent any spillover from Bahrain.

In the evening, we received word that some of the more hard-line Shia opposition groups were going to hold a march through Riffa to the Clock Tower roundabout the next day. Riffa is home to the Royal Court. It is where the regime and ruling family live. Essentially, the organizers wanted to drive a stake through the heart of the regime. It was a provocative move.

Other opposition groups pleaded for people not to attend and asked the organizers not to stage such a dangerous event. In response, pro-government demonstrators said they were going to hold a ceremonial sword dance at the roundabout. They said they would be out in the streets dancing with their swords and if anyone got hurt, well, they were just in the wrong place.

The tensions escalated to the point that Friday morning the government decided to intervene. They announced that the police would form a human barricade between the groups and prevent the marchers from reaching the Clock roundabout and the pro-government demonstrators.

As a result, the sword dance was canceled. Bummer, I love a good sword dance. Opposition groups felt that the police presence made the event safer (even though police had previously attacked demonstrators). So, people decided to come out in much larger numbers.

Around 2:30 p.m., people started to gather to march. Organizers spoke to the crowd and begged people to be peaceful. They said it was essential not to provoke the security forces. One man explained to me that he was urging calm, but also acknowledged that it was a decentralized movement, and it wasn't possible to control everyone.

Shortly after 3, the group began its march. About a thousand people (a massive group of men in front, and an almost equally massive group of black *abaya*-clad women in back) set off on a one-kilometer walk on a main highway to the line of police.

As the protesters marched off, the media scrambled to get up to the line of police ahead of the demonstrators. It was a powerful visual watching the horde of protestors slowly approach the police.

The police had deployed in multiple lines. The first was a wall of uniformed and unarmed officers with their arms interlocked. Behind them was a row of armed officers with shields and riot gear. About fifty feet behind them stood reserves—officers in riot gear, trucks, and some additional less-armed officers. The total number of security forces was well into the hundreds.

In addition to the police, there were a handful of men in plain clothes walking around, and many wore scarves or balaclavas to cover their faces. According to local journalists, they were pro-government thugs, most likely the aforementioned Syrians, Jordanians, or Pakistanis the government recruited to serve in the army, and according to some, carry out the government's dirty work.

One young man draped in a Bahraini flag walked out a few hundred feet ahead of the marchers. He stopped and sat down in the middle of the road about 100 feet from the line of police. It was a textbook move to create a great visual. Of course, the media, myself included, photographed the hell out of him.

A few minutes later, the throng caught up to him and organizers lined up holding hands and facing the protesters to create a barrier so they would not go any closer to the police.

That effort failed quickly as protesters pushed through and walked (somewhat gingerly at times) closer to the police. Organizers tried to slow the movement and keep a safe distance from the police. They were unsuccessful. Protesters gradually approached and came face-to-face with the front line of police.

Many of the demonstrators carried flowers and tried to hand them to the police officers—the classic protest cliche. There was some mild pushing and shoving, but it had more to do with the mass of the crowd converging on the police line rather than any attempts to cause trouble.

Some protesters sat down in front of the police to display passivity. Others continued to hold out flowers—some did so looking toward media cameras in a completely unsubtle effort to shape the narrative.

Eventually, the crowd massed to such a point that the cumulative crush of bodies pushed through the front line of police and pressed up against the riot shields of the second row. That's where things held for the next hour or more.

Demonstrators continued to arrive, and the crowd swarmed across both lanes of the highway. The police had laid giant coils of razor wire off to each side of the highway to prevent protesters from walking around them. Off to the right of the highway was an expansive, sandy farm plot covered with black irrigation hoses. Protesters overflowed into the field. To the left of the police was the wide highway median, and a handful of protesters walked up to the razor wire there.

People sang and chanted. They waved flags, gave speeches

over megaphones, and sang their own praises to the media for conducting such a large and peaceful rally.

The crowd had swelled easily into the thousands, possibly approaching ten thousand. We saw no evidence of clashes or people trying to cross through the riot police line or razor wire. There were certainly those who were agitated and yelling aggressively at the police, but no sign of improper behavior.

After about an hour, the crowd turned around and started to march away. People were joyous. One woman I talked to said they had delivered their message and the success of the event would inspire more people to join the movement.

The crowd headed down the highway, and we started to head out as well. Just then, we saw a group of boys running across the sandy field and heading back toward the right-most section of the razor-wire line.

More people started running. There was a road on the right side of the field, and a wall next to the road. People started tearing down the metal panels of the wall. Some were running into the construction site behind the wall, and it looked like they were trying to find a shortcut around the police line. Others continued to rush toward the front line.

Some men were violently agitated as they ran. Some picked up rocks, large sticks, or pieces of metal lying around. Others tried to restrain them.

We followed the crowd to determine what had set off the protesters. I came to the end of the fence and into a clearing not far from the police line. A man standing there was just starting to explain something about pro-government people attacking the protesters, when the bangs and pops of weapons pierced the air. Immediately, the horde of hundreds turned and ran.

It was suddenly like the running of the bulls—straight toward me. I turned and hauled ass. People were crushed together running from the security forces. Some tripped and fell while others picked them back up.

I felt increasingly panicked. I was not off to the side with a mob of press that would ideally be off limits to security forces. I was blended in with the fleeing protesters and as much a target as they. That was new and uncomfortable territory. I ran as quickly as I could in the sweaty, panicked mass of people. It took all my concentration not to trip and to keep pace without either knocking over anyone in front of me or getting trampled myself. The crowd became so thick and pressed together that I felt I could have lifted my legs and I would have been carried along in the mass of people.

As we ran, weapons fired, and tear gas canisters exploded over and in the crowd. The smell and burn of tear gas floated through the air. There was also a rain-like sound of something hitting the metal fence and other hard surfaces. I felt little bits of debris fall on me, fortunately with minimal force.

After about 45 seconds, I reached an open area out of the crush. Protesters were regrouping there. I could see several people holding scarves over their mouths and struggling to breathe. I saw men fall to the ground and go limp. Protesters picked them up and carried them to a clearing farther back and fanned air onto them.

There were easily 20 people who were incapacitated by the gas, although none looked seriously injured. A few people had fallen in the rush and had cuts and bruises. There were scattered piles of vomit on the pavement.

People in the crowd immediately wanted to talk to the reporters. They said it was the typical tactic—that the police waited until the end and attacked protesters when they were in the process of dispersing. That would result in some sort of scuffle or situation that the government could spin as the protesters starting a riot.

Multiple people said the same thing—that plain-clothed thugs were standing next to the police and started throwing rocks at the anti-government demonstrators as they walked away. The police did nothing to stop them, and as a result, demonstrators ran back to retaliate. That's when the police opened fire.

I received confirmation from a few photojournalists who were close to the incident that men standing with the police started throwing rocks at the demonstrators. That set off the chain reaction.

What began and almost concluded as a large, peaceful, and successful pro-democracy protest, ended as a clash between protesters and police that sent about twenty or more to the hospital for treatment from tear gas inhalation or other injuries. It was a case of a few minutes changing the entire character and narrative of a three-hour event.

Protesters gathered up the spent tear gas canisters and rubber bullets that had been fired. There were clearly identifiable tear gas and rubber bullet canisters from NonLethal Technologies, SAE Alsetex, and Federal Laboratories. They also picked up projectiles from SAPL Rubber Breakout Grenades. It was all U.S. and French stuff being fired at protesters.

Shortly after the smoke cleared and the dust settled, anti-government groups decided to stage an even bigger event the next day. And, since they were unsuccessful on Friday in marching through Riffa, they decided to pick another provocative and symbolic location: Safriya Palace.

That protest, which involved thousands of marchers, concluded peacefully. Protesters reached the palace, stopped to chant for a bit, and then marched off peacefully. No one on either side started any trouble.

The next day was the 13th when things escalated into the clash at the roundabout. While the situation quieted without loss of life, it was a short-lived pause. Word came that the conflict had moved to the University of Bahrain farther south. Details were murky. There were allegations of pro-government mobs attacking students, while anti-government students fought with police. Again, while the narrative was in question, the fact was that another batch of people ended up in the hospital, some with life-threatening injuries.

As the day wore on, rumors proliferated of marauding pro-government gangs attacking locals in the center of Manama. The following day, we would find some evidence, circumstantial as it might be, to support the rumors.

We visited Salmaniya hospital (which the government lambasted with unsubstantiated claims of bias towards protesters and failure to treat Sunnis and foreign nationals) on the morning of March 14. Doctors there claimed they treated 800 patients the previous day. Most arrived while the major clashes were taking place near the Pearl. However, doctors said that patients came in from the University and additional patients came in later in the evening—they tended to have some of the most severe injuries.

Those arriving later said that they had been attacked by Pakistanis and people from Bangladesh and India who they said wore police uniforms under their indigenous dress. A few of the Pakistanis came into the hospital with their own injuries, and hospital officials said the men claimed they were paid 20 Bahraini Dirhams (about $50) each to stir up trouble. However, no one could confirm who was paying the money, and no one I talked to spoke with any of the Pakistanis directly—everything was second or third hand.

Like so many conflicts or clashes, that was typical. It was almost impossible to verify anything you didn't see, and people paraded "facts" around that they did not witness. There were many plausible narratives at any given moment, and neither side had clean hands. Each was trying to wage and win a public relations war. The government blamed everything on the protesters, and the protesters said that the government and its thugs instigated everything. Would you expect either side to say otherwise?

The bottom line was, things had been ramping up, and it took another turn. It was almost metaphoric—the weather had been warm and mild the previous few days. But on the 14th, an edgy wind blew through the city. With it, came a cold, grey fatalistic energy. A convoy of Saudi troops in armored vehicles rumbled across the causeway and into the streets of Bahrain.

The arrival of the Saudi forces brought a sense of impending doom. The defiant fatalism of the previous days when protesters proudly chanted that they were ready to die for Bahrain had been replaced by resignation. Many protesters expressed a sense that the game was over and said they were expecting to be slaughtered. They were ready to be martyrs.

We retired to our hotel, which at that point was largely empty except for the staff and about a half-dozen foreign journalists. Around 11:30 p.m., I was trying to sleep, but my mind was racing as an Apache helicopter rumbled around outside the hotel window.

It was difficult to process how intense things had become in the few days we had been in Bahrain. There was a foreboding darkness that had taken hold, a knife-edge tension, and a feeling that floods and locusts were gathering on the horizon.

Susan and I were late to the party in Egypt and had missed the peak of the uprising that resulted in the fall of Mubarak. In Libya, we experienced the exuberance in Benghazi as people celebrated their freedom. We did see the reality of the fighting from the standpoint of the casualties coming into the hospital in Ajdabiya, but the mood was overall optimistic and positive that Gaddafi would fall, and Libya would be free.

In Bahrain, we were in the thick of it. The shit was going down in real time around us. Protests had been escalating, and now some 2,000 Saudi and Emirati troops were on the ground to make sure the regime survived. I was among a small group of foreign journalists there to witness it. Part of me couldn't help but hope for My Lai, Srebrenica, or Rwanda—something epic that could make my career. It was an ugly thought, but I was on the ground in a heady situation, so of course I was fantasizing about witnessing a life-changing story. Whether they will admit it or not, no journalist in a situation like this wouldn't be quietly pondering the cataclysmic possibilities.

The next morning, with martial law in effect in the immediate vicinity of the roundabout, the city was a ghost town. The roundabout was empty. Roads were blocked. The few people out driving couldn't pass through downtown.

It was an unnatural calm—zombie apocalypse stuff. Many offices and businesses were closed. The hotel went into lockdown. Only nine guests remained in a 250-room facility. The essential staff had moved into the hotel. Similar stories were circulating about other hotels. Some embassies started issuing advisories to their nationals to leave the country.

People on the streets that morning said that the world had turned against them. Just as one group of women told me how they were peaceful and armed only with flowers, I spied a couple of men holding large sticks and took a photo. The women complained and said I should not take pictures of the men. They didn't want anything to tarnish their image or message. I said it was my job to capture and report what was taking place. A local man in the crowd agreed and mansplained to the women that transparency was essential.

It simply couldn't be ignored that protesters were becoming agitated and started carrying hammers, knives, or anything else that could be used as a weapon. It felt like it had reached a point where both sides were spoiling for a fight, and the angry fringe of the protest movement could very easily have started any number of the recent clashes (again, the government claimed they started them all).

As of early afternoon on March 15, things were calm. That changed quickly as the phone started ringing. People at Salmaniya hospital called to say that casualties were coming in. They said that people were being shot with real bullets.

Since our visit the day before, the hospital had set up a new triage tent in the parking lot. There were around 100 people outside the hospital—medics, media, volunteers, and young men there to provide security, although their main weapon looked to be a human chain at the entrances.

Ambulances screamed in and hospital personnel dragged us inside to take pictures of the wounded. The first patient they brought us to was already dead. He looked to be about 20 and his skull had been split open, his brain visible. It wasn't clear whether he had been beaten or shot point-blank with a tear gas canister. Either way, the doctors wanted journalists to take pictures of his fatal head wound to document the alleged savagery of the government. Doctors and nurses broke into tears at the sight of his lifeless body.

I was a bit freaked out by it myself as I was still new to seeing mangled bodies. Fortunately, the chaotic scene reabsorbed me into my work, and I suppressed any further emotional reaction to the dead and wounded.

Hospital staff wheeled the dead boy off into a holding room as other live patients arrived. Many had pellet wounds—bird shot, or some sort of non-lethal shotgun rounds that sprayed small pellets all over them without penetrating too deeply. Those patients were alive, conscious and in pain. Many said they had been shot at close range. Furthermore, many were wheeled in lying on their stomachs—they were shot from behind.

All the injured patients gave the same story. They had been out in the streets of their villages and said they were out there to "protect their people," from pro-government thugs who had allegedly been attacking people in Shia communities. The victims claimed they were unarmed. They said that police vehicles drove up and people started shooting out of the cars. People said the shooters were wearing Bahraini police uniforms, but they were Pakistani or other nationalities.

Doctors and nurses ran about frantically triaging the patients. They had never experienced that volume of patients or those kinds of injuries. Some broke down in tears in the hallway. They begged the media to photograph every gruesome wound on every body.

Other patients came in suffering from tear gas inhalation or from beating wounds. One man was an ambulance driver who said his crew had been attacked while trying to rescue wounded.

Several doctors panicked when they heard that. They said that pro-government vigilantes would use ambulances as a Trojan rabbit to get attackers into neighborhoods or even the hospital itself.

As consistent and convincing as the narratives were, it was

impossible to verify it all. Everyone said that innocent, unarmed protesters had been out on the streets, and then suddenly convoys of riot police (all foreign nationals in police uniforms, and in some cases plain clothes) drove up and started shooting.

But we didn't see any of it happen, and no one provided any incontrovertible video evidence. We did not have anyone we felt could safely get us close enough to the action to see for ourselves. I wanted to see it firsthand, but I'll admit I wasn't sure I wanted to wade into it. It was the kind of situation that desperately needed independent witnesses, but I didn't know how to go about it safely. (I had yet to take that hostile environment training course, so I was lacking some knowledge and skills I needed to operate safely in the situation.) I was in a little over my head and chickened out. I was fine with the idea of rushing into combat while embedded with U.S. forces, but wading unsupervised into random violence when the security forces likely saw journalists as obstacles, I didn't have the balls for that.

A rumor emerged that the army had invaded a nearby hospital. Other rumors circulated that the ministry of health had been taken over by the army. People were gripped by panic. One doctor approached me in a state of utter fear and asked if I could deliver a message to the Red Cross for them to intervene.

We grew concerned about an attack on the hospital. The young men outside with sticks and rocks would hardly stop any armed forces who wanted to attack. While it seemed unlikely, we couldn't discount the possibility.

I called the U.S. embassy and spoke to the Marine on duty. I asked if the embassy was tracking any of the chaos. He said that they had no information of any violence happening anywhere in the country. According to his intelligence, all was calm in Bahrain. I informed him that something was causing hundreds of people with severe wounds to show up at the hospital, but he seemed unconcerned.

Frankly, I don't think he believed what I was telling him. It was more than disconcerting that I was staring at empirical evidence of violence—dozens of patients with pellet wounds, effects of tear gas inhalation, and other wounds consistent with baton strikes or rubber bullets—and the U.S. embassy said they had received no reports of any clashes or violence in the country. The image of Kevin Bacon at the end of *Animal House* came to mind.

Darkness was approaching and the government had already declared martial law (their press release called it a "State of National Safety"). There was a frenzied air, and people looked like they were out to kill or be killed. The typically friendly demeanor of the demonstrators was gone. Despite my bluster and desire to be in the shit, I was still on the risk-averse side of the journalist spectrum, as was Susan. We decided we did not want to be caught up in an angry mob carrying stone-age weapons fending off armed security forces.

To this day I regret the decision to leave and not see the story through. If I could do it all over again, I would have jumped in an ambulance and ridden to the scene of the violence to witness firsthand and then ride back with casualties and stay at the hospital until it was all clear. Alas…

A local woman who had been translating for us in the hospital us led us through a couple of streets full of rock-carrying young men rushing to the hospital. We jumped in her car.

There were protester-manned checkpoints all over the place. Protesters were trying to protect their neighborhoods from security forces and were improvising barricades. Some roads were completely blocked, others simply had dumpsters and tree trunks lying partially across them to slow traffic.

At each checkpoint, men stood with sticks and bricks and looks of fear and aggression. While we were not the enemy, and they had been kind to foreign press, we approached each checkpoint with a sense of unease. It felt like anyone could snap at any moment. Fortunately, they waved us through each one with little hesitation once they saw that we were American journalists.

We turned down a road and discovered it was blocked by scattered bricks, dumpsters, and tree trunks. We started to turn around to head back out to the main road and try a different route when we heard a loud bang nearby. It was difficult to tell whether it was gunfire or some type of explosive, or just a large dumpster being overturned. We saw several men running away from the direction of the sound—the direction we were about to head—and a couple of them yelled "Allah Akbar."

There had been unconfirmed reports of helicopters firing on protesters, and our driver thought that's what it could have been. Regardless, it was an "oh shit" moment, and we were all panicked that we were about to get caught up in something ugly. I could feel the adrenaline and my heart racing.

Men at the intersection of the main road and the side road we were on yelled at us to go. The woman driving decided to forge ahead. She cleared the bricks, made it around a couple of cement barriers, and almost made it through the dumpsters unscathed. She smacked one on the passenger side.

Fortunately, that side of her car had previous damage, so she wasn't too concerned. She adjusted course and cleared the dumpster, which fortunately did not catch on the car. We made it safely to the hotel after passing through three more checkpoints.

The next morning, we awoke to the sound of five Apache helicopters circling overhead. We made our way to the top of the hotel and found the best view of the Pearl in the women's exercise room. There, the half-dozen of us journalists stuck in the hotel camped out to watch events unfold.

We could see tear gas canisters flying into the roundabout. Huge plumes of white smoke rose and swept southward with the strong wind. Soon, black smoke began to mix with the white.

Troops moved in, and protesters pulled back from the roundabout. Some set small fires at the checkpoints. Additional plumes of black smoke emerged in surrounding neighborhoods.

Riot police gathered in a sand lot near the roundabout. Clad in dark blue uniforms and white helmets (they reminded me of the Robert Patrick Terminator T-1000), and accompanied by armored vehicles, they marched down the road in our direction.

At each intersection, they stopped and fired tear gas down the side streets. Protesters offered no resistance and retreated. A few officers stayed behind at each intersection and the others continued marching down the main street.

The helicopters circled and periodic shots rang through the air. They could have been live rounds or just blanks to scare away protesters.

A couple of hours after the operation began, the police had control of the roundabout and the adjacent streets. They held their positions until early afternoon. The streets were virtually empty and only a handful of people were visible in the surrounding neighborhoods.

After the physical "cleansing" of the area, as the government called it, the war of narratives began. The government released statements saying that it had successfully cleared the area without inflicting any casualties.

The government claimed that two policemen had been run over and killed by fleeing protesters. The official statement said that as police approached the roundabout, they were fired on and attacked with Molotov cocktails. The government said that protesters set fire to their tents as they fled the roundabout.

Each side released statements and videos—many of which immediately proliferated through social media—that highlighted their half of the story. But few, if any, videos or photos showed complete context and proved any evidence beyond a reasonable doubt.

The government announced a curfew for the immediate Pearl area running from 4 p.m. to 4 a.m. We remained in lockdown in the hotel the rest of the day.

The next morning, we could see Saudi tanks and armored personnel carriers deployed in the open field near the Pearl and in intersections near the hotel. With the roundabout cleared and the forces controlling the streets, it looked like the worst was over—for the time being.

Regardless, I had to continue with the rest of my reporting

trip. Even though I was in the middle of a major evolving story, I was working for a documentary program, and I wasn't there to cover the "news."

So, Susan and I arranged for a driver who could get to our hotel and then take a circuitous route around the area under martial law to get us to the airport. Airport security and immigration practically rolled out the red carpet for us to leave the country. Two fewer journalists who could bear witness and report on anything that might contradict the government narrative.

A couple of months later, I crashed into that narrative. The PR firm Qorvis invited me to a dinner with several Bahraini parliamentarians who were in D.C. doing some lobbying. I, along with two other journalists, attended the dinner with three members of the appointed upper house, or Shura, and two members of the elected lower house of Bahrain's parliament.

During the dinner, they let it all fly. They said that Iran was to blame for the uprising, and they had hard evidence to prove that. They said that several Bahraini Shia hardliners had meetings with Hezbollah and Iranian leadership. They made claims that there was evidence of the transfer of money (and possibly weapons) to opposition groups.

The delegation stated it was terrifying to see protesters armed with guns on the streets of a peaceful nation. They said that "operatives and insurgents" had taken over hospitals. They were running their operations out of hospitals and were storing weapons there. The protesters who claimed to have been injured were faking it with help from Iranian press, who were manufacturing scenes at hospitals and employing actors as doctors who made outrageous claims of injuries to protesters.

After the formal dinner presentation, I chatted with the young male MP who was most animated in painting the picture of Iranian-armed thugs running amuck in Bahrain. I mentioned to him that when I was on the ground covering the protests, I didn't see anyone carrying guns. He froze and went pale. "You were there?" he asked.

I told him that I was and asked about his evidence that protesters were armed. He sheepishly said that he heard there were guns on the streets, but he did not see for himself since he was not out on the streets. I also told him what I witnessed at the hospitals and how the facts on the ground did not match what he presented. He flopped about like a drunk teenager caught sneaking into the house after curfew. I felt the need to shower off his sleaze.

However, I had a much larger concern after leaving the dinner. I had been the only one in the room who had witnessed what happened on the ground. The other two reporters had not been to Bahrain. I could call the delegation out on some of their lies. However, I realized that they had given the same presentation to members of Congress, and probably State Department and think tank people. I highly doubt anyone else they spoke with in D.C. challenged them on anything they said, especially since it played into the narrative that Iran was the cause of the problems in the region.

My head started spinning as I thought through all the ramifications. How many international delegations paraded through D.C. each month to put on dog-and-pony shows for members of Congress or executive branch officials? How much PR-firm polished bullshit with significant consequences was peddled? How much policy was informed by lobbyists for suspect governments? How many regimes engaged in the oppression or abuse of their people came begging for weapons and aid to "maintain security and stability?"

I felt almost sick as I finally realized how fucked it all was. It also reinforced the essential importance of journalism. Bahrain was really the first time that I felt like a real-time witness to something of great importance where there was little coverage or awareness. It was terrifying to think how much went on around the world outside the view of journalists or "referees" who could call balls and strikes.

I got home from that dinner and sat on the couch in a mildly depressed funk drinking whiskey. I was torn between feeling that I needed to redouble my efforts to be out on the ground permanently crusading for truth and transparency or that I should just give up on humanity and move to an island and become a scuba instructor.

Chapter Fourteen
Beamed to the Mothership

March 2011

BEIRUT — Susan and I arrived after dark on March 17. We checked into the Golden Tulip Hotel de Ville in the Sodeco neighborhood, next to Ashrafieh. I didn't know anything about the hotel other than it had a reasonable reputation as a chain brand, was in a decent location, and the price was right.

We had of course reserved non-smoking rooms, and that was confirmed at check in and by the no-smoking signs on the doors of our rooms. As we entered our rooms, we were each overwhelmed by the eye-watering stench of cigarette smoke. I called the front desk to say that we were supposed to be in non-smoking rooms and that we wanted to be moved to non-smoking rooms. The man at the front desk stated that we were in non-smoking rooms and that none of the other non-smoking rooms would be any better. "This is Lebanon," he said. Fair enough. With that, I hopped on the painfully slow internet to find another hotel to check into the following day.

I went to bed that night with my mind racing. I was still processing everything that I had seen and experienced in Libya and Bahrain, and I was also dealing with the emotions of being back in the belly of the beast—the home of the woman who had broken me and sent me on my journey through the world's most dangerous places. It was coming up on four years since the end of the relationship and being in Beirut brought it all flooding back.

228

While I was over Layla as a person and didn't feel any longing to be back with her, I was still grieving the way I felt in that relationship. That feeling of being content, of being able to be myself and not wanting anything more. I did not feel that way with Anna, or anyone else I had dated since the breakup. I was worried that I might not feel that way again in a relationship, and that depressed me. I was in fear and loathing of through the rest of my life looking behind at the "high water mark—that place where the wave finally broke, and rolled back"—to borrow from Hunter S. Thompson. How could I commit to a long-term relationship with anyone else if it didn't feel like something more than I had before?

I was growing more convinced that I was only going to find what I needed in the work, in a tribe. At least that was something still in front of me that I could control to some degree. I had to keep my focus on achieving that goal.

The next morning, we met with our fixer and went about the usual business of visiting the Hezbollah press office and setting up interviews. I was back to focusing on the Iranian influence in the region story and so we were looking to speak with Hezbollah types about their connection to Iran and to interview regular people and analysts about Iran's role and influence in Lebanon.

That day as we were moving about the city, I was struck by how "normal" things were. People were out and about on the streets working, dining, and shopping. Traffic was normal, for Beirut (although these days thanks to the proliferation of rideshare services, the streets of D.C. aren't much safer or saner). There were no protests or explosions. In a weird way, it almost felt boring. You know you've been in some shit when Beirut seems boring by comparison.

We spent much of the next day in the Dahiya speaking to Hezbollah supporters. That night, we attended a speech by Hezbollah leader (and U.S. designated terrorist) Hassan Nasrallah. He spoke by video feed from his secret location to a hall packed with about 1,000 rabid followers and political elite. It was like a giant pep rally for one of the world's leading terrorists. It was icky—so was the fact that next to me was a young, very white American girl in a black hijab and abaya working for Iranian state television.

The next day, we took a field trip south into Hezbollah country. We spent much of the excursion at one of the weirdest attractions I have ever visited in the world (the weirdest was probably the Tiger Balm Park in Singapore, which was downright creepy with its disturbing dioramas about hell and damnation): the Hezbollah Museum.

Opened in May 2010, the war museum celebrates Hezbollah's resistance of Israel. The largely outdoor exhibit is a massive sculpture garden of sorts filled with destroyed Israeli tanks and Howitzers, shells, casings, helmets, ammo boxes, and other remnants of war.

There is a path that takes tourists to a hill and a series of caves and bunkers used by Hezbollah when it fought Israeli forces in southern Lebanon. Along the path and in the bunkers are exhibits displaying Hezbollah weapons, medical gear, communications systems, fighting positions, and living quarters.

There were dozens of visitors—mostly families with young children. Almost everyone there appeared to be under the age of 40. They came from across the country to see the exhibit. Some traveled from Syria.

Most were wary of a couple of American journalists approaching them to ask questions about Iran at a Hezbollah Museum—shocking. But a few were willing to speak. They gazed around nervously as they did. One man said that while he cared about Lebanon as a country because he was Lebanese, Iran was far more important to him. That stuck with me. It's a bad sign for a country when its natural-born citizens feel greater affection and affinity with another nation.

We left the museum and headed back north to Dahiya. There we had a bizarre interview with an arms dealer—well, is there any other kind of interview with an arms dealer?

It was dark and our fixer led us to an apartment building where we met a burly man wearing jeans and a black T-shirt that read "Break Rules Diesel." He led us to his van and allowed us to photograph the contents: pistols, mines, boxes and boxes of ammunition, explosives, and various sacks and bags containing who knows what.

We then followed him into an apartment where he had additional weapons on display for us: AKs, grenades, rocket launchers, and an assortment of vests and radios. He put on a balaclava and hat to conceal his identity and posed for pictures with his wares.

He proceeded to tell us about his business and his efforts to resist Israel. Interestingly, he was not Hezbollah. While he supported them in spirit, he was a member of the Amal movement, another Shia party and militia closely aligned with Syria.

In the middle of the conversation, a petite South Asian woman entered the room to give us some bottles of water. When she put them down on the coffee table, she moved some vases, so they didn't get damaged by the weapons placed on the table. She went about it in a casual way as if it went on in the apartment every day. I had to keep myself from laughing at the absurdity of it.

After we completed the interview, the man had my fixer and the two of us help him carry the weapons out to his car to get everything out in one trip. So, in violation of any number of laws and journalistic norms, I put on a vest full of gear, picked up an RPG, and grabbed some grenades. We then quietly, but as quickly as possible, ran down the stairs and out the side door of the building to the alley. We loaded everything in his van and left in our car.

The next day, our fixer got a call from Hezbollah. Apparently, we were spotted exiting the building carrying weapons belonging to someone who was a rival dealer. The fixer received a serious reprimand over the phone, but no further sanctions, and we were not in danger.

Still, it was an example of some of the blurry lines in journalism. Ethically speaking, we should not have assisted in carrying illegal weapons to the arms dealer's car. However, in a moment like that, you kind of feel like you're already in sketchy territory by meeting with a criminal, so what difference does it make?

It is difficult to sort out the lines in the heat of the moment. Certainly, for a story about Iranian influence in Lebanon it made sense to interview arms dealers and militants who had connections to Iran. We didn't help him sell or smuggle weapons or carry out an attack. His cause did not benefit from my reporting, I don't think. If anything, it shined light on one of the many symptoms of Lebanon's dysfunctions and the challenges of pacifying the region.

But moments like that do raise questions. Few journalists would balk at an opportunity to interview the likes of Osama bin Laden, Hassan Nasrallah, or a serial killer. Journalists routinely interview "enemies" and bad actors. It's essential to hear from the Taliban, the FARC, ISIS, and others of that ilk to understand their motivations and objectives and what drives people to join those groups. It's a creepy and dangerous part of the job, but essential. What are the reasonable rules of the road of doing that? I never had any legal or ethics training about that or guidance from an employer, so I improvised and interviewed anyone who would meet with me. I was never confronted with a situation of having to put a hood over my head and ride in the trunk of a car to a secret location for an interview. But I would have done it just as much for the value of the interview as the story to tell colleagues in a bar later.

In fact, I met with some U.S. diplomats in Beirut for a background conversation on Iranian influence, and I mentioned that I was interviewing some Hezbollah members. One diplomat excitedly and jealously blurted out, "you'll have to tell us everything you hear from them; we're not allowed to talk to them!"

So, as a journalist you have to make efforts to talk to all parties to a story, and sometimes that means getting into some weird situations and gray areas.

Our next sketchy interview was with an active Hezbollah fighter. Our fixer arranged a nighttime meeting with the man along the side of the highway south of Beirut airport, which Hezbollah controlled. We pulled up behind a dark gray van parked off the side of the road. We got out of the car and into the van—what's that wisdom about getting into a strange van at night?

A young man sat in the driver's seat with the interior lights off so we could not see his face from our seats behind him. He proceeded to discuss how he joined Hezbollah in 1997 because it was fighting Israel. His family was from southern Lebanon, and he had grown up in the Beirut area because Israel occupied his family's village. He first visited it in 2000 after Israel withdrew from Lebanon. He traveled to Iran numerous times for military training and religious and academic instruction. He was about as pro-Iran as anyone in Lebanon.

We concluded the interview, got back into our car, and returned to the city. After a few more days of roaming around interviewing politicians and citizens, and hooking up with a server from Kayan, I returned to D.C. That would turn out to be my last Middle East trip for *America Abroad*.

As I had been for much of the previous two years, I was keeping an eye out for an opportunity to jump ship. Ideally, I wanted a full-time overseas gig, but I would take anything at a more established news organization where there were fewer internal ethical conflicts.

I applied for a position at NPR as a producer on the Foreign Desk. I heard nothing for more than two months. Then, one Thursday in late June we had a staff meeting at *America Abroad* that put me over the edge. The organization had concluded that it was not journalistically unsound to take U.S. government money to produce public diplomacy programs for Afghanistan and other Muslim countries that the organization regularly reported on in its radio documentaries. I had lost the battle for journalistic and editorial integrity, and I was done.

After the meeting, I sent an email to the foreign editor at NPR to ask if the producer position had been filled. I received a response 30 minutes later. He said he was about to decide, and I still had time to come in and make a pitch.

The following Monday I met with him and presented my case for the job. On Wednesday, he offered me the gig, which I immediately accepted. I completed one last trip for *America Abroad* to report on the proliferation of counterfeit goods in Ghana (I got to watch the Boston Bruins win the Stanley Cup at a bar in Accra while sitting next to a fellow Kennedy school student on a summer internship), and then I joined the mothership.

While I had worked at an NPR station, WBUR, it was not NPR proper. It was a farm team. The mothership—NPR headquarters in D.C.—was the network, the major league. Landing that gig was the greatest source of professional pride in my life.

From the moment I walked into NPR, I was preparing to head to Libya. In between filling out HR forms and attending orientation and training sessions, NPR's version of Q kept popping into my office with body armor, satellite gear, and other bits of kit. It was such a drastic change from life at a tiny organization with little money where I had to manage logistics and acquire gear myself.

I was giddy. It was the same feeling as the first time flying first class on an international flight. The kid in you wants to yell, "yippee," but you have to act like it's no big deal, so you strut around like Richard Pryor in *Stir Crazy*—that's right, I'm bad.

Seriously, even though I had joined NPR as a producer, which I felt was a step backward from being an on-air correspondent, it was such an enormous leap forward in prestige and career standing to board the mothership. I had applied for at least half a dozen positions at NPR over the years and had never even merited an interview. Finally, I was onboard in one of the coolest positions in the organization—danger zone producer—because I had fucking earned it.

My years of toiling for a barely known organization, traveling around on a shoestring budget and having to figure it all out for myself had paid off. I belonged at the big kids' table, and shit it felt great to stop saying, "I work for an independent radio program distributed by Public Radio International," and say, "I work for NP fucking R, thank you very fucking much."

After three weeks of getting trained and outfitted (sadly without a tux or PPK), I was on my way into Libya to support Lulu Garcia-Navarro who had been covering the conflict much of the year. Rebel forces were marching on Tripoli, and Gaddafi was on the ropes.

Flush with $20,000 in cash, a bunch of kit, and five bottles of whiskey, I departed for Djerba, Tunisia. I spent a day there procuring food, water, a generator, and other supplies should we have to establish an expeditionary bureau. The next morning, I loaded everything into a minivan and the driver set off for Libya via Tataouine, Tunisia. Sadly, there was no time for Star Wars tourism. I was off to cover a full-on war.

Chapter Fifteen
Taking Over Tripoli

August 2011

ZAWIYAH, Libya — No sooner had I arrived at the refinery in Zawiyah then we were in the car zooming into Tripoli. Rebels had taken the city during my eight-hour road trip from Djerba, Tunisia to Zawiyah. Lulu and the pack of journalists who were camped out at the refinery guest quarters were rushing to the capital to cover the breaking news.

We pushed into the western neighborhoods of the capitol with little difficulty, stopping a couple of times along the way to speak with jubilant Libyans who had come out to celebrate the news. We reached a large traffic circle packed with cars and people. Some were celebrating, but the energy there was a bit twitchy. Shortly before we arrived, rebels there intercepted some Gaddafi fighters who were fleeing the city. Rebels warned us we should not stay long as they were expecting more fleeing soldiers and things could get dicey.

We spent about 10 minutes doing interviews and capturing the sights and sounds. A few of the men in our pack decided to press on deeper into the city while Lulu and I along with a couple of others returned to Zawiyah to file. After we finished working, I opened my bags to pull out one of the most important supplies I had hauled into Libya: whiskey. We had a nightcap and then I crashed in my reasonably comfortable room in the guest complex.

The next morning, our pack (which included Charles Levinson from the *Journal*, Italian journalist Rolla Scolari, Thomas Erdbrink with the *Washington Post*, and photographer Bryan Denton who was freelancing for the *New York Times* and was one of the cool people affiliated with the organization in Libya) drove into the capital.

Rebels had set up myriad checkpoints along the way, and at each one we received information on the conditions ahead. Basically, the routine in a situation like that was to go as far as you could until you reached a checkpoint where rebels told you that it wasn't safe to go any farther and that if you proceeded it was at your peril. To the credit of Libyan rebels, even though most of them had no prior military or tactical experience, they were good at setting up checkpoints and managing information. When they said it wasn't safe to pass, they were doing so on good intel and out of legitimate concern for our safety.

We advanced along the Gergarish Main Road through the Hai Alandalus neighborhood, which was one of the upscale sections of the city along the coast. The street, which was packed with shuttered shops and businesses, grew more crowded with jubilant Libyans and we found ourselves amid an ad hoc parade of rebels. They were driving along to the cheers of the people in the streets. But the battle was far from over. They were all making their way into the center of the city where the fighting was still intense, as evidenced by the distant gunfire and thuds of rockets.

We parked and walked along the streets to capture the scene and speak with the Libyans out celebrating. Men in casual clothes walked along carrying AKs and rocket launchers. Some had what looked like .22 caliber rifles—essentially whatever weapons they could get their hands on. Fighters waved and posed as they saw my camera. Toyota pickup trucks drove by filled with young fighters shouting and pumping their fists to the adoring crowd. Other trucks had heavy machine guns or anti-aircraft guns mounted in the back. It was the most rag-tag, chaotic looking "military" you could imagine. It was as if someone had dropped a pile of weapons in the middle of a mall and told all the young men shopping to grab something and run out into the streets to fight.

The convoy paraded east into downtown Tripoli until another checkpoint. From there, the main road was considered secure, but the side streets were not. As fighters advanced, small groups would break off and sweep the side streets for any signs of Gaddafi loyalists. We followed along staying a few blocks behind the lead patrols.

We walked up one side road to a body lying in the street covered by a fleece blanket. A trail of bloody footprints tracked across the street to where the man finally fell. One of the rebels lifted the blanket to show us the body. The man was dressed in green fatigues and white high-tops with green stripes. He looked African—probably one of the many mercenaries who had been recruited to fight for Gaddafi. It looked as though he had succumbed only hours before.

We proceeded slowly as rebels cleared each side street. They periodically took breaks and sat on the sidewalks of Gergarish Road. They made calls to rebels farther down the road to get intel on the status of security. Word was that it was safe to continue, so we drove until we reached a vast interchange of roads at a traffic circle nearly the size of a football field. Rebels held that territory and we could safely get out and explore.

It looked like a scene from *The Road Warrior*. Dozens of young men amped up and armed to the teeth were shouting and waving their Kalashnikovs in the air. A few wore pilfered military fatigues. The rest sported jeans, sweats, polos, Premier League jerseys, or T-shirts. Almost all wore flip flops. Some had thick, shaggy beards, others didn't look old enough to shave. One carried a Russian PK machine gun with an ammunition belt snaking around his torso. Several men manned an anti-aircraft gun precariously mounted to the back of a Toyota pickup truck crusted with dried mud. Gunfire cracked off from every direction.

These ragtag rebels were all standing watch at a traffic roundabout outside the women's military college compound in the center of Tripoli. The topaz-blue Mediterranean Sea shimmered 75 feet away. It was a beautiful summer day despite the war going on in the city.

A group of men had torn down and were jumping on signs picturing Gaddafi, who had been driven into hiding. Inside the white-walled compound, more ecstatic rebels were ransacking the facility, tearing down posters of Gaddafi and shredding them in the courtyard. Several men climbed to the antenna on top of the six-story watch tower. They removed the green Libyan flag and ceremoniously tossed it to the ground. To cheers from below, they raised the rebel flag—Libya's pre-Gaddafi flag.

There was an air of euphoria as decades worth of pent-up frustration and rage was being released, often punctuated with the firing of AK rounds into the air. Yet, the war was hardly over. These men were some of the front-line troops and fighting raged on only blocks away. Gunfire continued in the distance, drowned out by the periodic sounds of rockets and mortars exploding. The rebels wouldn't let us—a pack of close to a dozen journalists from different organizations—past this roundabout for our own safety.

Tripoli had technically fallen the night before, and we were only able to get just inside the city limits then. But on this day, rebels had made substantial progress clearing out neighborhoods as many of the pro-Gaddafi forces melted away. Although, there were countless soldiers still fighting to the death throughout the city.

As we stood at the roundabout recording and shooting photos of the celebrating rebels, one of the oldest of the fighters—a man in his forties with a thick black beard and a bandana around his head—stood up on the back of the gun truck and stared up the hill toward Gaddafi's compound. He was like a meerkat—ignoring the chaos immediately around him and focusing on the distant scent of a predator.

I fixated on him fixating on a potential threat and several of us determined it was in our best interest to retreat. Others in our pack decided to stay there. Four of us piled into a tan Ford Bronco with our twitchy rebel driver and sped off back into one of the neighborhoods that for the most part had been cleared.

We had heard about a house that had been converted into a field hospital of sorts. We decided to head there and report on that scene and gather more intel about how and where the fighting was moving across the city. We pulled off the main street that hours before had been the scene the parade. We drove up a hill into the narrow streets of a residential neighborhood.

We parked around the corner from the hospital house. As we were exiting the car, rebels in front of the house yelled to us that there were snipers in the neighborhood.

The rebels signaled for us to run, and we crouched and sprinted across the street and into the compound. Gunfire and explosions continued. Some sounded close by, but the walled compounds in the congested neighborhood played tricks with the sound, so it was hard to tell how close the fighting was.

The front room of the house had been cleared of furniture except for a few pillows and mattresses and a table cluttered with gauze pads, bandages, IV supplies, and various glass and plastic bottles of medicines and disinfectants. Three young Libyan doctors, one student, and some volunteers with varying levels of medical training were triaging wounded fighters.

They were all on edge because there had been some shooting in the neighborhood, and because they did not know if there were any Gaddafi loyalists still in the area. They were afraid of "fog of war" clashes between undisciplined rebels who didn't know the area or each other.

There were two young men mildly narced out and sprawled on mattresses. The doctors had already treated and bandaged their gunshot wounds. One had been hit in the left thigh, the other in the right calf. They would be fine.

The day before, the clinic treated 12 patients. Three didn't make it.

As we were speaking with the medics, rebels out front started firing their AKs as other rebels ran in with another wounded fighter. Two more journalists from our pack came in as well, unscathed, but barely so. The wounded fighter had been shot moments before at the traffic circle we had vacated.

Shortly after we left, a spray of heavy gunfire and rocket-propelled grenades rained down from the hill above the traffic circle, which confirmed the grizzled rebel's suspicions that they were in danger. One RPG struck the car of one of the journalists in our pack. The car burst into flames, destroying all his gear inside. Apparently, it wasn't the first time he had lost a car or his gear while covering a conflict.

The rebels took up positions and returned fire as several trucks came barreling down the hill. The journalists and translators ran inside the compound as RPGs struck the white walls and showered them with debris. They made their way inside one of the buildings and took refuge in a room as far from the fighting as they could find. Several of the young Libyan rebels who didn't quite have the mettle for a firefight huddled with them as the gunfire and explosions rang out.

The shooting drew closer. Gaddafi loyalists overran the rebels outside the compound. Our colleagues were pinned down and could do nothing other than stay quiet and wait.

Fortunately for all of us, after searching for a while, the loyalists apparently decided there were no more targets in the compound. They moved on and everyone made it out safely.

As our colleagues described what had happened, I found myself feeling jealous. Yes, we had to run to avoid possible sniper fire while entering the house, and we were getting important story details in the clinic, but they were really in the shit. That said, I probably would have shat had I been in the shit hiding in the compound hoping the Gaddafi soldiers wouldn't find us, but they came out the other side with an intense story.

Still, just a few weeks shy of the 10th anniversary of 9/11, I was realizing a dream that germinated in the ashes of the towers. After ten years of working my way up the journalism food chain and missing the most intense moments in Iraq and Afghanistan, I was finally a journalist on the front lines of a war.

We spent about an hour at the makeshift medical clinic and then determined we had pushed our luck enough for the day. According to the rebels, the way back out of the city was clear, so we loaded into our vehicles and returned to Zawiyah to file our stories and decompress with glasses of brown spirits—which seemed all the more appropriate after bathing in the brownish water coming out of my shower at the refinery.

The next day, we took the same route back into the city along Gergarish Road. However, one stretch of about a mile leading up to the rotary with the military college was no longer secure. Rebels said that snipers had taken up positions and if we wanted to pass, we did so at our own peril. Some rebels were refusing to drive that stretch, others did so only at extreme speed.

We conferred and decided to press on. We piled into the tan Bronco and huddled down on the floors. Our sketchy rebel driver gunned the truck and barreled along the residential street at more than 70 mph until we reached the rotary. While it lasted less than a minute, it was not fun. I felt helpless and in danger for one of the first times in my career.

Lulu, who had dodged bullets in many countries (although one of her laptops didn't), was calm and reassuring. She could tell that I was still a bit green when it came to active conflict experience, and she kept an eye on me to make sure I wasn't freaking out. Unlike some of the guys in our pack, she wasn't one to push the envelope just for the fuck of it, so our risk tolerance was well matched.

Dozens and dozens of rebels were massing at the roundabout as fighting raged on just over the hill in Bab al-Azizia, Gaddafi's compound. It was one of the last holdouts of Gaddafi loyalists, and the gunfire and explosions were relentless. We huddled under an overpass with fighters for some time waiting to see if we would be able to advance.

Occasionally, a truck would arrive with rebels taking a break from the fighting. A truck with fresh fighters would go tearing off up the hill to join the battle. Ambulances also sped up the hill from time to time.

One truck zoomed in from the front and a rebel overcome by the stress of battle clambered out and immediately vomited in the middle of the street. There was serious shit going on just over the hill.

We could see thick, black smoke rising behind the minaret of a mosque a couple of hundred yards away. The sound was overwhelming—constant gunfire and periodic thuds, some of which sounded uncomfortably close to our position. I twitched in response to each loud thud, and Lulu reassured me we were cool.

After a while, the mood lightened. Fighters came back from Bab al-Azizia cheering and indicating that the compound had fallen. The rebels said it was clear for us to proceed.

We drove up the hill and around a bend toward the compound. We passed crumbled buildings and tall metal walls riddled with holes from big-ass bullets. The gunfire was still relentless, but people claimed it was all celebratory.

Traffic slowed as we approached the compound. The streets were full of young rebels carrying weapons and other items they had just looted.

We pulled into a side street and parked. We got out of the cars and huddled next to a building as we assessed whether it was safe to proceed. The gunfire was relentless, but from what we could see, people were firing in the air—although those bullets had to come down somewhere.

We decided to venture in and crossed the street packed with rebels—both on foot and in vehicles—cheering, posing for photos, and firing their guns. We walked down the road to the compound and through the gates. There were more people leaving than entering. The remnants of a heavily bombed building stood in front of us. We turned to the right and came into a large park area on the right and a tall wall and building on the left. Directly in front of us was a throng of rebels congratulating each other and walking out with anything they could carry. One man was pushing a double stroller filled with rifle cases.

We pressed deeper into the compound. While most of the

gunfire was celebratory, I could see at least one rebel manning an anti-aircraft gun and firing horizontally away from the compound—not a good sign. Then, I heard a quick "whoosh" followed by an explosion just to my left. Little bits of debris rained down on us. Some dingbat fired an RPG at Gaddafi's house just for the fuck of it. That night I would have to carefully edit out myself yelling "shit!" at the moment of impact to use the audio in our story.

After a few minutes inside, Lulu and I decided we had enough and didn't have anything to gain by sticking around the chaos. Others in the pack wanted to continue, so we parted company.

On the way back out of the compound, we stopped at the metal entrance gate so Lulu could record a standup. We stood next to a large, smoking bullet hole in the gate. Then, some tracer rounds whistled past maybe 20 feet over our heads. That prompted us to pick up the pace.

We returned to the refinery and filed. A little later, our compatriots returned. They had gone deeper into the compound where TV news crews set up to shoot standups and film the madness. As they described what they had seen, I once again had that feeling of jealousy and slight inadequacy for not venturing farther. Granted, when working with a correspondent, it's a consensus decision and we had what we needed for our story. I certainly didn't feel safe going any farther than we did into the melee, but I couldn't help feeling like the others in our scrum had been ballsier and had better material—they certainly had a better war story.

Anyhow, our nightly whiskey ritual took my mind off that.

The next day, we did our morning calls to get intel on the state of fighting in the city, and we determined it was safe to move into the capital. While there were still pockets of fighting, we felt comfortable that the areas around the Corinthia and Radisson Blu hotels were secure, and we should break camp.

We packed up our gear and supplies and loaded into the cars. We spent the first part of the day driving around the city to explore the aftermath. Most of the streets in the west and downtown were clear and safe to travel. There were a few locals out in cars or on the streets cleaning up trash and debris. Every now and then we passed the burned-out carcass of a vehicle or a smoldering building. There were only a few roads where rebels still manned checkpoints and advised us it was unsafe to pass.

After a bit of driving around, we arrived at the Corinthia hotel. While open, they weren't ready for guests, so we continued down the road to the Radisson. Along the way, we passed more wrecked cars and small groups of people heading to the Martyr's Square area to celebrate.

Our dipshit rebel driver decided to celebrate as well and stuck his AK out the window and started firing rounds in the air. That was the moment we realized we were going to need to find another driver.

We entered the Radisson and encountered a young Libyan man in a suit. We asked if it was possible to get rooms. He said the computer system was down—shocking—but the hotel was empty. The only question was whether there were clean rooms since the staff and guests had fled the week before as the city was falling.

The gentleman escorted us up to the 14th floor, which was the VIP floor. We inspected the rooms to see if there were enough that were clean. Many were a mess as guests had fled and obviously housekeeping hadn't been back. A couple of the rooms had bullet holes. Fortunately, there were a bunch that were clean and made up and were otherwise in one piece. We returned to the front desk with the guy and provided him with the necessary information, agreed on rates (cash only), and he gave us keys.

As we were registering, a thong of other journalists flooded the lobby seeking rooms. Fortunately, we were first in and had the pick of the rooms.

And so, on August 24, three days after rebels stormed Tripoli, we settled into the hotel that would serve as our base for the next two months. The hotel was nice and modern, befitting the Radisson Blu line. While my room was comfortable, it got a lot smaller when filled with the bags and bags of food, water, and supplies. Even though we were in a hotel, we had no idea when it might have any food service, so we were going to be eating tuna and sweetcorn for a while.

We did some more reporting that afternoon and had to go into scramble mode to get our story done and filed before deadline. We barely made it. I was emailing back and forth with a panicked producer in Washington alerting him of the upload time on each piece of audio so he could pull it in on his end and mix the piece on a rolling basis. Par for the course when reporting from a war zone using satellite internet.

Before turning off work for the night, we fired our lunatic rebel driver and secured a new driver who had a Mercedes van, one of the nicest vehicles in the city, and perfect for hauling around six to eight journalists. Mahmoud was about six feet tall and husky. His hair was a tamer version of Inigo Montoya's, and he had a pronounced limp from a hip injury as a child. His English was good, but we still needed better-skilled translators much of the time.

That night, the press corps that had moved into the hotel all ended up outside by the deck of the pool partying. The bodies were still warm on the streets of the city, and there we were tossing back the whiskey and celebrating our move into the city and the new phase of the story. The life of the tribe…

The next day most of us started searching out the usual spots to find stories after the fall of a city: prisons and hospitals. We found multiple hospitals and a morgue, and I will spare you a description of the scene in the morgue, other than to say, not enough lockers. We gathered stories of how the conflict had progressed through the city from doctors and patients.

Then, we drove outside the city to investigate rumors about an alleged massacre. We drove through remote neighborhoods until we were in a somewhat rural area. Two rebels manning a checkpoint stopped us. One spoke a few words of English. The other spoke only Arabic and had what Josey Wales would call "crazy eyes."

As we explained that we were journalists and we were chasing a story in that area, the crazy-eyed rebel grew tense and twitchy. He started to raise his weapon. We realized we needed to flee and told Mahmoud to step on it.

We returned to the city and pulled up to an area next to Gaddafi's former compound. In the distance, we saw a couple of other cars belonging to journalists parked next to two giant dump trucks blocking the road. We approached. Mahmoud parked the van behind one of the other cars and we casually got out and approached the dump trucks. At the last second, we noticed a bunch of people on the ground huddled up next to the trucks. They motioned frantically for us to get down. We scrambled to the ground next to them as a few bullets whistled overhead.

There had been a clash just on the other side of the trucks and the journalists were pinned down. Snipers had killed rebels who lay dead in the street beyond the trucks. Those same snipers continued to fire shots in our direction.

We decided to make a run for it. We sprinted back to the van and Mahmoud hauled ass. We stopped at an intersection a few hundred yards down the road.

A handful of Libyans were out on the streets waving flags and trying to tear down a three-story fabric mural of Gaddafi hanging from the side of a building. A platoon of rebels driving black pickup trucks arrived. They posed for photos. The commander spoke with us about the fighting throughout the city.

Suddenly the rebels dove into their trucks and sped off. It took a moment for us to realize that snipers were firing at us. Once we processed that, we sprinted back to the van and dove into a pile on the floor as Mahmoud sped off again. I captured the chaos on tape, including an important rule of thumb Thomas Erdbrink uttered as we ran back to the van: "when the rebels leave, we leave!"

We regrouped for one more adventure that afternoon. A platoon of us, including the late Marie Colvin, drove into a pleasant, upscale neighborhood in the capital and stopped outside the entrance to a walled compound. It was the house of one of Gaddafi's sons, Mutassim.

Locals had backed a truck up to the 20-foot-high wall of the compound and then raised a ladder in the back of the truck. We hopped up on the truck, climbed the ladder, straddled over the wall, and climbed down a ladder on the other side.

Inside the walls was about a three-acre estate with a sprawling lawn surrounded by trees concealing the inside of the security wall. Across the lawn was an empty swimming pool and a large, tan, modern one-story house that looked like something you'd see in Taos or Sedona.

Many of the large windows were smashed, and the only things left inside the house were large pieces of furniture and gym equipment too heavy to carry out over the wall. We had missed the critical window after the fall of the city, and all the documents and personal items that could have told stories were long gone. Locals roaming around inside said that people had carted off crates of expensive champagne, nice watches, and other riches.

Inside the house was a large, vault-like door to a basement. Rebels were guarding it and would not let us enter. Presumably, there was useful or incriminating evidence there they wanted to preserve, but they would not give us any idea as to what, or who, was down there.

On the other side of the compound was a large, dried-up stone fountain, but more interestingly, a staircase heading underground. We descended into an enormous bunker. There was a long, white hallway heading to another open vault door. Inside were numerous sleeping and recreation rooms, as well as medical rooms with examination tables and medical office furniture. Like the house, the bunker had been thoroughly ransacked and pilfered. What was left was again furniture and the detritus from boxes, books and magazines, the insides of pillows, blankets, and catalog pictures of military vehicles and equipment—presumably the equivalent of porn to a Gaddafi.

We completed our tour of the bunker and climbed back out,

and then back over the wall of the compound. Journalistically it didn't yield much, but it was a fun, voyeuristic excursion.

That night, we gathered for drinks in one of the NPR hotel rooms. Marie and I sat on the balcony for a couple of hours watching the celebratory fire from the square and shooting the shit. I don't remember the details of the conversation, but I recall having a fit of insecurity and self-doubt—not uncommon for me, especially when I was surrounded by so many A-list journalists.

I was telling her about some idea or story that I was convinced I wasn't good enough to do. What I remember was her reaction to me criticizing myself. She was humble, reassuring, and supportive. She said she didn't know what she was doing early on and that if she could succeed, anyone could. She said to just focus on thinking through the elements of a story and the steps needed to get the material and put it together. She couldn't have been nicer or more generous. She easily could have walked away saying, "why am I wasting time listening to this limp dick," and gone to talk to one of the rock stars, but she didn't.

That was the only personal interaction I would end up having with Marie, and I am glad I had that opportunity to see her as a person rather than the icon she was from a distance. It was one of those moments that makes a lifelong impact.

The next day was a Friday and quiet in the morning. NPR correspondent Jason Beaubien and a security guy arrived from Tunisia to reinforce Lulu and me. They were able to take the shorter route to Tripoli as the border calmed down in the days after I traveled into Libya. I spent the afternoon driving around the city with the two of them to help orient them and scope out story ideas.

It was amazing how quickly the city was showing signs of normal life. We passed people out on the streets walking and shopping—granted, there wasn't much to shop for yet. Vendors were setting up makeshift stands to sell food and cigarettes—the two most important commodities in Libya. Stores were starting to reopen, although they had little on the shelves. Families were out with young children searching for food and water. Young men dressed in casual clothes and carrying AKs and pistols would pose for photos when they saw us passing by. People waved at us from their cars and flashed "victory" signs.

The reason people were out buying water was because the water supply to the city had run dry. A vast network of wells in the south of Libya sucked water from below the desert soil and pumped it to the urban areas in the north of the country. During the conflict, people abandoned their posts and the system shut down. After a few days, the taps ran dry in Tripoli. It wasn't just locals who were struggling with the lack of water, all of us were. The hotel had gone dry. While we had plenty of bottled water that I had procured in Tunisia, we had no showers and no working toilets.

Just imagine a hotel full of international journalists and security contractors with no running water. Plus, dozens of Libyan officials and rebels were using the hotel as a base of operations, and they needed bathrooms too. I will spare the really gory details of the situation, but we obviously did not want to use the toilets in our rooms since they would not flush. What ensued was basically an easter egg hunt for bathrooms throughout the hotel as the main ones in the lobby and public areas turned into cesspools. In addition, the hotel pool turned into a bathtub (I did not partake). After a couple of days, a mucus-green film grew and covered the pool, which put an end to the bathing.

At one point, the hotel hired a water truck to provide a brief supply that allowed most of us to fill our tubs with water. Then, we could pour buckets into the toilets to flush them. It wasn't pretty, but it got us through the week of no water that finally ended when the transitional government was able to dispatch people to the south to restart the wells and pumps.

On August 28, Jason and I stumbled across a troubling scene. We traveled to the Yarmouk-Salah Eddin area of southern Tripoli to inspect the scene of a recently discovered massacre. The site of the massacre sat behind the Brigade 32 compound—the base for the elite Khamis brigade of Gaddafi soldiers. Earlier in the year, NATO pounded the snot out of the base.

We arrived at the brigade compound at the same time as a few other western journalists. As we entered the facility, we saw several young rebels holding a group of terrified African men at gunpoint inside the guard office.

The scene was tense and chaotic. The rebels were shouting questions and accusations at the men. The rebels accused the men of being Gaddafi mercenaries, even though all the men were wearing casual clothes and did not look the least bit mercenary. The rebels had rounded them up on the street and corralled them in the small office and were preparing to carry out summary judgement.

We asked the rebels who the men were and how they determined that they were mercenaries. The answer, as I had encountered before, was that Gaddafi hired men from other African countries to serve as mercenaries. The men were African. Therefore, they were mercenaries.

We convinced the rebels to let us talk to the men, and they reluctantly agreed over the objections of one rebel who was amped up and arguing that they should shoot the men then and there. The men said they were migrants from Nigeria who had been working in Libya and were living in a makeshift camp nearby. They were not Gaddafi supporters and were simply in the country doing construction work to support their families back home.

A rebel came to the entrance of the office and started shouting "Allah Akbar." That terrified the African men. A couple of them began to weep, and they said they feared the rebels would kill them.

The Africans said they had just come out of their camp for the first time in days to find food. Their story made sense, and we saw no evidence to contradict their narrative. We then explained to the rebels that the men were no threat and should be let go.

The rebels conferred, and eventually talked down the one who was out for blood. The rebels let the men out of the office, let them rinse and drink from a nearby sprinkler, and then let the men sit outside. The rebels tried to reassure the Nigerians that no harm would come to them.

After the situation calmed down, I had time to process the fact that had we arrived a few minutes later, the African men would have been dead. There was no question the rebels were going to execute them. It was one of the scary realities of the conflict—the rebels were generally untrained young men often operating with no leadership or any sense of the laws of war. All it would take was one of them to start firing on a group of captives to unleash a war crime.

On top of it, we were in danger walking into situations like that. Just because the rebels were pro media and happy to have us around to document the atrocities of the regime, there was nothing to stop them from turning on us if they felt we were interfering or "taking the other side." Some of the guys were super twitchy and there was little stopping them from losing their shit on us.

We explored the compound and the wreckage caused by both NATO bombs and the looting by rebels. The base housed a dozen or more hangars that had been full of tanks, transport vehicles, and crates of weapons and ammunition. Several of the hangars had been shredded by explosions. Steel frames still stood, but all the walls and sheet-metal roofs had been blown to pieces and debris lay in heaps. Carcasses of tanks, stripped of anything that could be removed, sat looking like set pieces from the *Terminator* movies. Hundreds of weapons and ammo crates were scattered about, broken and empty. A few rebels were climbing through all the wreckage and debris looking for any remaining items that hadn't been pilfered, and others were simply having fun climbing through the tank skeletons and taking photos.

We finished our tour of the compound just as the rebels let the African men go free. From there, we drove around the Brigade 32 compound to the massacre site. Unlike the Nigerians, there was nothing we could do to help anyone at that compound.

During the fighting in Tripoli in the preceding days, the Gaddafi forces massacred the estimated 50 prisoners in the compound. At some point, a fire started, charring all the bodies. Inside a cinderblock building, the floor was covered with black ash and baked, white skeletal remains. Other journalists and human rights workers were at the scene chronicling the atrocity.

Outside that building, there were other bodies scattered about the compound. Those appeared to be Gaddafi forces killed by rebels during the fall of the city. Some of those bodies had been bound and brutally executed. It was a fucking grim scene. It was one of those moments where you compartmentalize and do the work: take pictures and interview people. But you can't unsee it. Scenes like that add to the wounds and scars on the Dorian Grey portrait in your emotional closet. Every horror that I saw, every atrocity, every tale of violence and depravity I heard about from victims, every example of people having no regard for the life and humanity of others, hardened me and convinced me that people are worse than animals.

Animals do savage and brutal things. They kill to survive. They will kill not just to eat, but to preserve access to food and territory. But they don't torture. They don't use sexual violence as a weapon of terror. They don't revel in sadism the way African militias or Syrian secret police do. People choose to inflict pain, suffering, and death on others for petty reasons, and sometimes for recreational purposes.

Over the last two decades, there has been plenty of discussion about PTSD among veterans and the need to provide treatment for the psychological and emotional impacts of their combat experiences. Unfortunately, there has been little to no discussion about journalists, humanitarians, and other civilians who work in hostile environments. You can argue that what we experience is as bad, and sometimes worse than what soldiers experience. We live and work not just in the conflicts, but in the aftermath. We see and try to pick up the broken pieces. We hear the stories of the survivors. We live among the suffering. And we often confront apathy and indifference to the plight of the Afghans, Libyans, Yemenis, and others who are the innocent victims of political choices of governments and leaders who rarely face any accountability for their actions.

Point is, being a journalist is one of the most amazing and fulfilling vocations and avocations, but nothing comes without a cost. I believe that giving victims a voice, informing the world about the human costs of wars and conflicts, is worth the toll it takes. However, news organizations and NGOs need to do far more to care for their people they send into apocalyptic settings, just as the military needs to do more for its people. Rant over.

Going forward, things gradually settled into a routine. We'd spend the days wandering the city finding stories. Security had reached a point that we were no longer traveling in packs with journalists from other organizations or wearing body armor. Officials from the transitional government were moving into Tripoli and holding press conferences. Nightly celebrations were taking place in Green Square. Unfortunately, those celebrations often included endless barrages of celebratory gunfire. Even though I knew the gunfire was theoretically harmless, it didn't make it any easier to sleep.

Stores reopened. Traffic increased. The hotel restaurant menu kept expanding. Even the hotel spa reopened, and I popped down for a massage. It was beyond surreal to me to be in an upscale hotel spa in Tripoli so soon after the fall of the city having a casual conversation with the Moroccan masseuse who had come back to work after hiding out in the city with some of the other foreign hotel workers.

The hotel internet came back to life. Cell service returned to normal. Gasoline supplies increased and the prices and lines decreased. A surprisingly good pizza restaurant opened behind the hotel, and it quickly became the most popular restaurant in the neighborhood.

During Eid, hundreds of people came out to worship in Green Square. It looked like Libyapalooza. Kids had Libyan flags painted on their faces. Families laughed and smiled. Yet, just blocks away there were streets still full of burned-out cars and shell casings. Reminders of death and destruction were everywhere, but the people were free and happy.

Taxis flooded the streets again. Some taxi drivers refused to charge westerners because they felt that they were serving their country by helping us. One evening I was out in Green Square covering the celebration and couldn't find a taxi back to the hotel. A couple of young Libyans riding motorcycles passed by and offered me a ride. I hopped on without any concern—things had become that secure and relaxed and the Libyans were so happy to have us there that there wasn't the slightest concern about hopping on a stranger's motorcycle.

Well, that's not entirely true. There wasn't a concern that they would kidnap or intentionally cause harm. However, as I mentioned in a previous chapter, Libyans were some of the batshit craziest drivers I had ever encountered. They loved driving at extreme speed and within electrons of the cars in front of them. They weaved in and out of traffic with such abandon it regularly made my testicles crawl up my abdomen.

The other concern was friendly fire. Rebels loved shooting off celebratory rounds, and they had to come down somewhere. In fact, in the first few days we were in the Radisson, a journalist was out by the pool and took a round in the leg. It's possible it was a sniper, but far more likely it was celebratory.

Plus, there were oodles of rebels who clearly had no training or muzzle discipline roaming around with guns. They were like cadet Leslie Barbara in *Police Academy* during shotgun training. I was convinced at some point one of them would accidentally discharge an AK in the hotel lobby.

To prevent that, the hotel added an X-ray machine at the entrance and required everyone to check their weapons in a large cardboard box at the door. Picture an enormous umbrella bin filled with machine guns. It was both comical and disconcerting.

A few weeks into my rotation, Lulu went out on R&R and Corey Flintoff arrived (toting some of the most random brands of whiskey I had ever seen). Rebels were trying to retake Bani Walid, a small city in the middle of the desert about an hour drive south of Tripoli. Every morning, journalists would drive south into the desert to spots along the road where large numbers of rebels would gather each day in preparation for a siege on Bani Walid.

It was all a bit *Waiting for Godot*. Day after day, bored rebels sat around awaiting the green light from their advance scouts, and we sat around bored trying to find other stories.

One day while we were in a giant throng of rebels as well as a line of press vehicles, bullets started whistling over our heads. Snipers had taken up positions in the desert hills near the road and were taking shots at us. In an exercise we hadn't practiced in a few weeks, we dove into our van and Mahmoud sped off up the road to another rebel checkpoint farther from the front.

Since the Bani Walid campaign wasn't going anywhere, Corey and I took a road trip to Misrata. The city had been taken by rebels in May, but loyalists had launched strikes and attacks throughout the summer. By mid-September, it was solidly under rebel control and the front line had moved east from there to Sirte. We went through a bureaucratic process of getting permission slips from the interim regime in Tripoli to allow us to travel through the multitude of checkpoints on the way to Misrata. Although rebels were in control of the city and the checkpoints, there were factions among the rebels, and each had their own turf and rules. So, we had to coordinate permission through the Misrata administration as well as officials in Tripoli to pass through the gauntlets.

With our papers and stamps in hand, we set off along the coast. As we neared Misrata, there was a change in appearance and demeanor of the men manning checkpoints. The Misrata rebels were beefier and gruffer. They were intimidating. Fortunately, they were reasonable once they saw we had the proper credentials. They made sure we got through to the city. Like most rebels, they wanted good press.

Misrata was beat to shit. There is no other way to describe it. Sections of the city had been fucking pounded. Along Tripoli Street, which endured the heaviest fighting, facades were falling off buildings. Large caliber bullet holes scarred the concrete walls. Shells had blasted gaping holes into buildings. Burned-out carcasses of cars were scattered around the streets. Enormous piles of debris clogged sections of road.

Locals were out doing war tourism. We passed a group of pre-teen and early teen boys, one carrying an AK, taking photos in front of burned-out buildings. They of course waved and posed so I could photograph them. We also passed young women in abayas and hijabs taking selfies among the wreckage.

On Tripoli Street, a man had set up a museum of munitions recovered after the fighting. The open-air display occupied about a 20' by 40' stretch of sidewalk. The "museum" was organized into sections based on the type of munition. There was everything from AK casings and bullets to 155mm shells. There were piles of mortar tubes and rocket launchers. There were giant wooden ammo crates and radio gear taken from regime armories. Next to the display was a disabled tank. A man was photographing his young children posing on top of the metal beast. What was a bit disconcerting was the fact that not all the munitions were spent or exploded. There was some live shit in the mix. A few dozen people crowded around the display ogling the remnants of the conflict and basking in the glow of a city overthrown.

We attended a meeting of the Misrata civil and military councils where the ad hoc interim government members discussed their efforts to maintain security and restore services in the ravaged city. One thing that was simmering during the meeting was something we were seeing bubble up in Tripoli: power struggles.

The Misrata militias had fought a brutal campaign to liberate the city and then moved on to help Tripoli fighters liberate the capital. They felt they had "done more" for the country than other militias had. They were hardly the only militia voicing such sentiments. The common enemy wasn't finished yet, and so there was much fighting to be done, but the fractures were emerging that would lead to the inevitable civil war among factions and militias who all felt they deserved the biggest piece of the post-Gaddafi pie.

Anyone who thought that a country awash in militias of heavily armed teenagers and twenty somethings was going to peacefully disarm and come together clearly had not spent any time on the ground. It was simply a matter of how quickly and violently the country would descend into chaos as old tribal animosities came to the fore and foreign powers started backing different horses.

We returned to Tripoli, and I started organizing the handover to my replacement. I had been in the country for almost six weeks, and it was time for me to take a break. I settled with the hotel to clear our tab. I plunked down stacks of cash on the front desk. By the time I left, I had paid more than $20,000 in cash to the hotel. Because they were not reconnected to the Radisson global network, they were not able to enter my rewards number. However, I took all the receipts home and faxed them to Radisson. They gave me the points for more than $20,000 in hotel expenses, which immediately gave me elite status. I then migrated the points to United Airlines for 96,000 redeemable miles. I was pretty certain I was the only journalist there who managed to play the points and miles game with the war.

On September 25, I caught a UN flight out of Tripoli as rebels pressed their offensives to the east and south and Gaddafi remained alive and in hiding. I touched down in Malta and spent a couple of days decompressing while eating expensive meals, drinking fine wine, going to the spa and casino, and exploring the historic city of Valletta by day and clubs full of British and Russian tourists by night. It was, as Chris Knight would say, a moral imperative to indulge in hedonism immediately upon exiting a war zone. Had I returned to D.C. without having done so, I would have been shamed by my foreign desk colleagues.

While I was in Libya, there was a lot of action and I rarely slowed down enough to reflect. Once I was out and taking some time off with Anna on Cape Cod, I was able to process the six weeks. The main takeaway for me was I was in my element and doing what I wanted to be doing and what I felt I was meant to be doing. While the moments of real danger (sniper fire, passing through insecure neighborhoods, hanging at checkpoints close to front lines) were fleeting, it was war reporting. We were covering a rapidly evolving and changing situation and reporting daily. That was all new to me. I had not done daily reporting in my travels until joining NPR. That increased the pressure and intensity of the work. It felt like the days after 9/11 at WBUR when we were in a flat-out sprint for weeks producing the daily talk show.

It was also new to me to be cavorting with the A-list foreign and war correspondents—to be sitting at the adult table. Many people initially saw me just as "NPR producer," which was a respected entity, but over time people saw me as a person and journalist and someone who was a peer based on skills, knowledge, my body of work, and my ability to troubleshoot and problem solve with the best (a number of journalists admired the cantilevered satellite internet perch I made on the balcony using a wicker table, an ironing board, and paracord—it was pure MacGyver). I was a Jedi master with satellite gear and often helped others with their kit. I managed bureaucracy well and I got shit done. That was in large part because of my years working for a small organization that provided me no air cover or backup—I had to fend for myself on the ground with few resources, and I got damn good at it.

It was also interesting to watch all the young freelancers flooding into Libya trying to make their mark as war reporters. A story like that attracted people from all over the world wanting what I had spent years chasing—a seat at the war table. Some of the freelancers had conflict experience, but many showed up lacking body armor, satellite gear, money for translators and drivers, or any kind of emergency support. It's kind of amazing that more reporters weren't killed in Libya in 2011 given how many were there and how many were either major risk takers or situationally unaware.

While I still had ambitions of returning to being a correspondent, I felt at home in those six weeks in Libya. The work was what I had been seeking, and the people were the tribe I had been seeking. It was stressful and draining, and at times emotionally punishing, but I loved every second of it and believed I was making a difference by helping to inform the world.

Chapter Sixteen
Turning out the Lights in Baghdad

December 2011

BAGHDAD — After a couple of days of sorting through years of accumulated and abandoned gear and junk in the Baghdad bureau, I embarked on my last embed in Iraq. It was an overnight junket for a few journalists to visit Camp Kalsu. The base was essentially a truck stop in Iskandariya, roughly 20 miles south of Baghdad. Convoys driving south on Highway 1 to Kuwait would stop for food and gas, a brief leg stretch, and maybe a bit of vehicle maintenance. The Army flew a few journalists from the Green Zone to the spartan base, which was getting threadbare as it was about a week from shuttering.

Convoys of MRAPs and other hulking vehicles would roll into the dusty outpost and line up in a staging yard. Soldiers would hop off, grab some food, smoke, and generally bask in the fact that they were bugging the fuck out of Iraq. While there was still the threat of attack on the drive out of Iraq, troops were starting to let loose and let it sink in that the war was over, and they were going home. While they were looking forward to heading home, some soldiers said it was bittersweet. There were aspects to being deployed that they were going to miss.

One lieutenant expressed something that resonated with me. He said that he was going to miss the camaraderie and the experience of living with the soldiers in his platoon. That was very different from the dynamic of living on bases back in the United States, he said.

What he was describing was a tribal connection that existed in the field, but not at home. It was exactly what I had seen and experienced over the years with journalists and expats living in places like Baghdad, Kabul, Sana'a, or Beirut. Tribes emerge in those downrange environments. And leaving, saying goodbye to a tribe is not easy.

I was getting a taste of the phenomenon of a news story ending and the tribe dissipating. When wars kick off, there is an influx of press. The initial phase is usually expeditionary and exciting (and potentially deadly)—following the front lines, chasing the story, setting up temporary bases of operations, moving together as a herd for safety and efficiency—like I experienced in Libya. Unless the conflict is something like Grenada, the war settles in and news organizations build up more substantial bureaus like in Lebanon, the Balkans, Afghanistan, and Iraq. A social scene inevitably develops. The work hard, play hard dynamic sets in. It turns into a mix of summer camp and college with death and destruction. What I mean is that the journalists based in places like Baghdad are out on their own in the wilderness—there are no parents, no adult supervision. Editors or managers might drop in now and then, but for the most part, the inmates run the asylums and navigate the local dynamics and decide on what to cover and how. If the work gets done, whatever hedonism or lunacy happens downrange stays downrange.

War reporting is a life and lifestyle. If you are a reporter based in Geneva, you work during the week filing your stories about international business or organizations, and then spend weekends relaxing or touring around Europe. When you are in a war zone, you are there 24/7 for weeks or months at a time. Even if you have a day or two of slow news, you are still in the bubble. It can be grinding and soul crushing at times, and that's why the social scenes that develop are so important, and often so decadent.

It's no different than human behavior in the run up to a major storm or in the early months of the COVID pandemic. Hoarding is a response to scarcity. In war zones, "normalcy" is scarce. Alcohol can be scarce. Sex can be scarce. Therefore, there is an inclination to hoard social interaction.

People gathered and partied more often than they would in a "normal" environment like New York or London. In those places, you know you can go out any time and there are always things you can do, so there is less pressure to go out all the time. In war zones, the sense of scarcity drives people to socialize and interact more often. That is one of the factors that forges a tighter community or tribe.

And back to the point of departure (pun intended)—leaving is difficult. As I have said before, the end of summer camp, the end of college, the end of any community or tribal experience is hard. Your very identity is tied to your tribe. Troops experience difficulties when returning from deployment and so do civilians.

When a war ends and it's time to go home, it can be disorienting and depressing. Where is the next rush? How do you relate to people at home who might have been your tribe once but no longer are because you have changed while you were away? How do you go from the exotic and dangerous to the seemingly mundane? How do you quietly process or lock away the horrors you have seen or experienced?

The Hurt Locker and *American Sniper* were typical Hollywood productions that got more wrong than right. However, each movie had elements and a scene where I felt they nailed it, and they were both subtle scenes that the general audience probably didn't think much of, but people who have been downrange can relate to.

In *The Hurt Locker*, it is the scene at the end when William James is in the grocery store. He had spent a year diffusing explosives in Iraq, one of the most stressful things anyone could endure. Then, he's home in a safe environment with his family, who can't begin to understand his experiences. He's staring at an entire aisle of cereals. You see how he is simply overwhelmed by all the choices. He's paralyzed by it. The next scene is him back in Iraq on another deployment—in his comfort zone. That moment in the grocery store captured what it's like leaving an intense environment and trying to relate to "normality."

Similarly, in *American Sniper*, there are several scenes where Chris Kyle is visibly elsewhere and unable to relate to and communicate with the people around him. He is distant, shut down, at times reliving moments downrange. To this day, those are the moments in the movie that I remember, in no small part because I still experience that feeling of distance from those outside the tribe.

The winding down in Iraq was perhaps more difficult, or at least more frustrating, for me because I had just gotten there. I spent a week at the NPR bureau in October before heading back into Libya for another couple of weeks. I liked the Baghdad bureau. The house was great. Kelly McEvers, the Energizer Bunny of correspondents, was great. The staff were great. The housemates, Roy Guttman with McClatchy and Inga Rogg with Neue Zürcher Zeitung, were great. The work was great. There were no parents looking over our shoulders. It was sleepover camp with car bombs. Even though I hadn't lived it full-time, I was experiencing a sense of loss with the war ending. I was on my last embed in Iraq. I was closing a bureau. The war that I never really experienced was over. A door was closing. I didn't want the embed to end, and I was soaking in every sight, smell, sound, and second of it.

At dusk, a couple of us loaded into MRAPs to tag along on a route security patrol. We drove out into surrounding villages as troops looked for any evidence of possible IEDs or attacks being staged. We dismounted a couple of times and walked through villages and meeting with Iraqi forces. The U.S. soldiers had cordial relations with the Iraqi troops in the area and they laughed with each other as they were all counting down the days before the Americans would be gone. Some of the Iraqis expressed that they were disappointed to see the Americans leaving, and there were a couple of reasons. First, they had formed friendships as typically happened during deployments to Iraq. Second, the Iraqis had concerns about security and stability in the country once the U.S. military was gone—a valid concern.

We spent a few hours driving and marching around the countryside. There was little danger that we would encounter any shit, but that didn't matter at that point. I was out with U.S. forces in Iraq walking around in the moonlight.

I can still picture the streets, the Iraqi police stations, the glow of the luminous rounds hovering in the sky; I can hear the MRAPs idling and our footsteps trudging along the pavement and dirt. I didn't want to come home for dinner. I wanted to stay out and play. I never fully appreciated Colonel Kilgore's lament in *Apocalypse Now* until that night on patrol south of Baghdad. "Someday this war's gonna end."

Alas, we had to wrap it up and return to the base. Dinner was dreadful. The dining hall was closed (for good), and the base was on MREs. In the public affairs office was a table covered with rat-fucked MREs. I think there were a few still unopened, but most had been picked through. We found some entrees and did our best with the chemical heating pouches. Thanks to the time I spent at COP Najil in Afghanistan when the kitchen was on lockdown, I was skilled in using the heating pouch. You had to add just the right amount of water to trigger the chemical reaction, and then slide in the packet with your entree, fold the top of the heating pouch, and then lean it against a wall at a 45-degree angle for a few minutes. If you do it right, you have a nice meal of hot chili mac (of course, all the chili mac was long gone, and we were slumming it with stroganoff and other undesirable entrees).

After dinner, we sat in the public affairs office uploading material from the day. I also sat there trying to figure out how to entice a very pretty and cool public affairs sergeant back to my CHU for some night maneuvers. Alas, I was too worried about coming across as a creeper or getting one or both of us into hot water, so I didn't make a move. It was yet another mission fail in the campaign to get in bed on an embed.

She and I have remained friends since then, and years later I asked her how she would have reacted had I made a play. She said she would have considered it but declined, in large part out of fear of the consequences of getting caught showing her military assets to a journalist.

Anyhow, the next morning, we wrapped up and flew back to Baghdad. That was it. My last Iraq embed was in the books. I returned to the bureau and filed my story about the truck stop on the way to Kuwait and how happy soldiers were to be heading home.

We spent another couple of days working on clearing out the house and preparing for a road trip to Kirkuk and Erbil. On December 9, we loaded into two cars and rolled north to Kirkuk. It was my first long road trip in Iraq, and it was enlightening to see how poor the infrastructure still was after eight years of "reconstruction." Once we were off the highway leading out of Baghdad, it narrowed to a two-lane road most of the way to Kirkuk. We passed rundown dusty villages, large expanses of desert, and industrial developments. Even though the distance was only a couple hundred miles, we had to leave early in the morning because we couldn't drive at highway speed the whole trip.

We rolled into Kirkuk and completed a couple of interviews, including with my buddy the deputy police commander who I had met during my embed in Kirkuk the previous year. We then visited the Kirkuk Citadel. It sat on a hill in the middle of the city. There were no guards or formal entrance. We simply pulled up and wandered the grounds. There were ruins of several ancient mosques as well as the ruins of the Chaldean Catholic Cathedral. The city sprawled out in each direction from the hill. It was fucking cool. We had the place to ourselves and roamed the ruins until it was time to head off for another interview.

We drove out into the middle of flat, brown farmland—the equivalent of drought-stricken Kansas. We interviewed a farmer about the tensions in Kirkuk and how the American withdrawal was going to affect the dynamics there. The sun began to set as we walked through bone-dry corn fields and vast expanses of flat, barren land. Another metaphor for Iraq in the coming years?

From there we rolled on to Erbil. We arrived in the city, checked into our hotel, and then went to the fucking mall. It was a completely different world than Baghdad or Kirkuk. Erbil was like a small Turkish city—clean, modern, safe. The mall was all decorated for Christmas with a two-story tree in the center. There were fashion and jewelry shops. There was a Levi's Store. I could not wrap my head around the fact that we were in Iraq.

The next day we attended a conference organized to gather leaders from Kirkuk and get them to sit and talk about resolving the status of the disputed city. After the event, we set out for Baghdad. The drive was downright metaphoric. Erbil was clean with new infrastructure. New buildings were under construction left and right. As we reached the midpoint to Baghdad, we entered a thick sandstorm. Visibility along the two-lane road dropped to 50 feet in spots as traffic crawled along. Basically, it kept getting shittier—the weather, the villages along the sides of the road, the traffic, as we closed in on Baghdad. The northern part of the city was poor and industrial. It was congested and dirty. There were large dirt berms on the side of the road. It was unpleasant.

We made it back to the bureau and spent another couple of days packing and cleaning. An Iraqi interpreter who had been waiting for several years for a Special Immigrant Visa came to the bureau so I could interview him. He was one of far too many Iraqis who had worked for U.S. forces and then applied for the promised visa, only to have the process drawn out for years while he and his family faced threats. His brother was shot and disabled. The interpreter, who went by the name Johnnie, said that had he known he was going to have such a hard time getting his visa and having to go into hiding in the meantime, he probably wouldn't have offered to work for the U.S. military. Powerful lesson—if you don't honor promises, good luck getting people to trust you in the future.

On December 15, we drove to a remaining section of the U.S. military base at Baghdad Airport for the end of the war. The ceremony took place in an open space about the size of a hockey rink. Blast walls and HESCO barriers surrounded the stage and seating area. Chairs were set up for U.S. military personnel and Iraqi dignitaries—such as the Prime Minister, who did not attend the event. A color guard marched through the two-hundred or so attendees to the stage. Secretary of Defense Leon Panetta, Ambassador James Jeffreys, and U.S. Forces-Iraq commander General Lloyd Austin stood before the crowd. There was music, fanfare, speeches, and then General Austin rolled up the flag.

Kelly and I sat at a table covered with coffee cups and food wrappers at the back of the ceremony. We cranked away on our laptops and launched sound and pictures over our portable satellite internet terminal. We filed our story, watched the U.S. dignitaries board a C-17, and then we drove back out of the base though trash-covered fields where seagulls and vultures feasted. There were no metaphors to be found there...

And, just like that, the war was over. Kelly rocked off to roll out of Iraq and into Kuwait with some of the last troops to leave, and I stayed behind in Baghdad continuing the bureau shutdown and covering the political crisis that kicked off the moment the last U.S. troops crossed into Kuwait.

The Iraqi prime minister wasted no time in launching a campaign to consolidate power and hobble his rivals. I ended up much busier than I expected reporting on explosions in the city, efforts to arrest government officials, and attending a press conference held by the prime minister. His security was so tight that reporters were not even allowed to bring pens into the event, let alone recording devices. You were provided with pens and notebooks once inside. Tight security was understandable, but the level of paranoia was downright Nixonian. Granted, Maliki was Saddam-light in terms of his authoritarian ways, so there were plenty who wanted to see him swinging from a streetlamp—pardon the mixed metaphor from Afghanistan.

Maliki sent his goons to arrest or intimidate his Sunni rivals in the government. He accused the vice president of running death squads and orchestrating bombings in Kabul. It was like parents going away for the weekend and leaving feisty teenagers alone for the first time. The moment the car was out of the driveway, the kids started fighting over the remote control and what to eat for dinner. While it was predictable to a certain degree, it was faster and more thuggish than some expected.

The city shook almost daily as powerful bombs detonated. Often after a powerful rumble I would run to the roof of the house to look for smoke plumes to see the location of the blasts and assess the intensity. One car bomb struck less than a mile from the bureau and shattered windows for blocks from the site of the blast.

In a sideshow to all of it, Anna came to Baghdad. It was her first visit to Iraq since she left in 1991. We had been discussing the idea with Kelly for some time. The plan was for Anna to make the visit when Kelly was in Iraq so she could report the story of Anna's return after 20 years. The timing and logistics never aligned and the only opportunity for Anna to visit Baghdad before we closed the bureau was while Kelly was out.

Our driver and I picked up Anna at the airport and we spent a few days roaming the city, including touring her family's abandoned house. I ended up reporting the story about my girlfriend's *Alice in Wonderland*-like return to her home after 20 years of war, sanctions, and another war.

It was awkward because our relationship was in another ambiguous phase (meaning I was questioning things again, or more accurately, continuing to try to make something work that deep down I knew was close, but not the right fit for me). However, we got through it, and it turned into a compelling story, even though she was emotionally guarded the whole time and never let herself have a truly vulnerable moment in reaction to being back in Baghdad. I think she was also justifiably keeping her guard up around me since I was continuing to give her mixed signals. Anna departed and I spent a few more days packing and celebrating the season.

On Christmas morning, I attended a Catholic mass in Baghdad to report on how Iraqi Christians were reacting to the departure of the U.S. military and the political crisis. The mass was jubilant and ended with a rousing performance of Christmas carols in Arabic. The men and women in the choir wore Santa hats with flashing LED stars and sang along to cheesy synthesizer and drum machine accompaniment.

It was one of those moments that sticks with you—Iraqi Christians celebrating mass and enjoying a campy singalong against a backdrop of daily bombings and political combat. People I interviewed after the mass said they were just trying to feel normal and enjoy a moment of celebration and community. It was a respite from the daily news and violence that was like a vice squeezing the will out of people. Many I spoke to said they were contemplating leaving the country. With the moderating influence of the American military gone, they did not want to be casualties of the Sunni-Shia power struggle.

That night, we enjoyed Christmas dinner at the neighboring *New York Times* house. It was my first downrange holiday, and it was a feast. It was a tribe moment—a dozen or so of us celebrating together in that strange place and time. Some of us would be leaving, others staying on. For that night, we were a family.

On December 27, I said my goodbyes to the local staff and left the bureau for the last time. I exited Iraq hauling a giant road case of electronic detritus and a lot of mixed emotions.

I flew home through Istanbul on a Turkish Air flight in business class. I wined and dined my way back to D.C., all the while contemplating the fact that the war was over. That month living in the bureau and being in the moment—covering a major story and living the war correspondent life of parties and dinners (and doing important journalism)—seduced me as Libya had. I wanted that life more than anything. And that was what it was—a life. It was a complete structure.

While there was downtime, you were always embedded in the story. Your whole life was Iraq. Your entire social life was the tribe. There was a simplicity to it. You didn't spend the day wondering about what you were going to do at night, where you were going to eat or what you would do for entertainment. You had a staff that cooked meals. You had nights when you would go to dinner at an embassy or another bureau. It was all programmed in a way. I wasn't there long enough for that to get boring or feel like a straitjacket. It was a life that I needed. Living in a strange place with like-minded people who had to band together for security and psychological and emotional stability. Once Baghdad shut down, there was only one place left where you could find that: Kabul.

Chapter Seventeen
Staring at Syria

February 2012

BEIRUT — Late in the month, NPR shipped me off to the Middle East to pinball around Lebanon, Turkey, Jordan, Iraq, and Israel—basically everywhere except Syria, which was the main story we were working on at that time. Kelly McEvers had resettled in Beirut, and we were mapping out plans to sneak into Syria—something she had done previously, and I was eager to do. Syrian opposition members had established underground railroads to get journalists in and out of the country to report on the atrocities being carried out by the Assad regime.

It was high stakes danger. The routes were fleetingly secure. It was kind of like the *Harry Potter* staircases—the routes could shift in front of you and behind you in an instant. Not all the Syrian rebels could be trusted along the way. Add to that a sadistic regime carrying out heinous attacks on civilian infrastructure, and it was about the hairiest war reporting out there.

Sneaking into Syria to cover the civil war was something I had to do. Yes, there was a part of me that wanted the bragging rights, but honestly it was a case of a story that I really wanted to see for myself. It was the same feeling I had about Afghanistan in fall 2001.

The NPR security manager, Kelly, and I had been laying the groundwork and mapping out a plan. We would be following the approach that other journalists had been using to infiltrate from Lebanon.

However, tragedy intervened. Just as I was leaving Washington for Beirut, the Assad regime murdered Marie Colvin and Remi Ochlik. The government deliberately targeted the building in Homs that had been serving as a media center. It sent a shockwave through the entire tribe.

I arrived in Beirut to a community of journalists in pain. One of the luminaries of the industry, a woman who had been at the front lines of countless conflicts and done some of the most important reporting of a generation, was gone. The Beirut-based tribe members gathered for a wake at Bread Republic in West Beirut. Some two dozen of us drank in disbelief. Among the group were some who had been in Syria with Marie and left shortly before the attack that killed her and Remi. It had been a difficult decision to leave, and their survivor's guilt was palpable.

It was the second straight gut-punch to the tribe. A week before Marie and Remi's death, Anthony Shadid, another leading war reporter of the generation, died after suffering an asthma attack on the trek back out of Syria. His death was a mindfuck. One of the most accomplished war correspondents who had seen and survived as much shit as anyone died on his way out of Syria from a cause that had nothing to do with conflict or violence.

In a dark way, you are prepared for and accept the possibility that war correspondents will be killed in action. It's an unfortunate consequence of getting as close to danger as possible. It had been happening for decades and would continue to—reporters would be in the wrong place at the wrong time. Marie's death—which initially seemed to be accidental but was later deemed to be deliberate—was tragic and painful but not surprising. The possibility was always there. Anthony's death was incomprehensible. Of all fucking things, an asthma attack when he was in the middle of nowhere and unable to get medical care.

I can't claim to have known either Anthony or Marie well, but I knew them and spent time with each of them. In each case, I was green both with professional envy and inexperience. I sought wisdom and counsel from them, and they were both humble and generous. Anthony helped me out with my first time free-range reporting in Baghdad in 2009. Marie calmed me when I was having a fit of insecurity and self-doubt in my first real war-zone deployment in Libya in 2011.

Due to the loss of Marie and Remi, NPR put a freeze on any incursions into Syria. Since any stealth trip was indefinitely on hold, I applied for a visa to go into regime-controlled Syria via legitimate means. It was a long shot, and I never got the visa, but had to cover all options.

In the meantime, I diverted to Istanbul to join up with Peter Kenyon for a trip to Hatay province to report on activity at the Turkish-Syrian border. Due to flooding at the Hatay Airport, we had to fly to Adana and drive for several hours to Hatay—in a Toyota, not a Rolls-Royce Phantom II, sadly. The route passed through Iskenderun, formerly Alexandretta. Alas, we didn't have time for a crusade.

We rolled into a hospital on the outskirts of Antakya. Syrian rebels were convalescing in one of the wards. We interviewed an 18-year-old who had lost his right leg below the knee from an artillery blast near the Syrian city of Hama. Shrapnel had ripped through his arms and hands. He said he used to sing to boost the morale of demonstrators in his village. He broke into a verse while lying under the pink sheets on his hospital bed. His voice quavered as he sang about avenging martyrs and liberating Syria. It was a moving bit of audio in the story Peter later reported.

The man in the bed next to him had a medieval looking contraption of pins and rods screwed into his leg above and below the knee and tubes draining infected goo from the wounds. They were just two of countless casualties of the war that was a year old then and still roiling eleven years later as I write this.

Syrians had set up a network of small clinics in rented apartments in the province. Once patients had been stabilized in Turkish hospitals, Syrian doctors would move them to the clinics to continue their care and recovery. We visited clinics where doctors and volunteers struggled to get the necessary supplies to treat all the wounded. Doctors described how they were also supporting clinics inside Syria. In some cases, Syrian dentists were performing surgeries with remote supervision and direction from doctors. The improvisation going on to respond to the humanitarian disaster caused by the regime's attacks on civilians, including medical facilities, was stunning.

The next day, we drove to Guvecci, a village on the Syrian border, and met with a group of resistance fighters coordinating logistics to transport refugees out of Syria and weapons, food, journalists, and medical supplies into the country. At a smoke-filled house, they said the cat and mouse game with the Syrian regime was growing more complicated as government forces were stepping up efforts to stop cross-border activity. They were begging for assistance from the international community so they could continue the fight against the Assad regime.

That night, we joined a small convoy of journalists on a trip to the banks of a river separating Syria and Turkey. It was maybe 50 yards across and rocky and shallow. Syrians would sneak across in the darkness.

We gathered along the road right next to the bank as families gingerly crossed the river. It wasn't long before several Turkish military trucks rolled up and ruined our night. I had walked up the road a bit and was off to the side behind a tree when the trucks arrived. The Syrian families and the journalists were all caught. I debated whether to stay in hiding and then continue to gather material once the Turks left with everyone else. However, I decided to stick with Peter and the others, and I walked back to the group standing in the headlights of the trucks. The Turks said they were not going to detain us, but we were not allowed to be out there. The Turkish forces said that they would be taking the Syrians to a camp for processing, and we could follow them there and if we wanted to interview the families. Basically, we got off with a warning.

The next day, I visited a school that refugees had established in a farmhouse. The founders discussed how they were trying to continue educating the children by setting up small schools in apartments, public parks, or wherever else they could. Like the medical clinics, the schools were improvised to meet the growing needs of a refugee population that had no idea if or when it might be able to return to Syria.

That uncertainty was weighing on a lot of the Turks helping the Syrians. I interviewed Turks who said that they had been providing financial assistance, signing leases for Syrians, and providing discounted food and supplies for refugees. But they felt the Syrians were starting to take it for granted. They were packing families into apartments and disrupting neighbors and neighborhoods. Turks were saying that they were eager for the war to end in Syria so things could return to normal. Again, those sentiments were brewing one year into a conflict and crisis that is nowhere near resolved.

A few days later, we spent an afternoon at the sprawling Boynuyogan refugee camp speaking with recent arrivals as well as some who had been in the camp for months. The camp was one of the most clean, uniform, and organized refugee or IDP camps I had visited. Rows of white tents with Turkish Red Crescent logos stretched in all directions. Satellite TV dishes clung to the utility poles running through the camp. White minivans drove around delivering food and supplies. Children roamed playing while some helped clean the streets between the tents.

We wrapped up our reporting and returned to Istanbul. From there I flew to Amman to link back up with Kelly to report on the plight of Syrians who had fled to their neighbor to the south.

After a night in Amman that of course included a visit to Trader Vic's for Mai Tais, we drove north to the small city of Irbid. Compared to modern, clean, and cosmopolitan Amman (well, west Amman, that is), Irbid was poor, gritty, and conservative. While headscarves are optional in west Amman, the women of Irbid were all covered—at least those who were out on the streets.

There were far more men than women out and about in Irbid. Large groups of young men caroused the streets at night looking for entertainment.

What I saw there was terrorism in the making. Young men in a very conservative city with a weak economy and few healthy social outlets—it was a recruiting pool. Over the years, Jordanian men from Irbid and other cities such as Zarqa traveled to Syria to join ISIS and other terrorist groups. In 2016, Jordanian security forces conducted a raid against an ISIS cell in Irbid. Again, it was evident to me within minutes of walking the streets of Irbid at night that the city was teeming with potential jihadists.

We spent the next couple of days visiting groups of Syrians in apartments and houses. We snuck around refugee camps to conduct surreptitious interviews with some of the activists who helped ignite the Syrian uprising. We passively smoked packs of cigarettes in our meetings with refugees and activists.

Jordan was overwhelmed by the burden of the refugees. It was scrambling to build new camps and absorb refugees into private homes. We visited the arid grounds where Jordan and the United Nations were constructing the Zaatari camp, which would open four months later and become home to 80,000 Syrians.

After completing the refugee tourism and reporting in Jordan, I hopped over the border to spend a couple of days at the NPR bureau in Jerusalem. It was my first time in Israel, and I received the usual "warm" welcome that included 45 minutes of grilling—and we're not talking the kebab kind—in a small room at the Allenby Bridge border crossing. Once they completed the virtual colonoscopy and let me in the country, I enjoyed a couple of days of great food, touring the Old City, and a visit to the Hebrew University to produce a story on the display of Einstein's handwritten documents and letters.

From there it was back to Beirut. We continued some Syria reporting and secured Iraqi visas. Three months after shuttering the bureau, we were heading back to cover the Arab League Summit. It was the first time Baghdad had hosted the event since

1990. It was a coming out party for Iraq. The country spent hundreds of millions on painting and other projects to spruce up the country.

Iraq was also spending a fortune on security for the summit. Baghdad was a fortress. Security forces from around the country descended on Baghdad to lock down the city and prevent violence. Such was the Iraq paradox—the summit showed that the city was safe, but the city was safe because just about the entire military had been deployed to protect Baghdad from threats. There were curfews and street closures. Still, there was one rocket attack during the summit, but nothing landed within the grounds.

We camped out at the *New York Times* bureau for the five days we were in Iraq. It was next door to our old house, which had been taken over by DynCorp and they had installed all sorts of strange electronic gadgetry in the compound.

The summit itself was grandiose and vacuous. The palace was all decked out for the event with top notch catering and reasonably well-organized media events. There was little, if any, news to cover. The only interesting nugget was the empty seat for Syria as Bashar al-Assad was not invited since he was busy slaughtering his citizens. Given the sketchy nature of some of the regimes and rulers, you had to be doing some evil shit to be excluded from the Arab League Summit.

While it was nice to be back in Iraq, it was an artificial trip. We were there to cover a choreographed event that generated no news, and the city was shut down. I was able to get out and walk around a little and interview some people on the street, but it was a boring trip. Yes, it was good to see some of the tribe and our local team, but it wasn't the same. It was a reminder that the Iraq war chapter had closed, and you could never go back to that world.

After a month of living out of my suitcase in Beirut, Istanbul, Antakya, Amman, Irbid, Jerusalem, and Baghdad, I returned to D.C. for a couple of months of boredom while waiting for my next deployment.

Chapter Eighteen
Temping in Kabul

June 2012

DULLES AIRPORT, Virginia — On June 3, I settled into my business-class seat on the United contractor shuttle and started downing champagne. Twelve hours, countless drinks, and an Ambien later, I landed in Dubai and checked into an upgraded room at Radisson Royal. I strolled over to the Emirates Towers for a massage at the 1847 spa, and then dined on crispy duck and Mai Tais at Trader Vic's.

The next morning, I went from one extreme to the other as I flew into the Kabul dustbowl. The NPR driver, Ataullah, picked me up—in a silver Corolla of course—and drove me through a Kabul far more congested and complicated than the city I last saw in October 2009.

I arrived at the bureau and started my five-day handover with Quil Lawrence, the outgoing correspondent. His two-year stint was up, and NPR had decided to send people in for two-month rotations for the rest of the year. I got the first call up for Kabul duty.

The house was delightful—not a word I use often, but sometimes it fits. It was a single-story three-bed with a large eat-in kitchen, comfortable living room, and small dining room with floor to ceiling windows. The real treasure, though, was the patio and yard. The shaded stone patio seated six people and looked over a small but immaculately manicured lawn and garden with hedges, flowers, and vegetables. The yard was not a large space, maybe 700 sq ft, but it was serene. The high walls around the compound dampened the Kabul cacophony and provided just enough privacy.

Behind the main house was a second house. The first floor was the office and a guest bedroom (where I stayed the first five nights) and the second floor was a complete apartment rented by McClatchy.

I spent a few days getting acclimated to the staff, the neighborhood, and the social scene. There were dinner and drink gatherings at news bureaus and NGO houses, which I expected. What I didn't expect was the Venue—an Afghan-run restaurant and music club with a large garden and a small indoor performance space. I had an immediate need to dust off my guitar playing chops for the frequent jam sessions.

Another surprise was that there were "big" grocery stores (Finest and Spinneys) that had an ample supply of American and international foods, including frozen meets and seafood.

Quil and his wife completed the handoff and sailed off into the sunset. I moved into the house and got down to work. Since I had only spent a few days in Kabul in 2009, almost everything in the city was new or different to me. The overcrowded, underdeveloped city was a story itself. The electricity cut out several times a day and our small but unapologetically loud generator cranked out the amps for hours a day. The plumbing in the house was a mess, and bathing entailed a waltz under the shower head as the water temperature and pressure oscillated from hot to cold and back.

Traffic was bonkers. The main roads were mostly paved, although some had already reverted to Toyota-swallowing craters. The NPR bureau was on a residential cross street between two main roads, and our street, Taimani 1, was undulating dirt. It was a great neighborhood, though. There were expats living across the street and Sufi, one of the best restaurants in the city, was a couple of doors down. A block over was the Flower Street Cafe. At each end of our street were little shops and markets and a Finest grocery store was a five-minute walk away.

I was comfortable walking around the neighborhood by day. Most NGO workers were not allowed to walk the streets, but for journalists it was generally up to our discretion. I sometimes walked the neighborhood at night to go to the clubs and restaurants a few blocks away. I had both daytime and nighttime drivers, so I didn't go too crazy walking long distances and exposing myself to threats.

My first trip out of the city was to Baghlan province to the north. It is home to the perilous Salang Tunnel. The Soviets built the 1.6-mile-long engineering marvel in 1964. Unfortunately, the harsh geology of the 11,000-foot mountain pass had been taking its toll on the tunnel ever since.

Due to a spat over a U.S. drone strike that killed Pakistani civilians, Islamabad had closed its borders to NATO convoys. That forced convoys bringing in fresh supplies and hauling out gear from downsizing bases to take a longer route through the Stans to the north. That route passed through the decrepit tunnel that was never designed for the volume of traffic it was handling. Truck traffic could only flow one direction at a time, and it alternated every 12 hours. That was causing backups lasting for days in some cases.

The drive up to the tunnel was scenic as we gradually climbed through river valleys up the mountains still capped with snow in mid-June. The road switched back and forth, at times barely clinging to the sides of the rocky mountains. There was evidence of recent slides. Things got hairier the closer we got to the tunnel. My testicles spent the rest of the drive hiding in my abdomen.

Eventually, we penetrated the opening and spent 20 minutes transiting the 1.6 miles of wet, cratered pavement as exhaust fumes hung in the air and water leaked into the tunnel from all sides. Trucks leaned precariously inside the narrow tunnel. We emerged safely on the other side and stopped to clear our lungs and interview the Afghan official in charge of the tunnel. Despite a $5 million investment from USAID the year before to repave, fix the lights, and seal some of the leaks, the tunnel had shaken off those repairs and was in life-threatening condition.

Had there been an alternative route back to Kabul, I would have taken it as once through the tunnel of horrors was enough. We steeled ourselves and got back in the car for the return trip. It turned out we had timed things well. Traffic flowed reasonably well heading south, but the northbound lane had been blocked by a truck that had dipped into one of the deep craters and wedged itself against the tunnel wall. There was no way in hell I would have sat in the car in blocked traffic in the tunnel. I would have had the driver turn around and get out as quickly as possible. You did not want to spend a second more than necessary in that large intestine. Driving through that tunnel was probably the most dangerous thing I did during that two-month stint in Kabul.

The next couple of weeks I spent the days roaming the city interviewing citizens and officials for stories about the lack of electricity, the overpopulation and underdevelopment of the city, and a firing range near Bagram Airfield that dated back to the Soviets and where Afghans were getting killed by unexploded ordnance.

I traveled to a village outside the base where Afghan *kuchis*, or nomads, had settled in crumbling mud compounds. A family invited me into their house, and we sat on a rug in a large room furnished with only a couple of pillows.

I interviewed a father and son, both of whom had been maimed by explosives in the range. The main problem was that the area was not completely fenced off and not well marked. People would graze their animals, as the father had done, and cross into the range. The father lost his leg when he stepped on a mine.

Months after that, the 16-year-old son was roaming around the area picking up scrap metal to sell. He picked up a grenade that blew off both of his arms.

I could understand the injury to the father, but I was baffled by what happened to the son. I asked the son, "Your father lost his leg and another relative was killed in the range, why were you in an area that had explosives and why did you pick up a strange piece of metal? Didn't you think it was too dangerous?"

His response was worded in a specific way that gave me my introduction to Afghan empirical logic. He said, "If I had known it was going to blow my arms off, I would not have touched it for a million dollars."

I sat there as the response sank in. I asked the question again in a slightly different way. I was trying to tease out why the injuries and deaths to his family didn't make him think twice and not pick up strange things in a firing range. But he answered the same way. What he was saying was that if he had known the specific object he picked up was going to maim him, he would not have picked up that specific item. However, the broader danger did not register to him that anything in the area was potentially dangerous, and he shouldn't touch anything metallic, and frankly should not have been there to begin with.

I then asked his father if he warned his son about the dangers after his own incident. The father said he did not. I was absolutely gob smacked. What kind of father doesn't say, "Son, you know that area where I lost my leg and where your uncle was killed? Stay the fuck out of there!"?

Over the years, I would come to learn that kind of reductive empirical thinking was intrinsically Afghan, but in that moment, I simply couldn't believe that a 16-year-old was sitting there with no arms because he could not infer danger from clear information and circumstances prior to his decision to pick up an unidentified object in a firing range. I was also blind to their plight—that they were so poor and desperate that they didn't have alternatives to rummaging through a firing range to find scrap metal to sell.

I stuffed my reaction away and finished the interview. My incredulousness oozed into the story I wrote, to which my editor remarked that I had a "very western perspective." He wasn't wrong, and it made me stop and think about how hard it still was to step outside my values and views and understand things in the local context. The funny thing is that I regularly criticized (and continue to) the American government for not taking Afghan culture, values, interests, and capacities into account when formulating the policies that failed so miserably, and I often struggled to see and understand the Afghan (or Iraqi or Pakistani) perspective.

The family was polite and generous and of course offered me something to eat. One of them came into the room with a wooden plate with a mound of off-white goo on it. Flies were landing on the substance. One of them said it was a homemade cheese and they wanted me to try it.

It was one of the greatest dilemmas of my reporting career. How did I say no to that hospitality? I felt myself getting food poisoning just looking at the oozing mound of warm cheese. There was no way in hell I was going to touch it. Yet, I couldn't simply refuse as that would have been offensive.

Fortunately, I came up with a quick excuse. I didn't know if it would translate or not, but I told my producer to thank the hosts and explain that I had a lactose allergy and dairy products made me sick. However he translated it, the people in the room nodded with understanding and withdrew the goo. Crisis narrowly averted. The flies certainly seemed to enjoy the stuff, though.

I survived that junket and returned to Kabul where the nights were filled with dinners and parties at embassies and news bureaus. There were jam sessions at the Venue. It was the tribal life I had been seeking.

There were expats from all over the world, but we shared the same identity—adventurous internationalists. We were travelers, seekers, misfits, and marrow-suckers. We spoke the same language. We didn't have to bother with small talk or trying to impress each other. We were brothers and sisters.

And like any family, some of the members were batshit crazy. There were people who partied to extremes that would give Charlie Sheen pause. There were backstabbers, manipulators, and liars. There were some hard-core narcissists. "I'm not a journalist, I'm a writer," one used to say as he hit on the young women.

Others couldn't stop bragging about the places they had been and stories they had covered—please, save it for your book!

But they were in the minority. Most of the people were smart, passionate, and hot. Why I picked those two months to be faithful to Anna, I'll never fully understand.

Because I wore the NPR seal of approval, I had nothing to prove, no one to impress, and no need to justify my presence. Even though I wasn't a household name when I arrived, I was a household brand and therefore was a full partner in the tribe. In fact, I remember one of the stringers based in the city telling me at a party that his mother was an enormous NPR fan. He said she was more impressed that he was partying with an NPR correspondent than impressed with the fact that her son was reporting in Afghanistan.

I had always known how passionate the NPR audience was, but I wasn't used to being the subject of it. I was just happy being in the tribe and automatically being on the invite list to all the cool dinners, parties, press events, and poker nights.

Not every night was fun, though. There was the late night covering a Taliban attack on Afghan civilians at Lake Qargha just outside Kabul. It was a popular recreation and resort area where people picnicked, boated, and dined at a large restaurant. On Thursday June 21, militants killed the security guards and stormed the resort area. The Taliban assailants shot up the restaurant where hundreds were dining. According to a Taliban statement, the attack was targeting adulterers and people drinking and engaging in other immoral behavior.

The assailants dug in at the restaurant and held diners hostage as they fought with Afghan and NATO forces. After a 12-hour battle, the Afghan and NATO forces killed the attackers. Seventeen civilians and four Afghan security forces died in the attack.

It was the first complex attack that I covered in Afghanistan, and I was up most of the night getting updates and reporting for NPR's newscast at the top and bottom of each hour. The next morning, I filed a short report on the attack. What was disturbing was that it deliberately targeted civilians and the Taliban was accusing Afghans of engaging in immoral behavior. Deliberate attacks on civilians were the exception. Typically, civilians died as collateral damage during attacks on military or government targets, or by accidentally striking IEDs.

Reporting on the attack consumed much of my Friday and my Afghan producers were disturbed by the incident since their friends and families, and sometimes they, visited the area that was attacked.

That night, I attended an enormous embassy party. I can't remember which embassy it was, a European one, but it was a midsummer bacchanalian themed thing at a ginormous compound not far from my house. I was pretty crispy from covering the attack all night and most of the day. I walked into the compound and saw probably 100 or more young westerners in festive and skimpy dress. They were pounding drinks, grinding to loud music, and generally being bacchanalian and hedonistic. Under normal circumstances, I would have started drinking and carousing. But it was too soon.

Instead, I felt a revulsion. I was disgusted and angry to see jaded diplomats and NGO workers in short dresses and tight clothing drinking and groping in the middle of a city where innocent Afghans had just been slaughtered for having a nice dinner by a lake. I mean, the Taliban said they were attacking the lake resort to kill adulterers and immoral people, and less than 24 hours later, the bulk of the westerners in Kabul were engaging in a prelude to an orgy. Holy fuck if the Taliban had any idea that was going on. I realized that the party had been planned long in advance, but it came across as so utterly tone deaf and offensive in the context of the attack. Granted, half the people there probably had no idea about the attack and the message the Taliban was trying to send, but still, it made me feel ill.

That was by far the most decadent party I attended in a war zone or place where locals lived in horrible or dangerous conditions. Had the attack not happened the night before, I'm sure I would have gotten hammered and naked at the first opportunity. Instead, I had a couple of drinks and left early before any more bile churned in my gut.

I calmed down a couple of days later and then started regretting the fact that I didn't cut loose at the party. Such was the emotional rollercoaster of war reporting.

For the 4th of July, I flew to Kandahar with a team from the embassy to cover a swearing-in ceremony for 44 soldiers and Marines being naturalized as U.S. citizens. It was as perfect a July 4th story as you could ask for. A hanger full of young men and women in uniform holding little American flags and reciting the oath. I stuffed my cynicism aside for the day and produced a heartwarming piece about the ceremony and some of the new young Americans.

A couple of days later Secretary of State Hillary Clinton made a surprise visit to Kabul. Since NPR did not have an embedded reporter on the trip, the State Department and embassy allowed me to enter the bubble to cover the visit.

The secretary held an event at the embassy to rally the folks there and then held a meeting and press conference with President Karzai. That was my first visit to the Afghan presidential palace. A dark gray stone fortress-like wall surrounded the palace grounds. Inside was a large, verdant courtyard and patio surrounded by offices and residential buildings. Because I was entering with the delegation from the embassy, I didn't go through the complete security colonoscopy that I would experience in subsequent visits.

The press conference was cordial. The secretary announced that the United States had granted Afghanistan "major non-NATO ally" status. While it was news, it was also little more than a diplomatic blow job to placate the increasingly cantankerous Karzai. Relations between Karzai and Washington were at a nadir that summer as the Afghan president railed against the United States for killing civilians during air strikes and night raids in villages. Karzai was rightfully pissed that foreign troops in his country were carrying out operations—often unilaterally—that were killing innocent Afghans. That was fueling anti-U.S. and Afghan government sentiment and undermining the whole hearts and minds thing. Frankly, it was also making Karzai look impotent that he didn't have sovereign control of his country.

For the record, Karzai was corrupt and whiny and blamed the United States and Pakistan for every problem in Afghanistan. He took no responsibility for his failures or his self-enrichment at the expense of U.S. troops and taxpayers. Still, he had some valid complaints from time to time. Hence, the gesture from the United States to confer fancy-sounding but mostly meaningless ally status to Afghanistan. Hey, it got me into the palace to see some political theater, so it worked for me.

After that, it was back to war, death, destruction, and dysfunction. For good measure, I came down with a case of food poisoning after dining at the Lebanese Taverna, one of the most popular restaurants for expats. I had to cross food poisoning off the to-do list for the deployment.

The ISAF public affairs office put together two mini-embeds while I was in country. I didn't have time to do a long or complicated embed, so the two junkets provided opportunities to get out of Kabul for a few days and see other cities.

The first trip was to Mazar-i-Sharif, and by virtue of being fresh meat in town, I was invited to join a few journalists coming in from Europe for a short, guided tour by ISAF public affairs. We flew up to Camp Marmal, which was the German-run hub for northern Afghanistan. We visited an explosive ordnance disposal training class for Afghan soldiers. We toured a maintenance shop where Afghan soldiers were climbing all over Humvees and Ford Rangers trying to repair the damage they had done to them. As I would see and hear many times over the years, Afghans were not big on routine and preventative maintenance. They used things until they stopped working, and they tried to revive them. Every Afghan base had yards full of damaged, destroyed, or otherwise scrapped vehicles.

We then hopped into German armored vehicles and rolled into the city. The ISAF folks let us loose to walk the streets and visit the stunning Hazrat Ali Mazar mosque, otherwise known as the Blue Mosque. The sprawling mosque complex of turquoise blue domes and elaborate mosaic walls and arches sat in the center of a large plaza covered by white doves. It was one of those structures that when you looked closely at the intricacy of the mosaic covering the structure, you couldn't help but think, "How the fuck did they build this?"

After admiring the mosque, we strolled back down the street past smiling children and friendly vendors inviting us into their shops. We partook of some ice cream bars from one of the ubiquitous little red plastic carts. All summer long, vendors pushed them through Afghan streets, blaring electronic melodies like Happy Birthday, Celine Dion's "My Heart Will Go On," and other earworms to attract attention. By the time I left Afghanistan I was having fantasies of recreating the *Office Space* scene of demolishing the printer, except with an Afghan ice cream cart.

We returned to the base and dined in the German beer hall where we were allowed two steins apiece. Across the plaza in the center of the base was the sad American club, which did not serve alcohol.

The next day the embed crew visited some other organizations in the city, but I split off and went for a road trip with members of the controversial Task Force for Business and Stability Operations. It was a Defense Department initiative that started in Iraq to develop private-sector enterprises to boost the economy and thereby improve security. It expanded to Afghanistan in 2009. Over the years it would become a lightning rod. Some praised it as an innovative model to promote business and investment, others viewed it as an opaque, shady initiative that enriched staff and contractors at taxpayer expense but did little to promote economic growth and security. I leaned toward the latter view.

Anyhow, they were taking me out to Jowzjan province to the west to view a new initiative—a compressed natural gas fueling station. The task force had funded the creation of the station and a garage to convert taxis to run on CNG. It was an interesting little facility, but it was hard to see how it would have any significant impact on the local economy or security. In addition, the project involved rehabilitating a gas plant and pipeline and constructing a new pipeline to transport gas to Mazar.

The whole thing was an ambitious and expensive project that amounted to little more than another scathing report by the Special Inspector General for Afghanistan Reconstruction that slammed the project as yet another boondoggle. SIGAR also slammed the task force for spending way too much on housing in private villas. I spent that night in their villa in Mazar, and it was clearly expensive and much nicer than the housing most other organizations had in Afghanistan. While SIGAR was usually justified in its scathing criticisms of wasteful project, it often inflated the numbers, ignored relevant context, and otherwise overstated some things. Still, their frequent exposes of waste and stupidity weren't enough to drive multiple administrations or Congress to change course.

I returned to Kabul and spent a couple of days gathering material on unexploded ordnance and de-mining before heading out on another ISAF junket. On that trip, I joined three other Kabul-based reporters as opposed to the European-based gang on the Mazar trip.

We traveled to Herat in western Afghanistan and stayed at Camp Arena, the Italian and Spanish run base chock full of pork and alcohol. After dinner on our first night on the base, I visited one of the outdoor bars where non-American soldiers sat at picnic tables with ice buckets full of cans of beer. Unlike the German base, there did not appear to be any quota at the Spanish-Italian compound.

The next morning at breakfast, the two women reporters in our group described the scene in the bathroom of their dorm building. Apparently, some of the Italian Carabinieri women were hot, stacked, and liked to help bathe and groom each other. Nothing like a little lesbian military porn to start the morning off right.

That day, we roamed Herat doing a mix of tourism and reporting. We visited the hulking citadel that dates to Alexander the

Great. After, I interviewed people on the street for my story about Iranian influence in Afghanistan since the province bordered Iran and had a lot of trade and interaction.

Herat was bustling and had a relaxed vibe. People were friendly and at worst indifferent to a random American guy wandering around the streets.

We then sat down with leading women's rights activists who painted a bleak picture. Despite the so-called gains for women in Afghanistan, young girls were still being sold off, married young, or otherwise abused—often by relatives. The police and courts were corrupt and often sent female rape victims to prison on adultery charges while letting the perpetrators go. The lone female prosecutor general in the country received death threats for prosecuting men for committing acts of violence against women.

One of the women made a comment that stuck with me—she said that women's rights had been treated as a cause by the international community rather than a pillar of Afghan society. In that regard, women's rights were a political item to be negotiated and bargained for, and if the international community backed off, then women's rights would suffer.

That was spot on for many reasons and is relevant today in how things played out in Afghanistan. Women's rights in Afghanistan came at the point of the gun and were backed by bullets and billions of dollars. Programs created quotas for women in government. Initiatives focused on educating and empowering women. Women clearly benefitted from those programs. However, the initiatives were barely addressing the real barrier to women's rights and progress in Afghanistan: Afghan men.

Many women who were attending trainings, joining the government or security services, or starting businesses were going home to husbands and male relatives who did not support women's empowerment. The patriarchy persisted. While the Taliban was extreme in its views toward women, the average rural Afghan man wasn't all that different.

And so, women's rights were overlain on a rotten foundation of toxic patriarchy. Women's rights were never woven into the fabric of Afghan society and culture. Therefore, as the guns and greenbacks from the international community dialed back, so did the rights and protections for Afghan women.

Had the Afghan government been able to negotiate a peace deal and a power-sharing arrangement with the Taliban, it is possible that the plight of women would have been somewhat better than it is now under a Taliban regime. But people should not delude themselves into thinking that the U.S.-supported Afghan government and security forces were going to lay down their lives for Afghan women.

Had the international community shifted 75 percent of the funds it spent on empowering women to programs on educating Afghan men about the value and rights of women, maybe there would have been some lasting gains for Afghan women. Instead, the international community built up the expectations of women, and countless women who bought into it had to flee their own families who opposed their liberation.

Anyhow, back off my soapbox. After meeting with the activists, we toured an ice cream factory. It was a state-of-the-art facility where Afghan men and women wearing lab coats, hairnets, and face masks toiled around exotic stainless-steel machines churning out popsicles and ice cream bars. Along with the bowling alley in Kabul, it was probably the most state-of-the-art facility I ever saw in Afghanistan.

That night we dined at one of the restaurants on the base. We feasted on charcuterie and red wine. Unfortunately, the bubble of normalcy and civility was burst when the base went into lockdown due to a nearby security incident. We relocated to the media center where we were sequestered for a couple of hours.

Initially, we received little information. All we knew was that there were casualties brought into the base's trauma center that we had toured earlier in the day. It was unclear for some time whether there was any threat to the base, or us. The ISAF public affairs people minding us gradually received and provided details.

A member of the Afghan police attacked NATO contractors at a training base near Camp Arena. The assailant killed three contractors and wounded a fourth. The perpetrator was killed in the incident. It was the 21st "green on blue" or insider attack of the year. Insider attacks surged in 2012 and I reported on five or six of them during my summer deployment.

It was sometime after 11 p.m. when the lockdown ended, and we could leave the media center. The bars on the base had closed at that time. However, I had anticipated that and right before we were put in lockdown, I stopped at one of the bars and got a double shot of whiskey to go and stashed it in my bunk. As was often the case in Afghanistan, that whiskey was essential to calm the adrenaline rush of frantically filing news spots on the attack late into the night.

The next day, we took a field trip to a small Spanish base in Badghis province. It was a rare opportunity to visit one of the more remote and unknown provinces. We went out on a foot patrol through the village of Muqur with Spanish and Afghan troops. I kept a more watchful eye on the Afghans that day than I otherwise would have because of the incident the night before.

The terrain was a vast expanse of rolling desert with periodic mud compounds with domed roofs and scattered green vegetation. It was primitive. There was no pavement to be seen in the tiny village. After the patrol, we met with some local elders at the base who said security in the area had been getting worse. The violence there was mostly hit-and-run attacks on NATO and Afghan forces and scattered IEDs.

After the meeting, a U.S. Black Hawk swooped into the base to evacuate an Afghan civilian who had stepped on an IED near the base. Fortunately for us, we didn't encounter it on the foot patrol. It was another reminder that you were never safe anywhere at any time in Afghanistan.

We then drove to a nearby Afghan base for a staged demonstration of Howitzer training for Afghan forces—after all, we were on an ISAF-run junket, so it was largely a PR effort designed to show off the growing capabilities of the Afghans and how they were taking on responsibility for security. I will just say that the assembled Afghan troops and their demonstration did not inspire confidence. There were a lot of mouth breathers in ill-fitting uniforms who looked like they could barely tie their boots let alone operate artillery—to be clear, that is not a racist statement, just observational. Over the years, I saw plenty of American troops who could fit that description too.

We flew back to Camp Arena for one last demonstration. We gathered with a unit of U.S. and NATO forces and walked to the entrance gate to the Afghan compound attached to the NATO base. On bases in Afghanistan (and Iraq), weapons were carried unloaded. There were clearing barrels at all base entrances. Anyone returning from a mission had to stop and unload all weapons before entering the base. I was used to that protocol from all my embeds to that point.

That was why I was taken aback when the U.S. and NATO troops stopped at the gate to the Afghan compound and loaded their weapons. In addition, there was a platoon of security guys, or Guardian Angels, that surrounded us as we entered and walked around the Afghan compound. That was one of the protocols that had been enacted in the wake of the insider attacks.

Think about that. U.S. and NATO forces could no longer trust their Afghan partners and had to treat them as a security threat. That was the situation—American troops were training Afghans who at any moment could turn their weapons on the Americans. That right there was another snapshot of how fucked up the whole enterprise was. With friends like that...

We spent 20 minutes visiting with Afghan forces who demonstrated some of the hand-to-hand combat skills they were learning. They also demonstrated some counter-IED tactics. While the engagement was designed to show us the progress the Afghans were making, the whole display was undermined by the fact that we had an armed security detail surrounding us to protect us from the Afghan soldiers.

We returned to Kabul, and I spent the next week finishing up stories and enjoying the nightlife. The last night of my deployment I finally tried my hand with the brick-and-stone pizza oven at the NPR bureau. I invited the tribe over and we plowed through piles of homemade pizza and countless bottles of wine. It was a perfect final night.

Then next morning I buzzed around the city on the back of a friend's motorcycle gathering material on the Bush Bazaar, the market that had sprung up years before selling all sorts of stolen and counterfeit U.S. military and tactical gear. You could buy military clothing and accessories, MREs, and giant size cans and packages of food meant for dining facilities, all of which had "fallen off the back of a truck" or some such bullshit. It was yet another sign of the rampant corruption in Afghanistan.

After gathering the last bits of sound I needed, I returned to the bureau, grabbed my bags, and the driver took me to the airport. When he dropped me off, he said he hoped that I would return as the full-time correspondent. I did too. Kabul was the tribe and home I had spent the previous five years seeking. It was my new Layla.

A couple of days after returning from my two-month stint in Kabul, I popped into the mothership. I met with the head of the foreign desk and mentioned the comment made by the driver in Kabul. I said I was interested in the full-time gig. I was informed that it would likely be January 2012 when the new correspondent hit the ground.

It didn't take that long. A few days later, the boss called me into her office and said I would be going to Kabul on October 1, 2012 and staying until the end of 2014 when NPR was going to close the bureau. At the time, the expectation was that U.S. troops would leave at the end of 2014 and Afghanistan would be a peaceful, flourishing democracy (and *Saturday Night Live* was going to be edgy again and we'd all have hoverboards).

The terms (salary, length of rotations, expenses covered) were not ideal but were "take it or leave it," so I took it. I did not consult with Anna before agreeing. There were a couple of reasons.

First, well, I had spent years working my way to that moment. I wasn't going to pass up the opportunity so there wasn't any point in discussing it with my partner. Second, I had been ambivalent about the relationship for much of its two-and-a-half years. Moving to Afghanistan would force and end to a situation that I had been unable to end on my own.

That of course made me both a spineless cad and a cliche. There was a joke about people working in war zones that they were all running from marriage, mortgage, or murder. I was running from a relationship that was never bad enough for me to end it, but never good enough (or at least never made me feel the way I did with Layla) to go all in.

I was also running *to* something. I was running to the job, the life, and the tribe that I had been yearning for. It was a win-win in my mind. I finally had the job I had been seeking for 11 years, and I could start fresh and hopefully meet a woman among the tribe.

On October 1, 2012, I boarded the United contractor shuttle (upgraded to first class) with two hockey goalie bags as suitcases (each a few ounces below the 100 lb. threshold), two regular suitcases, two guitars, and a carry-on backpack. On October 3, all my shit and I arrived at the bureau, and I settled in for a two-year and three-month tour.

Chapter Nineteen
The Dream Comes True, Briefly

October 2012

KABUL — It was a warm, sunny afternoon shortly after I moved into the bureau. One of Kabul's greatest attributes is the weather in October and early November. The afternoon sun radiates through the dusty, mountain air and beckons you to work outside.

On that afternoon as I basked on my patio, a ragged street cat appeared in the backyard with two kittens in tow. They were scrawny and dirty grey tabbies with white underbellies. They passed through the yard and disappeared before I could open a can of tuna.

A week later, the mother returned, escorting a single kitten. I put out a plate of tuna, and the cats scampered onto the porch and gorged. That ritual continued every few days for the next couple of weeks.

Then, the mother started turning on the kitten. The mother started hissing and swatting at the dusty little fur ball when she approached the food dish. Only after the mother had eaten her fill would she allow her offspring to dine. I'm guessing the kitten had reached an age or size that the mother deemed her a competitor.

I figured the kitten's days were numbered. I mean, I knew the odds were against any kitten living on the streets of Kabul. After all, what had become of the second one that I saw just that one time?

297

I had only been in Kabul a few weeks and was still settling into my routine. Adopting a street animal hadn't crossed my mind even though it was common practice among the tribe. I had not yet contemplated the implications of rescuing a critter and caring for it over the next 26 months I would be living in Afghanistan, let alone what would happen after I completed my assignment.

However, I took pity on the kitten. Despite being dirty and likely full of worms, she was cute. There was an innocence and vulnerability to her—she was a metaphor for the children of Afghanistan living through war and hardship. Her meow was so high-pitched and, well, squeaky, that I dubbed her Squeak.

On November 3, 2012, exactly a month after moving to Kabul, I made the decision to rescue the Afghan street kitten. To this day, it is one of the best decisions I have made in my life. Squeak became my wing-cat and battle buddy on my Afghanistan adventure. She was my muse. She made me smile at the end of some of the most intense days of my life. Well, there was the time she knocked the giant vase off the top of the kitchen cabinet, which sounded like a bomb going off in the house and scared the living shit out of me. Still, she provided much needed companionship and comic relief.

During my first 10-week rotation I went on an embed to three bases in Logar province. One was FOB Shank, which took incoming fire daily. In the middle of interviewing a colonel at the base, the alarm went off and we hit the floor. The mortar struck the nearby DFAC and injured some Jordanian troops.

At the other two, smaller bases, I went out on foot patrols through remote villages. While there wasn't any contact—other than a warning shot fired when a motorcycle approached too quickly—I still loved it. Sure, for years I had wanted to experience combat (not unlike many of the troops I embedded with), but I simply enjoyed the embed experience.

Even if there wasn't any "action," there was always a story and something to learn. Granted, the food was often unremarkable at best, and terrifying at worst, and showers and latrines could be unpleasant, but there was always a feeling of adventure. That said, there could often be boredom and frustration as I experienced in my 2009 embeds in Afghanistan.

Still, there was the "weekend warrior" appeal of wearing tactical gear, crashing in sleeping bags in tents or primitive buildings, and otherwise roughing it. Then, there was the adventure of marching through farms, forests, and villages. There was the anthropology of studying not just "typical Afghans" in remote areas, but the anthropology of observing U.S. troops. I loved spending time with both grunts and officers and learning about their backgrounds and experiences and their perspectives on their missions and the war.

I met some amazing and some dicey troops. Most were receptive to hanging out with a journalist—for many I was the only reporter they had met in the flesh, and it presented them an opportunity to ask everything they ever wanted to know about the media. Others were borderline hostile and kept their distance. Some of them blamed the media for the problems in Afghanistan—sometimes I would engage in discussions to point out that successive administrations and their senior officials were to blame. Occasionally I had some success in opening minds in those conversations.

While embedded, I saw and heard things that had nothing to do with my reporting assignments but were informative and both uplifting and disheartening. There were committed troops who wanted to help Afghanistan (or Iraq) and protect America. There were others who were sociopathic xenophobes who wanted to kill "hajis."

The military is a tribe, which was another reason I enjoyed embeds. It was an opportunity to hang with a tribe, and in some cases become an associate member. It was like the lieutenant said on my last embed in Iraq in 2011, being deployed created a different bond and relationship among troops that wasn't the same back home. There are some members of the military with whom I have lifelong bonds because of time I spent with their units.

Lastly, I loved embeds because they were a free-range activity when you could ignore your editor, email, and phone. That was the summer camp aspect of it

In addition to the Logar embed, in my first rotation I attended a boxing match; nearly got alcohol poisoning at a Halloween party; visited the striking Panjshir Valley; came in third at my first "Mujahadinner" cooking competition; spent an afternoon with the Afghan women's soccer team for a U.S. embassy-sponsored feel-good story that perpetuated the myth that Afghanistan was a changed place and life was good for women; attended the Ashura festival where men lashed themselves with metal blades to the point of collapse; played loud, stupid guitar at the Venue; reported on the exodus of Afghans who believed the country was doomed; regularly drank too much at embassy dinners and parties at news bureaus and NGO houses; and stupidly concluded that the expat women in Kabul were too young or otherwise not relationship candidates and orchestrated an elaborate proposal to Anna during my first break in D.C. It was a decision I regretted the following day when she said we had to start trying to have kids, one of my red lines in life. The relationship fizzled out by the following summer in part because of that, but also because as I became more immersed in the Kabul tribe, I found that a relationship with someone outside the tribe wasn't working for me. The distance between Kabul and D.C. didn't exactly help either.

2013 was filled with more embeds and jam sessions, major attacks in Kabul, stories about the Afghan security forces supposedly getting better, transition ceremonies of bases and PRTs shutting down, another trip to Panjshir, a multi-day music festival, a trip to Doha to cover the Taliban office opening fiasco, an international MRE tasting dinner, Afghan kids juggling, flash flooding in Kabul, stories about identity, the delivery of C-130s to the Afghan Air

Force (another great folly), a visit by John Kerry to broker a security agreement to keep troops in Afghanistan after 2014, President Karzai's refusal to sign the deal he agreed to with John Kerry, an Afghan wedding, a trip to Helmand to report on poppy growing, more food poisoning, epic parties, a new girlfriend in Kabul, and lots of whiskey, Xanax, and Ambien (which were available over the counter at the drug store at the end of my street, along with opioids, but they were constantly sold out because the contractors living at the Green Village compound always bought up the available stash in the city).

In February 2013, I went on an embed to FOB Frontenac in Shah Wali Kot, Kandahar. Since there were few missions going out, I had to kill time and find things to report on around the base. That yielded stories about retrograde (U.S. forces packing up their shit to close and transition bases) and the K-9 unit.

One afternoon, I toured the scrap yard where a couple of specialists were sorting through junk and throwing shit out. I asked what the weirdest thing was they had seen in the trash. One specialist paused and looked at me with an awkward expression. I reminded him that my recorder wasn't broadcasting live so he could say whatever he wanted. He then said that the most unusual things he had seen people throw out were "pocket pussies and dildos, sir."

I'm not sure what I was expecting him to say, but sex toys wasn't it. That said, on further reflection, it made sense.

I got outside the wire twice during the embed. The first mission was to the Shah Wali Kot district center to listen to a bunch of Afghan district government officials talk about how they had to step up and deliver for the people to improve security. It was one of the countless examples of a lot of talk with no follow through. The few Afghan bureaucrats who really did want to make the country better could accomplish little as the central government couldn't deliver the goods and services that the district governments needed to improve the lives of their people. That's why Afghans kept turning to U.S. forces to fill the gaps. At that meeting, the Americans were trying to deliver the message that the gravy train was packing up to head home.

The other mission was a short trip to check in on Afghan police at a small post overlooking the Dahla Dam. During the drive to the post, U.S. soldiers quipped that it was early in the morning and the Afghans might not have had time to "wake and bake" before we arrived. It was another of those awkward behind-the-scenes moments when U.S. troops joked about how the Afghan police—forces the United States was training and relying on to secure the country—were useless stoners. The handful of Afghans at the post, none of whom had uniforms of any kind, did little to dispel the notion that they were useless stoners.

After the embed I flew back to Kabul on a C-130. I was the only "voluntary" passenger. After I strapped in, several soldiers marched a shackled young Afghan man wearing a white *shalwar khamees* and a black hood into the back of the plane. They put him on his knees in the middle of the cargo bay and chained him to the floor.

I watched with morbid curiosity as the plane took off and the disoriented detainee wobbled and grew ill. The soldiers had to lift the bag from his head enough that he could vomit into a trash bag. Shit, flying in a C-130 is rough enough when you aren't hooded and tied down. Hell of a first, and probably only, flight for that Talib…

In August, I embedded with Marines at FOB Nolay in Helmand's Sangin district. Sangin was one of the deadliest places in Afghanistan. Explosions and gunfire cracked off near the base daily, and I didn't see any of it.

My story from that embed started with the sound of an explosion and gunfire in the distance, and the Marines doing nothing in response. That was the story—the Afghans were in charge and the Marines were not running out of the gates to fight every time something went boom, which was often.

I spent five days with Marines in Helmand and didn't go outside the wire the entire time. Instead, I watched U.S. troops trying to explain the basics of a diesel generator to indifferent young Afghan soldiers, the brightest of whom would take the knowledge and bail on the Afghan Army and work in the private sector repairing generators. I came back from the embed with a story that reflected the reality—the Marines were handing the fight to the Afghans and trying to build up their ability to support themselves. It didn't inspire optimism. I also got to fly in an Osprey and earn that merit badge.

While I was a little disappointed to again go to a dangerous place and not see action, to feel like I had missed it all, I was getting over all of that. That wasn't the story anymore. It was all about whether the Afghans could take over the war. The story was the training and transition effort. The challenge was cutting through the spin from the U.S. military and painting an accurate picture of the capabilities and limitations of the Afghans. I think the media came up short on conveying to the American people just how unable the Afghans were to sustain the fight and that the effort to build an Afghan military that could defeat the Taliban was throwing money in a latrine. I did what I could to show the effort was futile, but I certainly could have done more—not that it would have made much difference. There was no lack of clear evidence of failures over the years, but Washington's instinct—until President Trump came along—was to change tactics and metrics, but not change policy and strategy.

After I completed the embed and filed the story, I went on my two-week break and feasted on seafood, truffles, and barbecue in Croatia and Greece. In Croatia I spent some time with a smart and beautiful grad-school classmate who unfortunately had no romantic interest in a cranky American war correspondent. I can't imagine why...

In Greece I stayed with Patrick Quinn, the AP bureau chief in Kabul. He was another of the journalists who had seen and done the shit that had seduced me into becoming a war correspondent.

Over the summer of 2013 he had become my big brother, mentor, and main drinking buddy in Kabul. His partner had moved from Kabul to Beirut, and my engagement was over, so we were Kabul bachelors of sorts. We regularly spent evenings at his house cooking dinner, drinking gin and tonic, and venting about the weird or stressful days we had. We were like Alan Shore and Denny Crane without the homoerotic undertones, or the bloat.

That friendship was a microcosm of life in the tribe. We had a bond and relationship forged in the common experience of life in Kabul, but also shaped by the separate experiences we had reporting in other conflict zones. Even though Patrick had far more experience than I and had covered the Balkans, Iraq, and other places during the peaks of conflict, we were cut from similar cloth—as were most of our friends and colleagues in Afghanistan.

The Kabul tribe consisted of staff and stringers for AP, Reuters, AFP, BBC, *Wall Street Journal*, *Washington Post*, *LA Times*, *Guardian*, *The Times*, and *New York Times* (although like in other places, the NYT crew were more insular than others in the press corps and focused more on protecting their stories and their brand). There were also freelancers, documentarians, NGO workers, and to a lesser extent diplomats in the core social tribe. NGO workers and diplomats typically had more security restrictions and couldn't move about and socialize as freely as the journalists did. Some resorted to subterfuge to evade their security personnel, which of course was cool—merit badges for them.

At least once a week there would be some sort of social engagement that would bring together anywhere from a handful to dozens of tribe members. It could be a small embassy dinner where diplomats would invite journalists for an off-the-record chat or one of the many themed parties or events like Mujahadinner, a *Big Lebowski* party, or a pizza party at my house.

Over the course of 2013, my ties to the tribe deepened and my connection to Anna faded. Hence, in the summer of 2013, I let go of that relationship, and in September started seeing someone in Kabul. She worked for an NGO with rigid security restrictions, so she couldn't get out as much as some others, but her organization approved my house as a secure location where she could visit.

Through 2013, the parties continued, and we were able to socialize and carry on with little difficulty. The only really dark moment I remember from 2013 was when a young American foreign service officer was killed by a car bomb. Anne Smedinghoff was a model diplomat—smart, idealistic, hard-working, and eager to make a difference.

Her death was a tragedy on multiple levels. I liked her—no, there was nothing romantic, she was way too young for me and had a boyfriend. She was the anti-me in some ways. There wasn't a cynical bone in her body. She always met you with a smile. I admired her ethic. Her death was painful and shook all of us.

It's a touchy subject, but I have to say her death angered me. I don't believe that the public diplomacy mission she was on when she was killed was necessary. It was high risk and low reward. She should still be alive.

So, that was a significant black mark on what in general was a fun year of doing the job and living the life. I was in the moment. I was the full-time correspondent I had sought to be for years. I was ensconced in a job and a tribe. I was home. Even though it was enervating and dangerous and frankly an unhealthy existence, I could have stayed there for years (or at least until my liver failed). It was a dusty and rundown version of the Nexus in *Star Trek Generations*.

Everything changed in 2014.

The downward spiral began on a Friday night in January. Several of us were settling into a round of gin and tonics at the AP house before heading to the Abba party at the Russian embassy. The alcohol hadn't begun to wash away the stress of another week in Afghanistan when there was the sound.

It was that low-frequency mix between a boom and a rumble that made your stomach drop when you heard it. Immediately, your brain started scrolling through the menu of possible causes like Iron Man performing a system scan. The options, from most palatable to least, were a door slamming downstairs, an earthquake, a controlled detonation by Afghan security forces, a gas canister blowing up in an Afghan's home, a rocket or mortar, or a suicide bomb. All but the last two were generally singular events after which there was silence.

We all paused after the sound, waiting for another boom or gunfire. It was maybe 5 or 10 seconds—time always seemed to freeze in those moments—and then there was a loud burst gunfire. It was close, maybe two or three blocks away.

A few of us ran out to the balcony to see if we could locate the attack. It wasn't the smartest thing to do, but running toward danger is the norm for journalists. The initial burst of gunfire only lasted a few seconds, probably not an entire magazine of an AK-47.

The silence after the volley of gunfire gave us time to continue processing—it was clearly nearby, but was the gunfire just a nervous Afghan security person firing in panic or was it an attacker storming a compound after a suicide bomb blasted an opening in a door or wall?

After another 10 or 20 seconds, there was another burst of gunfire. It was farther away, maybe a mile, maybe more. That firing lasted longer—several sustained bursts.

That seemed to indicate we were dealing with multiple coordinated attacks across the city. That was rare in the Afghan capital. It hadn't happened in my brief tenure there. But it was always a possibility, and frankly I sometimes wondered why that didn't happen more often given the enormity of Kabul, the inconsistent quality of Afghan forces, and the ease with which militants could move around the city.

After that second volley of gunfire, we abandoned our drinks and any thoughts of attending the embassy party. We began calling our Afghan producers and fixers.

It was a well-rehearsed routine, unfortunately. Our local staff would start calling contacts in the Ministry of Interior, the Kabul police, and the intelligence service. We'd scan Twitter for tweets that might reveal the locations, targets, and victims of the attacks. We would alert our newsrooms and tweet initial details ourselves.

The *New York Times* correspondent left to go work the story on his own, as NYT correspondents usually did. Jessica Donati with Reuters, Yaroslav Trofimov with the *Wall Street Journal*, and I stayed at the AP house with Patrick and continued working the story. The practical reality was in a situation of an ongoing attack, you were all going to end up with the same information and story. No one was likely to scoop anyone else, so there was an incentive to pool resources and share information—to a certain degree. Sure, Reuters and AP were going to compete to be first and fastest, and each of us was looking for an exclusive angle, but when you were all together to start with in a situation like that, it just made sense to collaborate on piecing together the basic details. It was also a matter of safety in numbers.

I can't recall how long it took before details triangulated and we determined that there was at least one attack taking place just down the street in the Wazir Akbar Khan neighborhood that was home to embassies, news organizations, NGOs, and upper-class Afghans. It was a target-rich environment. We also all knew a lot of people living in that area, so there was immediate concern that friends could have been involved.

Jessica, Yaro, and I walked 100 feet down the street to the *Journal*'s compound to grab body armor from their stash. We donned vests and then set out farther down the street until we arrived at a crowd of Afghan and expat journalists who security forces had corralled at the end of one of the main streets in Wazir.

One of my Afghan producers was there, and he filled me in. It appeared the attack was taking place at one of the popular restaurants in the city frequented by the international community. The Lebanese Taverna was one of our regular haunts. I had dined there with friends about a week prior.

We plied security officers for information, and initially "very bad" was about the extent of what they would say. Pickup trucks full Afghan forces drove in and out of the street. Ambulances screamed by.

I didn't have my full radio kit with me as I was off the clock when I left my house earlier to head to the AP. But as I typically did, I had a small recorder with me that I regularly carried "just in case." It was kind of the equivalent of an ankle piece carried by a cop.

Since there was little new information, we turned to the next tack in a situation like that—head to hospitals to interview survivors and doctors.

Outside the Wazir Akhbar Khan hospital were crying family members of Afghan victims. Doctors said they treated one Afghan worker from the restaurant for injuries from the blast. Two bodies came into the hospital. At least one body was brought to another hospital.

Over the next hour, the details came together. A suicide bomber approached the security gate outside the restaurant and blew himself up, killing security guards and a driver sitting outside the restaurant. Then, two gunmen entered the restaurant and started shooting the guests. Victims included four UN staff, the International Monetary Fund representative, two EU police trainers, two teachers from the American University in Kabul, and the Lebanese owner of the restaurant. In total, 21 people died: 8 Afghan, 13 foreign.

There was no military or Afghan government value to the restaurant as a target. It was a haunt for international civilians—something that generally had been considered off limits for Taliban attacks.

The Taliban released a statement claiming the attack was retribution for an alleged airstrike earlier in the week that killed Afghan civilians. The Taliban statement said they were targeting a restaurant "frequented by high-ranking foreigners where they used to dine with booze and liquor in the plenty."

While that was true—we drank plenty there—it was still an unprecedented attack. Plus, it was unlikely that an attack of that complexity could have been planned and carried out in a matter of days, so the explanation that it was retribution for the airstrike was dubious.

Whatever the motivation was, it was immaterial to the outcome. Friends had been killed.

I returned to the AP bureau and continued working from there. One of the victims was one of Patrick's closest friends, and he was fighting through the pain to continue filing the story. Such was the nature of reporting on the death of a friend or colleague—file first, grieve second.

Sometime after 3 a.m. we finished filing and poured drinks. We sat in shock, overcome by grief and shaking from adrenaline. Around 5:30 a.m. the alcohol numbed the shock and pain enough so we could crash.

None of our lives were the same after that. The rules changed. Expats no longer had immunity in Kabul (even though the immunity we previously had was more perceived than real). We didn't have to just worry about being unlucky. We had to worry about being targeted.

At lot of things soaked in the days after the Taverna attack. One thing sticks with me to this day—partly I guess because of being a radio and audio person who has a heightened sense of sound—that second round of gunfire.

That gunfire that I described as sounding like it was a mile away was not. It was muted, and therefore sounded distant, because it was inside the restaurant. I can still hear that sound in my head and know that was the sound of the people in the restaurant being executed.

I visited the scene of the attack the following afternoon. A few men were shoveling debris from in front of the restaurant. A silver Toyota Corolla that had been parked out front was sitting in the street with the front end mangled and all the glass blown out. One of the victims was the driver who was sitting in his car in at the time of the blast.

The giant steel door to the restaurant was crumpled like a ball of paper. Blood stained the street outside. Windows were shattered on the houses nearby. Bits of flesh clung to nearby tree branches 20 feet in the air. It was sickening.

As if that weren't enough trauma to process, another shoe dropped. The AP had been overdue in reassigning Patrick. He should have been out of Kabul months before. After the attack, the AP told him to pack up and get ready to leave.

It was a good thing for him, but terrible for me. With Patrick departing, I was losing my primary (human) battle buddy. While I was happy for him that he was finally getting out, I was devastated that I was losing one of the best parts of my life in Kabul.

It all triggered a flood of complicated and unprocessed emotions. The Dorian Grey portrait was trying to sneak out of the closet. I fought it off the best I could for the next few weeks until my break.

While in D.C. in February, NPR gave me another gut punch. Due to ongoing budget woes, there was going to be downsizing. What that meant for me was there would be no position after I closed the Kabul bureau at the end of the year. While it stung at the time, I was hopeful that over the course of the year circumstances would change and an opportunity to stay on, ideally overseas, would present itself. Still, I felt a little betrayed that I had taken on the most dangerous assignment for the organization, and I was not going to be rewarded for it.

I returned to Kabul at the beginning of March with my head in a bit of a fog over it all. David Gilkey, the NPR photojournalist, arrived a few days later.

David was one of the most regarded and decorated photojournalists in the business. He and I had traveled to a lot of the same places, knew a lot of the same people, but had not met until I entered the mothership in summer 2011.

On my first day at NPR, he sauntered into my office to introduce himself. He was husky with his trademark shaved head, jeans,

Oxford shirt, and Blundstone boots. We got on like brothers from the get-go.

He was usually low-key and often quiet as he soaked everything in, but he could unleash some of the most trenchant, sardonic, and appropriately inappropriate comments I'd ever heard. He was one of the few people I met who could be darker, more cynical, and more foul-mouthed than I am. I've never been accused of being warm and fuzzy, but next to him I came across as Ned Flanders. That said, he was a generous, caring, and vulnerable person when you got to know him.

David and I stayed in regular contact during my time in Kabul. He checked in whenever he heard about anything going boom (or when westerners were kidnapped in my neighborhood) to make sure I was cool. We talked often about him coming over and spending a month or two with me and the stories we wanted to cover.

Finally, as Afghanistan's presidential election neared in the spring of 2014, David got word he could deploy to Kabul for a couple of months. He would split time between me and *Morning Edition* host Renee Montagne and her producer Peter Breslow, who would be traveling to Afghanistan for two weeks to cover the election.

That was an example of something that drives a lot of foreign correspondents nuts. It happens mostly in broadcast, but sometimes in print. Whenever there is a high-profile story—an election, disaster, conflict—the big dogs want to get out of the studio or home office and cover the action. When you see people like Anderson Cooper, Christiane Amanpour, Geraldo, or Brian Williams (before he was grounded) in the field, you know some shit is going down. They, understandably, want a piece of the action and want to put their stamp on the story.

The flip side of that is that it takes stories and airtime from the in-country correspondent. It's referred to "big footing" in the industry, and it sucks when you're getting the foot in the ass. With Renee coming to town, it meant I was going to have to surrender some election stories, and it meant she was going to get face time and interviews with the commanding generals who typically would not grant me interviews anyhow since they would do interviews with the program hosts, not the lowly correspondent.

Anyhow, David arrived in early March and our field adventure together was finally underway. The next day, it almost stopped in its tracks.

We were in the house discussing plans when I heard a commotion outside. I thought that some of the Afghan domestic staff were arguing, and I went to calm things down. But I discovered it was a more serious problem—the fucking garage was on fire.

Flames were belching out of the garage where we stored our firewood. The garage was attached to the house by a small bathroom for the staff and it was not much of a buffer.

My Afghan producer Sultan called the fire department while the other local staff and I emptied our fire extinguishers on the flames to no avail. David was convinced we were going to lose the house. We ran inside and began throwing everything important into suitcases and hauled what we could carry out into the yard away from the house.

It was sheer panic. I couldn't find Squeak and was convinced she ran outside and was gone for good. It was probably the only moment of chaos that David experienced where he was too focused on responding to the crisis to take any pictures—sadly, as there were some great visuals of the flames belching out of the garage. I had just enough composure to turn on an audio recorder and leave it rolling in the courtyard near the fire.

Fortunately, the Kabul fire department came and extinguished the blaze just as flames were starting to lap against the side of the house. Crisis resolved; but it left us with no electricity, and no generator for a couple of days (it was our old generator that apparently started the fire to begin with). At least Squeak reappeared from whatever hiding place she had found in the house. And I had great sound that ended up in a story about how well trained and equipped the Kabul fire department was. Nothing like a story that thrusts itself on you. Turned out the fire department was one of the most functional things in Kabul, in no small part because of a foundation built by the Soviets when they tried to master Afghanistan.

Perhaps the fire was an omen, as the next month turned out to be one of the more chaotic, stressful, and violent ones in Kabul. The city and the international community were still reeling from the Taverna attack. About a week after David arrived, a Swedish journalist was shot dead in the street in the Wazir Akhbar Khan neighborhood.

A little more than a week later, militants attacked the heavily fortified Serena Hotel in Kabul. Almost all the other journalists in town were at a party that night that David and I somehow didn't get invited to (I'm not bitter), so we drove downtown to cover the attack. We nearly got shot by an Afghan special forces soldier manning a checkpoint. David sat calmly in the back of the car as I screamed at the driver to slow down as the soldier took a knee and aimed at us as we approached.

We survived that encounter and spent a couple of hours on the streets covering the attack. The news was once again tragic. A beloved Afghan journalist and his family and several international civilians were gunned down in the hotel as they ate dinner.

After that, a couple of election monitoring organizations pulled their people out of the country, and some of the NGOs also pulled staff out. Almost every international organization enacted some sort of lockdown protocol.

At the end of March there were multiple complex attacks on election offices. Militants attacked a guesthouse in Kabul, hoping to kill Christian missionaries, but instead hit the neighboring house. They failed to kill anyone inside, but the initial explosion killed an Afghan girl on the street.

In each case, David and I rushed to the scene to gather all the audio and photos we could. Bullets would whistle overhead as panicked Afghan forces scurried about firing wildly in the direction of the perpetrators. With each attack, the sense of doom about the future of the country and the safety of foreigners grew.

The Afghan government shut down hotels and guest houses in Kabul that it considered vulnerable to attack. One of the hotels it closed was Gandamak, the legendary and popular expat hotel and bar in Kabul. It was where Renee and Peter were staying.

When the government announced the closure, they gave a couple of hours for all the guests to evacuate. David, Renee, and Peter were traveling with presidential candidate Ashraf Ghani that day and unable to clear out of Gandamak before Afghan forces seized it. That meant that my Afghan producers and I had to rush to the hotel and pack up and clear out all of Renee and Peter's stuff. I literally had to pack up Renee's wet underwear and other laundry hanging out to dry in her room. It was one thing to deal with being big-footed and giving up some stories, it was another thing to carry the host's underwear. Who said the life of a war correspondent was glamorous?

Renee and Peter moved into the Serena Hotel (despite the recent attack it was still considered the most secure in the city), and David and I remained at the NPR bureau. He and I talked for hours about the situation in the country. We spent a lot of time just saying, "what the fuck?" to each other. What conclusions could we draw from the attacks? Were they blips, or trend lines? What stories could we safely cover? How much should we restrict our movements? Since the beginning of 2014, more and more attacks targeted foreign civilians, which was a sea change. Were we heading towards a Baghdad-style locked down existence?

David had been covering Afghanistan since 2001 and had seen just about everything, but what was going on then had him unnerved—which was unnerving to me. If he was starting to feel that things were getting dark and dangerous in Kabul, then it must be bad.

I was grateful to have him there. It was a tough period having to cover all the violence and report on the deaths of friends and people I knew, and it was also stressful to figure out how to react to the increasing danger in the city. Having a guy in the house who had lived through the worst of Iraq and Afghanistan helped keep me somewhat grounded. Squeak, whiskey, Ambien, and Xanax also helped.

We talked about friends and colleagues we had lost over the years. We talked about why we did the work. We questioned whether Afghanistan was worth our lives. We joked about how it would be OK for NPR if either he or I got killed in Afghanistan, but if something happened to Renee it would be a tragedy of epic proportions. "Imagine the shit show if a host bites it," he said.

As a photographer for a radio organization, he always felt he was expendable, and his job could be yanked out from under him at any point. He never quite accepted that he was a brilliant photographer and a tremendous asset to NPR. That said, there were those in the organization who wondered what the point was of having a photographer on staff, which added to David's existential angst.

I was the one who was expendable. That was weighing heavily on me as David and I clawed our way through the days of death and grief. He knew how long and hard I had worked to get to Afghanistan and that it was crushing to know my ride was ending.

We talked about that pain and frustration. We discussed PTS and self-medication (and prescription meds too—David was on some heavy stuff to battle the ravages brought on by a life of covering the shit and near-death experiences). There wasn't anything we couldn't discuss candidly and without judgment. David became my tribe within the tribe.

We realized that no matter how bad it got, we had to stick it out, for the sake of the story. David had been there from the beginning. He rode in with U.S. Special Forces in 2001. He had spent more time in the country, mostly with the U.S. military, than a lot of troops did. He had seen more shit in Afghanistan than anyone I knew.

He said he had to see the story through for the Afghan people and the members of the military and their families. It wasn't about him, and he sure as shit wasn't in it for the glory and awards. He was committed to making sure the world never forgot about the plight of everyone on the ground in Afghanistan.

Despite all the attacks and pre-election violence, we were able to travel around a bit and cross some stories off our list. We reported on the growing number of internally displaced Afghans in desolate camps in and around Kabul. David's photos captured the harsh conditions and the resolve of the Afghans who just wanted to return to their homes and have peaceful, quiet lives.

We traveled to Kandahar to the Panjwai district for a quick mini-embed. We took a daytrip to the Panjshir Valley. But our greatest adventure was our trip to Northern Afghanistan to attend a Buzkashi match. That's Afghanistan's national sport where men on horses try to pick up the carcass of a goat or calf and carry it across a field and drop it in a circle. It's a gruesome and violent sport.

David, our Afghan producer Sultan Faizy, and I flew up to Mazar-i-Sharif. We traveled by car to Sheberghan to the west. It was about a three-hour drive, but it took a little longer than planned.

An hour into the drive, as we were in the middle of nowhere, I was just turning to David to point out that we had made a rookie mistake. We had failed to inspect the car before leaving the airport to make sure it was in good condition and had a spare tire and tools. And at that moment, the front right tire blew.

We ground to a halt on the side of the road—completely exposed to all passing traffic. We feared the worst as the driver opened the trunk. AAA was not going to save our bacon. Fortunately, there was a full-size spare tire and a jack. We were quickly back on our way laughing about how it was a total failure on our part to get in the car without inspecting it first. We got lucky.

In Sheberghan we stayed in the ornate and utterly tacky guest compound of notorious warlord and then vice-presidential candidate Abdul Rashid Dostum. We spent a couple of days with Afghanistan's leading Buzkashi players—seeing them prepare their horses for competition and watching them get ready for the match.

The match itself took place on a chilly, rainy day. The spectators sat in covered stands while David and I spent the whole time on the muddy playing field capturing the action. He of course waded far closer to the action than I did. David was not a fan of telephoto lenses—quite the opposite, he preferred wide angle and getting ridiculously close to the subjects of his photos.

I stood farther back and yelled warnings at him when a horseman was about to run him over or sideswipe him with the dead calf. That trip was the highlight of 2014.

After that adventure, we returned to Kabul for the election. The day before the vote, two AP journalists were deliberately shot by an Afghan police officer. One, Kathy Gannon, was critically wounded, and the other, photojournalist Anja Niedringhaus, was killed. It was another kick in the balls. We were in shock. We had to process another personal loss and carry on covering the election the following day.

Originally, the plan was for David to stick around another month so we could report on the process of tallying the results and cover some other stories on our long list. But his team back in D.C. was getting antsy. There were other projects on his itinerary, and there were persistent security concerns in Kabul, so the feeling was we wouldn't be able to get out as much as we wanted, and his time would be better spent elsewhere.

In mid-April, David departed. I soldiered on until the completion of my eight-week rotation at the end of April. The day before I left on my break, an Afghan police officer shot and killed three American medical workers as they entered a hospital in Kabul.

That was the most intense and emotionally draining of my rotations in Kabul. During that break I considered quitting. Why should I go back to Kabul again and risk life and limb for an organization that was going to cut me loose? Friends, and some coworkers, advised me to bail. I thought about it.

However, I wanted to finish out the year in Afghanistan and see the story and my assignment through before moving on (and I wanted to hang with the Kabul tribe as long as I could). I thought that finishing and acquitting myself well would demonstrate my professionalism and loyalty and someone at NPR would see that I deserved to be rewarded for that.

I knew I wasn't Kelly, or Lulu, or Jason, but I had done damn solid work, was well regarded by officials and media in Kabul, never said no to the NPR programs or news desk, and I saved NPR a ton of money by switching to GEICO. Seriously, I made staffing changes, switched our satellite internet service, and negotiated down the rent, which saved at least $60k in bureau expenses while I was there. I thought that should have been worth something.

The summer was a hell of its own with the disputed presidential election consuming every moment. It was impossible to do enterprise reporting as each day there was a new twist in the pathetic drama—a new objection filed, a threat to form a parallel government, a call to arms. It was like a dress rehearsal for the 2020 U.S. presidential election. At one point I was nearly assaulted by supporters of Ashraf Ghani during the vote auditing process in Kabul. They thought I was spending too much time observing election officials evaluating a box of fraudulent votes for Ghani. There were knife fights that broke out at the elections compound. It was a complete and utter shit show.

It came to a head for me on July 4th. I was drained from working all day and arrived late to a party. I started drinking heavily. I felt myself getting into a weird headspace. There was simply too much stress in my life to process.

I got trapped in a conversation with a former Croatian special forces guy who was working as a security contractor. He proceeded to badger me and push my buttons. He maligned journalists. It was a bullshit discussion, but I was so drained and stressed from work, the election, and the frustration and disappointment I was carrying from knowing that my ride was ending, that I couldn't tune the guy out. He burrowed deeper and deeper under my skin. I kept drinking and getting angrier about everything.

Eventually, it was too much. I left the party around 1 a.m. and instead of calling a car, I staggered drunk for two miles through the dark, empty streets of Kabul back to my house. I was flicking open my automatic knife as I walked along in a state of rage I had never felt before. I was looking for a fight. I wanted to kill or be killed. Everything was coming to a head inside me and I was blowing up.

I made it home safely. I spent about 30 minutes in my living room throwing my knife at the wall. I wanted to break shit. I felt like doing harm to myself. Picture Martin Sheen's meltdown in the hotel room at the beginning of *Apocalypse Now*. That was my headspace.

I was scaring the crap out of Squeak. That realization was what finally pulled me back from the edge. I had an innocent cat, a life that I had chosen to save from predators, cars, and all sorts of other calamities on the streets of Kabul. I couldn't give up or do myself in because I was responsible for her. In that moment, my decision to save her saved me. I don't know that I would have made it through that night without her tethering me to the land of the living.

I drugged myself to sleep. The next day I re-immersed myself in the slow-moving train wreck that was the presidential election. I hid inside of work and whiskey for the next ten days until my next break.

I dropped off Squeak at the Nowzad kennel in Kabul—where she had to stay in solitary as she did not play well with others—and went to Beirut for a week and stayed at Patrick and Rachel's apartment. It was my first vacation in Beirut. I ate, drank, went to spas, and partied with tribe members. I barely thought about Layla the whole time I was in Beirut. I was past that. I could be in Lebanon and enjoy it for what it was and who was there rather than think of it as some portal to an alternate life or reality. Besides, I had far more immediate concerns—like, where the hell was my life heading? I had no answer to that question.

After Beirut, I spent a week in Cyprus scuba diving. Under the water is one of my happy places. Feeling somewhat refreshed, I returned to Kabul at the end of July and jumped right back into the Groundhog Day that was the disputed presidential election.

I made it through the eight weeks and then traveled to Bonaire for two weeks of diving, eating seafood, and more diving. That trip got me in about the best headspace I could possibly be in to return to Afghanistan for my final rotation.

In late October, I traveled with a small pack of journalists to Helmand to cover the U.S. withdrawal from Camp Leatherneck, the sprawling Marine base that once hosted tens of thousands of troops and had been stripped down to something resembling the set for a zombie apocalypse movie. The remaining Marines cased the colors, raised an Afghan flag, and then got the fuck out of there as quickly as possible in fear the Taliban would overwhelm the Afghan forces and take the base. It was another vote of no confidence in the Afghan forces and another omen that the whole U.S. endeavor in Afghanistan was doomed to fail.

After that it was a mix of parties, jam sessions, cranking out stories about the uncertain future, and packing and throwing away shit. I was a master of emotional suppression during that time. The thought of leaving, of leaving the tribe, was killing me, so I did everything to deflect, deny, suppress, sublimate, self-medicate, and every other psychological trick to avoid feeling the sadness and pain.

Thanksgiving was a disaster. I went to a base in Kabul to do the usual saccharine "Thanksgiving for troops on deployment" story. Unfortunately, I couldn't file that story because the Taliban launched an attack in Kabul. They were targeting a CIA compound but hit the wrong house. Regardless, it kicked off a fierce battle that raged until after midnight.

I was supposed to have dinner at a friend's house across the street but never made it. I had to report on the attack. Gunfire rang out nonstop for hours. At one point I walked out of the house to go into the office in back and record an interview with *All Things Considered*. Bullets whistled over my head.

I ran back into the house and shut off the lights. I had heard gunfire that sounded close to the house, and I wasn't sure if the battle had moved from Swimming Pool hill in Wazir where the attack kicked off. It was possible there was shooting going on nearby. It was also possible it was gunfire from the battle in Wazir. The Afghan forces had taken up positions on top of the hill and were firing down on the attackers at the house below. Likely, the Afghans were spraying the entire city with gunfire from that perch. Despite all the training they had received, their instinct was to shoot as many bullets as possible at a threat with no regard for where they were aiming.

Anyhow, hearing bullets whizz directly overhead was beyond disconcerting, and I bunkered in the house for a while with Squeak until things calmed down enough that I felt reasonably safe walking into the recording booth in the back office. The fighting ended after midnight, and sometime around 2 a.m. I drank myself to sleep to the sound of U.S. warplanes circling above the city.

December came. I had to close another NPR bureau. Unlike in 2011 when I was the producer helping the correspondent shut things down, I was flying solo. David was hoping to spend December with me knocking out some more stories and helping me turn out the lights. Unfortunately, his masters would not OK the trip.

I packed up containers to ship back to Washington. I gave piles of clothing, furniture, and other household items to my local staff. I burned stacks of documents. I sold off the obscene amount of alcohol I had accumulated (scarcity mentality). I attended a few farewell events.

I was devastated inside. I was leaving the Nexus. I had only spent a couple of years in the place I had longed to be for more than a decade, and it was coming to an end.

On December 13, 2014, I said goodbye to the bureau staff and left for the airport hauling four giant suitcases, a couple of guitars, and a backpack. Squeak stayed behind at the Nowzad shelter as I wasn't sure I was going to settle in D.C. and only wanted to move her once.

The expensive sushi dinner and massage in Dubai were cold comfort. I flew back to D.C. on the contractor shuttle and drank just about the entire booze stash in first class.

I wanted to be numb.

At 8:30 a.m. on December 14, I walked into the living room of my D.C. condo. I hauled the bags into the middle of the room and sat down on the couch. I stared at the empty shelves. They were a metaphor. I was back where I started, but I had less than when I left. I had no job, no significant other, and no path to get back to the Nexus. I had achieved my dream, only to have it slip through my fingers. It felt like the moment when Layla packed her stuff and walked out of my life. Back to zero.

Chapter Twenty
Aftermath

December 2014

WASHINGTON D.C. — As I sat staring at the empty walls of my living room, I knew I was damaged, but I wasn't remotely aware of just how broken I was. Some of the damage had set in long before NPR and Afghanistan. The years of traveling to dangerous places had been slowly altering my DNA in ways that I am still sorting out many years later.

While NPR had an arrangement with a counselor with whom staff could speak, it wasn't mandatory. There was no formal reentry process. There was no evaluation of my mental health. It was up to me to decide whether to seek help. As is the case with most people in need of help, they aren't aware that they need it, or don't think they need it, and therefore don't get it.

I thought I was "OK" when I got home in the sense that I wasn't having traumatic nightmares or anxiety attacks or any of the more acute PTS symptoms. I appeared to be functional in general.

Over the years, I realized that I was not OK and that NPR, like just about every media organization at the time, was ignorant (if not negligent) when it came to the mental health of its staff who lived in dangerous places and covered traumatic subjects. While there has been extensive discussion in recent years about how the military fails to take mental health seriously and needs to do better, news organizations and NGOs have been even worse than the military in this regard.

What I noticed immediately when I got back to D.C. was that I couldn't walk around outside without feeling anxious. My Spidey-sense was so dialed up that I perceived everything as a potential threat. If anyone was walking behind me within about 15 feet, I had to move to the side and let them pass. I could not tolerate having people in my blind spots. I was constantly listening for footsteps behind me or watching shadows to see if anyone was close. Loud noises—like trucks unloading heavy items, car horns, doors slamming, basically anything somewhat percussive and unexpected—made me jump and shot adrenaline through me.

I couldn't sit in a bar or restaurant without my back to the wall in a seat with full visibility of the room and all entrances and exits. Being in crowds freaked me out.

I also felt a ton of anger. People complaining about mundane first-world problems pissed me off to no end. D.C. just felt more entitled and frankly selfish after I returned. In Afghanistan, drivers and pedestrians were batshit crazy and I got used to it. But in D.C., when drivers ran lights, cyclists rode on the sidewalk, or pedestrians stopped traffic, it sent me into a rage. Any lack of courtesy or consideration made me want to punch people in the head. It just felt like no one cared anymore and giving a shit about how your actions affected others went out the door.

The smallest things like that set me off. Everywhere I looked, someone was doing something inconsiderate or selfish, and it ate at me. For whatever reason, my time in the shit had made me hyper cognizant of people doing anything "wrong" that affected others, and I couldn't walk a block without observing five things that made me want to punch someone in the head.

I was feeling like a fish out of water and simply unable to process being back in a place where people were addicted to TV shows about spoiled, narcissistic, toxic housewives pulling each other's hair out or backstabbing bimbos trying to win the affection of some dude-bro asshat bachelor. And then there was the embarrassing political discourse with elected officials from both parties who couldn't find Afghanistan on a map.

Basically, I noticed that I hated everyone who had it easy. I didn't want to talk to anyone or couldn't relate to anyone who hadn't experienced real shit.

And the shit wasn't just the accumulated stress of being in dangerous environs and the threats to your safety. It was all the things I saw, heard, and smelled: countless bodies and body parts; shattered and broken bodies, still clinging to life; people ravaged by violence, disease, and other hardships they could do nothing about; refugee and IDP camps overflowing with desperate people driven there by ruthless and sadistically violent militias and warlords; corruption, malfeasance, greed, and selfishness on an unbelievable scale; and shattered, burned, bullet-riddled, and ransacked homes and full of destroyed personal effects—the reminders of lives people would never be able to get back.

In my travels from the fall 2007 until the end of 2014, I saw the absolute worst of humanity. It was like Leeloo in *The Fifth Element* watching the montages of war and violence, or *The Abyss*, or countless other sci-fi movies where aliens view the history of violence and cruelty and determine that humanity should be eliminated.

While I saw examples of bravery, kindness, resilience, and people being amazing when they had every right to be hateful and vengeful, those moments didn't outweigh the horrors. It was traumatizing to see so many examples of just how fucking awful people can be. By the time I returned to D.C. in December 2014, my brain had been hard-wired to see and expect the worst from people. It takes a hell of a lot more than whiskey and black humor to process the horrible shit that humans do to each other.

Plus, it makes it harder to be around other people and not be a constant downer. When you're in a place where you see humans as a malign species, beings who will do unspeakably horrible things to each other—sometimes out of a perceived need to survive, but often because of greed and lust for power—it's difficult to contain that and not be a black cloud around other people. No one wants to be around someone who is constantly venting about how vile and awful people are.

Again, I was only slightly conscious of how altered I was by my experiences when I returned from Afghanistan. No question I needed help processing it all, but what I needed first was help in getting to a place where I understood that I needed help. Given that I had no significant other and no job at the end of 2014, there really wasn't anyone or anything that could help me. I was on my own, and nothing good would come of that.

On February 6, 2015, Squeak finally arrived in D.C. and that was transformative. I had my battle buddy back. I felt some purpose again—I had "someone" to take care of. There is no question in my mind that you would not be reading this if it weren't for her. To this day, every time I entertain the notion of checking out, I look at her and realize I have to keep going.

Things just kept getting worse and more difficult. I was not having any traction in my job search. I was sending out scores of resumes and doing constant networking. I was getting no response. I mean, on top of everything else I had done in my career, I had just spent the better part of two-and-a-half years in Afghanistan reporting for NPR doing very solid and at times heralded work, and yet the D.C. industry didn't seem to care.

I was running into a few barriers. Because I had been let go by NPR, other organizations assumed that meant there was something wrong with me. They didn't see it for what it was, which was that there were management changes and the people who had my back left while I was in Afghanistan, and new people had to make their mark and put "their people" in place. I was a victim of organizational politics, but people didn't realize the scarlet letter I would be stuck with. So, when I had interviews for other positions, I faced two pointy lines of inquiry. One, why did you leave NPR (answer was that my position ended and there wasn't a slot for me, which was true, but not a satisfying answer). Two, can you write? Since the only jobs in international reporting out there were in print, I had to deal with the bias/assumption that radio journalists can't write print stories—it's complete horseshit to assume that, but I could see where it was coming from. So, potential employers viewed me as problematic because NPR laid me off and they assumed I couldn't do print work. Basically, the gigs I wanted were closed off to me.

It ate away at me. Maybe I wasn't good enough. Maybe there was no need for me in the journalism world. If not, who was I? What was I? I was sinking into a funk of self-doubt and depression.

Being out of the Nexus and not having a full-time job gave me far too much time to think and wallow. When I was downrange and immersed in the work and life, I was one step ahead of whatever I was feeling, most of the time. I tried not to slow down enough to let the wounds and scars on my Dorian Grey portrait catch up with me. Once I was back in D.C. the portrait was hanging on the wall staring at me.

Then, there was another problem that grew out of my damaged mental state in 2015. It started on a Tuesday afternoon in February. I was bored and the notion popped into my head that Maryland might have opened a casino or two while I was in Afghanistan. Google confirmed my suspicion, and with that I was in the car heading to Maryland Live Casino. Like many bad things, it started innocently enough. I would go periodically and play 25-cent video poker. I had plenty of money in the bank and was playing maybe $200 to $300 during a visit. It was a cure for boredom, and it was also something edgy and dangerous that was filling that void in my life.

Of course, you already know where this is going, and I started going more often and gambling larger amounts. Sure, I was taking advantage of all the perks and getting as much entertainment value as I could out of it (I rationalized to myself), but safe to say that an unemployed former war correspondent with untreated depression, anxiety, and PTS going to a casino on a regular basis was not going to end well.

Oddly, I found a new tribe at the casino. I developed an

alternate life there where I felt safe, welcomed, and valued. I forged bonds with staff and some of the players. Being treated as a high roller compensated for some of the pain and emptiness I was feeling in the rest of my life. Still, it turned into a financial wrecking ball.

As if getting into gambling wasn't enough of a problem, I fell into a toxic and abusive relationship with a younger woman. It was a cliche on every level. Lonely, damaged, underemployed man in his 40s takes up tennis lessons and ends up falling for young instructor who was the only woman to show interest at the time.

We had outrageous physical chemistry, and that blinded me to all the negatives—the fact that we had almost nothing in common, and she an emotional extortionist who had unprovoked episodes of anger and jealousy.

There were plenty of warning signs early on that would have driven away a reasonable person, but I wasn't reasonable then. The physical relationship was yet another form of excitement and danger that I needed to fill the void.

Aside from Squeak, I had one other thing working in my favor: David Gilkey. David had been living in Portland, but NPR decided they wanted him based in D.C. He wasn't thrilled about that, but I was. I was going to have the person I considered my most important friend in the same city. He would be traveling a lot for work, but he would be around enough that I would have a support system in D.C.

He purchased a condo, and we started mapping out plans to help him move to D.C. We would get that all done after his annual big reporting trip to Afghanistan with Tom Bowman, the NPR Pentagon correspondent.

David was increasingly stressing about the trip and the pressure to get great material that would justify future trips. The previous year, they struggled to get stories due to the drawdown of U.S. forces and the lack of embed opportunities with the U.S. military. They had a close shave or two but ended up with enough material to make the case to go again in 2016.

We talked before his trip about the challenges and dangers of embedding with Afghan forces. It was far riskier than being with U.S. forces for a multitude of reasons, and he was quite sober about it.

Anyhow, David and the rest of the NPR team (Tom and a young producer with no war zone experience) set off for Afghanistan in late May 2016.

We chatted a few times while he was there. He was feeling stressed about some of their reporting plans falling through. He was growing concerned they were not going to get the material they were seeking.

On the morning (my time) of June 5, I sent him a text. "How's asscrackistan treating you?" I wrote. It didn't go through as an iMessage, so I figured they were somewhere out in rural Afghanistan, and I would hear back later when they returned to a base or a city.

I didn't hear back.

I was at a cookout next to the Potomac with friends that afternoon when I received a text from my former Afghan producer who was still in Kabul. "We lost David," the message read.

Everything came to a halt. Yes, it was always a possibility something like that could happen. David and I discussed it many times. We knew the risks, but he wasn't a cowboy. He didn't love the bang bang; he just saw it as part of the story, and it was his job to tell the story.

All the knowing and understanding of the danger did not prepare me for that moment. I walked away from the picnic table and stood by the river. There had to be some mistake. It was the fog of war and information got scrambled.

I received more messages from Kabul. There was no way around it. The most important person in my life was gone, killed by the Taliban.

I wanted to pull a Cameron Frye and jump into the water and sink to the bottom. What was the point of continuing? David had been my life vest keeping me afloat and now he was another cinderblock pulling me down.

David's death hit me harder than the nuke Layla dropped on me nine years earlier. No other death has hit me like that. It's rare a day goes by without him crossing my mind.

His death left me rudderless. I believe that had he completed the move to D.C., his presence in my life would have prevented me from going as far as I did in my relationship and gambling. I don't know if anyone could have talked any sense into me at that point, but I think he would have tried like hell to stop me from continuing down the path that I was on, he was the kind of guy who would do that for a friend.

Unfortunately, I fell victim to emotional manipulation and married my girlfriend. I snapped and proposed to end another pointless argument. It was a Marty McFly moment—she was essentially calling me an emotional chicken. I took the bait.

Sadly, marriage and applying for her green card did not solve the problem. Within weeks, she returned to constantly accusing me of having affairs. She would interrogate me about women who followed me on social media. She would wake me up in the middle of the night demanding passwords to my email and phone so she could investigate for signs of an affair. We would have a week of calm and fun, and then something would trigger her like a post-hypnotic suggestion, and she'd start accusing me again. She got violent periodically. She'd break things.

There was nothing I could do. Despite my spotty relationship history, I took marriage seriously. I was faithful. I was more transparent with her than anyone I had been with. I allowed her far too much access to my email and phone records than I should have, but I had nothing to hide.

It didn't matter. It was as if showing her I was innocent only made her more determined to find evidence of guilt. When she was in one of her states, she would unleash venom at me that made Alex Forrest seem quaint. I mean, hateful, hurtful, nasty shit. It was pure emotional terrorism.

It got to the point where I was afraid all the time that she was going to snap and start breaking things or assault me. It was like living in Kabul again—there was always the possibility that something could blow up at any time. Except, the explosive was living in my home.

Six months after our Vegas wedding, I had to throw her out. The psychological, emotional, and physical abuse pushed me to my breaking point, and I had to save myself. I think I still have as much PTS from that relationship as I do from Afghanistan.

A few months later, I started a job at the Defense Department Office of Inspector General. It was a good gig, but it was a desk job in a soulless office complex in the ass of nowhere in Alexandria.

Taking that job felt like an admission of failure, that I wasn't going to get back out in the field. I was less and less grieving the losses of other people and increasingly grieving the loss of myself. The person I was—the adventurer, traveler, chronicler, and storyteller—was gone. Hearing even a few seconds of NPR gnawed at my wounds.

For my entire adult life, I had animating purposes. First, it was to be a recording engineer and musician. I pursued that into my early 30s when I transitioned to journalism. Then, being a war/foreign correspondent was my passion and pursuit.

While many people derive their identity from their jobs, I realized that I wasn't who I was because I was a journalist, I was a journalist because of who I am. Being a journalist traveling the world was an expression of who I am as a person. No longer doing that and seeing no path to return to that left me feeling like I was a dead man walking. It didn't help that every day I entered an office through a prison-like entryway and vault doors.

The other side of that coin is that sitting in an office is not my highest and best use. Plenty of people can edit government reports. Fewer can find their way around weird and dangerous places and observe, absorb, process, and then communicate what is going on. I contribute more to humanity by being out there roaming though jungles and villages of far-off places. I'm like the Sundance Kid, I'm better when I move.

Not surprisingly, my gambling increased in intensity the moment I started my government job. The gambling was the only sense of danger and excitement in my life, and it was the only thing resembling a tribe. By then, most of my tribe mates from Kabul who had also returned to D.C. had moved on, and I was alone. My life had peaked at 45 and I couldn't see anything to look forward to anymore. I was Willy Fucking Loman.

This is one of the primary drivers of the suicide epidemic of middle-age (mostly white) men. It's the same for coal miners, athletes, soldiers, and men in white collar jobs. When it's no longer possible to do what you did, to be who you are, what is there to live for? What do you do? Many people reinvent and have second acts. Others cannot and cannot process or live with the grief. They cannot handle going forward with a life of looking back and mourning.

I never expected to be in that position, but that's where I ended up. I grew convinced that the world had no interest in what I had to offer and that there was no reason to continue. It was a rare to get through a day without contemplating ending it.

I stuck it out in my government job until October 2020. COVID, the growing frustrations of the job, and my loneliness drove me to the point of self-destruction. I was gambling harder and going through too much whiskey. I hated my life and myself.

I started thinking about the logistics of checking out—updating my will, selling off crap and getting rid of things so family would have less to deal with, organizing my computer files so it would be easier for people to go through my stuff.

I started considering how I would go about it. I mapped out a few different scenarios and approaches. I was trying to decide how much of a statement I wanted to make. Do I quietly sneak off into the woods? Do I do it outside the NPR building in D.C. to say, "Hey, you did this to me, it's on you!"? I've always had a bit of a flair for the dramatic, so if I was going to check out, I would want it to generate discussion and soul searching and hopefully help the next person who ended up in my predicament.

Either way, I reached a point where I felt there wasn't any reason to stick around. I had experienced all the death, loss, grief, rejection, and emptiness I could handle.

Epilogue

So, by virtue of the fact that you've read this book, you know I didn't pull the plug. I was close, and closer than anyone in my life realized—no, people, I wasn't being melodramatic.

There was one thing I couldn't get past, well maybe two. I was, and am, terrified of it all going dark. Despite my efforts to get as close to death as possible, and moments when I felt like I didn't care to stick around anymore, I have a hard time with the notion of the lights going out. When you have what I refer to as a hyper conscious mind and heightened sense of awareness, it's really scary to imagine it coming to an end.

However, the more immediate thing that kept me tethered to the land of the living was Squeak. I couldn't think of anyone who I could leave her to who would care for her as I do. She and I have a bond. In a weird way, we're soulmates. She doesn't relate to others like she does with me. She's a one-person cat, and the thought of abandoning her was what ultimately kept me from checking out.

So, I took an extended mental health leave from my job. I wanted to find an inpatient facility that does intensive PTS and mid-life crisis work—kind of a reboot facility—but realized that doesn't seem to exist. Inpatient facilities are either for substance abuse or severe mental illness. There really needs to be a category of inpatient facilities for near-suicidal depression and PTS that gives people the time and space to step away from negative stimuli and do intensive work.

I entered therapy and did a lot of soul searching. By the middle of November 2020, I had a plan. I was going to quit my job, cash out everything I could, and go write the book about my adventures that friends and family had been urging me to write for years.

It was something I knew I needed to do for years but had been afraid—too intimidated by the task of writing a book and somewhat afraid to root through the memories I would have to so I could tell the tale. I decided I was ready to confront everything, and I needed to in order to continue healing and to help find a healthier path forward.

In March 2021, I handed in my ID card and ended my career in government—don't get me started on what I think about inter-agency programs.

Squeak and I moved to Cape Cod to sit by a lake and write—well, I wrote, and she critiqued. No question I am lucky and priv-ileged to have a family that owns a house on Cape Cod where I could step away from everything and heal.

Kayaking, fishing, grilling on the deck, senior softball, and restorative yoga (and chasing a whack nut cat around the house) served as my therapy, along with writing, of course.

It was cathartic to step away and process the last 15 years or so. At the same time, it was difficult to look back on the moments when I was happy and in my element and wonder if there will be such moments again.

In a way, I came full circle. It was 9/11 that lit the fire in me to become a war correspondent. Then, it was a series of losses—the woman I loved, my step-grandmother, and my original music—that set me on a path to confront death and find a place and a tribe where I felt at home.

I found it. I lived it. I loved it. And it was gone again in the blink of an eye. That started the cycle all over again.

Twenty years after it all began, I am back on the outside. I've watched in envy as reporters, friends who were once my tribe, have covered the fallout of the Taliban takeover of Afghanistan and the war in Ukraine. Sitting on the sidelines watching those events reignited the feelings I had in fall 2001.

I continue grieving losses: the loss of a happy relationship, the loss of the life I built after that, the loss of pieces of my humanity that died on the battlefields, the loss of David, and the loss of my tribe. Every day I have to find reasons to keep going. Fortunately, when I can't come up with one, I look at Squeak and remember she's counting on me.

I am still broken and full of holes. I've come to realize we never fill the holes. At best we learn to live with them. At least I was able to turn mine into the book that you just read.

Now, I hope to continue this conversation about the psychological and emotional impact of working in war zones and hostile environments. There are thousands of civilians—journalists, aid and development workers, diplomats—who are deployed to dangerous places to do important work saving lives and informing the world.

Most did not receive any counseling or training before deploying. They, like I experienced, did not have any monitoring while deployed. I did not receive any reentry or reintegration counseling or care, and neither will most people out there now.

Some have worked through it, others not. Some will suffer and struggle the rest of their lives—either remaining in dangerous places because that's the only world that makes sense or flailing around "polite society" trying to make sense of it.

I'm shocked that there haven't been more suicides by journalists or aid workers. I think that's the only reason that the military started paying attention to mental health (not that it is doing nearly enough). The epidemic of suicides among veterans is tragic and a sign that it is foolish to think that you can ask young men and women to go to strange places and put their lives on the line to kill people for sometimes ambiguous reasons and not have them experience psychological or emotional trauma.

But the civilian sector is far behind. Humanitarian and development organizations and news organizations are just starting to realize that their people experience all sorts of psychological and emotional stress and trauma. Some are adding resilience training programs. It's a start, but not nearly enough.

Organizations that send people to work in hostile environments have a duty of care to their people. While most organizations recognize the physical threats and take security seriously, they are failing their people in terms of mental and emotional health. Just like most organizations have in-house staff to evaluate, monitor, and mitigate security risks, they need in-house staff who look out for and respond to psychological and emotional dangers.

The war in Ukraine highlights all this. It's a catastrophe that humanitarian community, already strained from years of responding to Afghanistan, Syria, Yemen, Ethiopia, and other crises, is surging to address. And journalists have flocked to the front lines with tragic results. The world needs to know the human toll of the conflict. Some of that toll will be on the journalists and humanitarians. Hopefully they will have more than cats to serve as their mental health support.

Acknowledgments

Thanks to John Carberry and Margaret Watkins for all the love, support, and generosity over the years and for letting me run up the heating bill at the Cape Cod house while I wrote this book. Rudy Burwell, Wendy Carberry, and Steve West—thank you for you love, friendship, and belief in this project and the help getting across the finish line. Eric Webber—thank you for the brainstorming session that led to the title and helped with the framing of the book. Dick Gordon and Brian Murphy—I'm grateful for your friendship and the time you put in reading the draft and providing the editorial feedback that made this a better book. Professor Rick Matthews at Lehigh University—thanks for stimulating the writing node in my brain way back when. To the federal interagency process—thank you for making me realize that I needed to quit my government job and write a book. Jacki Lyden—thank you for the encouragement and for connecting me with Bob Kunzinger who connected me with Madville Publishing. Finally, Kim Davis and the Madville team—thanks for believing and getting behind this project.

About the Author

Sean Carberry is an award-winning journalist, writer, and editor. In his more than 15 years as a radio and print journalist, he has traveled to dozens of countries, including the Democratic Republic of the Congo, Iraq, Libya, Sudan, Syria, and Yemen. He was NPR's last Kabul-based correspondent in 2012 through 2014. After that, he spent several years working for the Defense Department Office of Inspector General, writing and editing oversight reports on counterterrorism operations, before returning to journalism. In a previous life, he was a Gold Record-winning recording engineer and producer. He has a B.A. from Lehigh University and an M.P.A. from the Harvard Kennedy School. He lives in Washington, D.C. with his cat Squeak who he rescued from the streets of Kabul.

Printed in the USA
CPSIA information can be obtained
at www.ICGtesting.com
LVHW090419080823
754551LV00009B/643